Linguistics and the Language

Edinburgh Textbooks in Applied Linguistics

Titles in the series include:

An Introduction to Applied Linguistics
From Practice to Theory
by Alan Davies

Teaching Literature in a Second Language
by Brian Parkinson and Helen Reid Thomas

Materials Evaluation and Design for Language Teaching
by Ian McGrath

The Social Turn in Second Language Acquisition
by David Block

Language Assessment and Program Evaluation
by Brian Lynch

Edinburgh Textbooks in Applied Linguistics
Series Editors: Alan Davies and Keith Mitchell

Linguistics and the Language of Translation

Kirsten Malmkjær

Edinburgh University Press

© Kirsten Malmkjær, 2005

Transferred to Digital Print 2012

Edinburgh University Press Ltd
22 George Square, Edinburgh

Typeset in Garamond
by Norman Tilley Graphics, Northampton,
and printed and bound
by CPI Group (UK) Ltd, Croydon, CR0 4YY

A CIP record for this book is available from
the British Library

ISBN 0 7486 2055 9 (hardback)
ISBN 0 7486 2056 7 (paperback)

Contents

Series Editors' Preface vii
Preface ix
Acknowledgements xi
Dedication xii

1 From writings on translation to translation studies 1

2 Mapping and approaching translation studies 17

3 Translation and language 42

4 Sounds and rhythms in translation 70

5 Words and meanings in translation 86

6 Words in company 115

7 From words to texts 134

8 Perspectives and reflections in clauses and texts in translation 168

Conclusion 185
References 186
Index 197

Series Editors' Preface

This series of single-author volumes published by Edinburgh University Press takes a contemporary view of applied linguistics. The intention is to make provision for the wide range of interests in contemporary applied linguistics which are provided for at the Master's level.

The expansion of Master's postgraduate courses in recent years has had two effects:

1. What began almost half a century ago as a wholly cross-disciplinary subject has found a measure of coherence so that now most training courses in Applied Linguistics have similar core content.
2. At the same time the range of specialisms has grown, as in any developing discipline. Training courses (and professional needs) vary in the extent to which these specialisms are included and taught.

Some volumes in the series will address the first development noted above, while the others will explore the second. It is hoped that the series as a whole will provide students beginning postgraduate courses in Applied Linguistics, as well as language teachers and other professionals wishing to become acquainted with the subject, with a sufficient introduction for them to develop their own thinking in applied linguistics and to build further into specialist areas of their own choosing.

The view taken of applied linguistics in the Edinburgh Textbooks in Applied Linguistics Series is that of a theorising approach to practical experience in the language professions, notably, but not exclusively, those concerned with language learning and teaching. It is concerned with the problems, the processes, the mechanisms and the purposes of language in use.

Like any other applied discipline, applied linguistics draws on theories from related disciplines with which it explores the professional experience of its practitioners and which in turn are themselves illuminated by that experience. This two-way relationship between theory and practice is what we mean by a theorising discipline.

The volumes in the series are all premised on this view of Applied Linguistics as a theorising discipline which is developing its own coherence. At the same time, in order to present as complete a contemporary view of applied linguistics as possible other approaches will occasionally be expressed.

Each volume presents its author's own view of the state of the art in his or her topic. Volumes will be similar in length and in format, and, as is usual in a textbook series, each will contain exercise material for use in class or in private study.

Alan Davies
W. Keith Mitchell

Preface

This book is for students of translation, languages and linguistics who would like to enhance their understanding of the relationships between translation studies and linguistics – of how linguistics can be applied to the creation, description and constructive criticism of translations.

The book can be used at undergraduate and postgraduate levels. It includes a chapter on the development of translation studies in the west (Chapter 1) and one on contemporary approaches to the discipline (Chapter 2). These provide the disciplinary context within which the processes and products of translating are studied; it is useful to be familiar with this context before tackling the more applied parts of the book.

The third chapter outlines the theory of meaning underlying the book and the mode of application of linguistics to translation studies adopted here. It is interesting that in the relatively recent past, 'linguistic science' as a whole, or at least comparative linguistics, has been viewed as what might justifiably be called 'applied translation studies' by one set of scholars (see especially Roman Jakobson 1959: 233–4, see Chapter 3, section 3.6.i), while translation theory, almost simultaneously, has been viewed as an area within applied linguistics by another group of scholars (see especially Ian Catford, 1965, who subtitles his book on translation theory *An Essay in Applied Linguistics*; see Chapter 2, section 2.3.i). This book adopts neither of these stances: There is obviously more to linguistics than the comparison of expressions and texts in different languages; and the discipline of translation studies can no more be exhausted by applying linguistics to it than disciplines such as literary studies, journalism, or dramatology. Here, linguistics is applied to translation studies as a way of attending to the language used in translations and their source texts: linguistic insights, theoretical concepts and descriptive categories are drawn on in discussion of the creation, description and constructive criticism of such texts. Chapter 3 thus provides a broader theoretical and academic context for the chapters where application is focal; this will be helpful especially at postgraduate level. Under-graduate students may find the chapter challenging, and prefer to move straight to the remaining chapters (Chapters 4–8) which apply more directly descriptive and theoretical linguistic notions to original texts and their translations.

The rationale for this application is that texts, whether translated or not, are made up, concretely, of language. Texts have power to evoke a multitude of cognitive and emotional responses to the ways in which language shapes them, and aspects of these responses must be assumed to be sharable; if they were not, there would not be communication through language. However, degrees of sharability are likely to be affected by linguistic, cultural and temporal distances between the participants in speech events, and, at points where these distances become too great for mutual comprehension to be immediately possible it may be restored through the mediation of a translator.

Whereas a first writer is relatively free to write what they desire, a translator may be thought to be doubly bound: bound to produce a text that is based more or less closely on the original, translators' choices of what to say are restricted; and bound by the relationships between the languages and cultures involved, translators' choices of how to say it are restricted too. On the other hand, this also presents translators with tremendous opportunities to be creative: The double bind becomes a double delight at shaping a text world (Werth 1999) to suit a community of readers.

Translators act as reader/writers who respond to a text and who produce a text for others, in turn, to respond to. In some cases, translators hope for a high degree of overlap between readers' responses to the translation and the first writer's presumed intentions. In other cases, translators seek to produce somewhat different responses in their readers than those which they assume that the first writer desired to produce. In either case, it is as well for translators to be conscious of what they are doing and for observers to be conscious of what is going on, so that they can function creatively in translating and in reacting to translations. It is my hope that this book will enhance its readers' creativeness by fine-tuning their awareness of the language of contextualised translation.

Acknowledgements

I would like to thank Keith Mitchell, Alan Davies, Sarah Edwards, James Dale and the anonymous reviewers who have helped the book along its way. It would never have seen the light of day without them.

Grateful acknowledgement is made to the following sources for permission to reproduce material previously published elsewhere. Every effort has been made to trace the copyright holders, but if any have been inadvertently overlooked, the publisher will be pleased to make the necessary arrangements at the first opportunity.

AKAL, Madrid (trans. by Francisco Torres Oliver of Lewis Carroll's 'Jabberwocky').
The Banker (text by Kathy Evans, 'Kuwait Economy at the Crossroads').
Eva Lene Kristensen (extracts from Tom Kristensen's *Hærværk*, 1930).
Wicked Paint (e-mail sales promotion letters).

The examples from Peter Low (2003), 'Translating poetic song: An attempt at a functional account of strategies', *Target*, 15:1, and the examples from Kirsten Malmkjær (2004), 'Censorship or error', in *Claims, Changes and Challenges in Translation Studies*, Gyde Hansen, Kirsten Malmkjær and Daniel Gile (eds) are reproduced with kind permission by John Benjamins Publishing Company, Amsterdam/Philadelphia. www.benjamins.com

The figures from Melissa Bowerman (1996), 'The origins of children's spatial semantic categories: Cognitive versus linguistic determinants', in John J. Gumperz and Stephen C. Levinson (eds), *Rethinking Linguistic Relativity* are reproduced with kind permission by Cambridge University Press.

The extracts from Tom Kristensen (1968), *Havoc*, tr. Carl Malmberg are reproduced with kind permission by The University of Wisconsin Press.

We have made every effort to obtain permission from:

Diario de Poesia (trans. by Mirta Rosenberg and Daniel Samoilovich of Lewis Carroll's 'Jabberwocky').
Der Kinderbuckverlag (trans. by Liselotte and Martin Remaine of Lewis Carroll's 'Jabberwocky').
Flammarion (trans. Henri Parisot of Lewis Carroll's poem 'Jabberwocky').

Dedication

This book is for students of translation – those who appear in it as well as those who do not – and especially those who have helped me develop its content and been exposed to its numerous permutations.

Chapter 1

From writings on translation to translation studies

1.1 INTRODUCTION

This chapter highlights a number of important steps in the development of the European tradition of translation studies from its inception in Greece and Rome to the important 'Target Text Turn' within the discipline in the last quarter of the twentieth century. Then, a number of theorists began to advocate a shift of attention away from an exclusive occupation with discovering ways of representing a Source Text faithfully in a translation, towards viewing a translation as a factual phenomenon displaying a number of relationships, which might be called relationships of translation equivalence, with the Source Text.

This turn paved the way for the discipline to secure its place within academia, because it established that translations were legitimate objects of description, so that a set of descriptive statements could be developed and used to foster and test theory. The substantial body of empirically based research which has developed since this turn took place also opened the way for the division of the discipline into a number of sub-areas and for a number of approaches to translation, which will be introduced in Chapter 2.

The discussion will move along European lines, not because of any disrespect for other traditions of thought about translation, but because this book is not primarily historical in orientation. It could not hope to do justice to several traditions.[1] What is provided here is far less a history than an account of how a number of issues which have remained of concern in translation studies were introduced to the discipline. Some of these issues have been focal in other traditions of thought about translation too, and some remain among the concerns of a discipline which is itself becoming increasingly international in nature, scope and aims.

1.2 THE ROMANS

In Europe it is common to write as if translation theory begins with the Romans, Marcus Tullius Cicero (106 to 43 BC) and Horace (65 to 8 BC) in particular. For example, Steiner ([1975] 1992: 248) identifies Cicero's *Libellus de optimo genere oratorum* of 46 BC and Horace's *Ars poetica* of circa 20 BC as the starting points for theorising about translation, and most other European theorists follow suit (see e.g. Bassnett-McGuire [1980] 1991; Qvale [1998] 2003).

The reason is that these are among the earliest writings about translation still extant and that they have had a significant effect on the development of translation theory in the West. But it is important to be aware that translation is likely to have been taking place for as long as languages have been written down, and that traces of translational activities dating from long before Cicero was born have been found in several parts of the world outside Europe. For example, Hung and Pollard (1998: 366) note that there were government officials with special responsibility for translation during the time of the Zhou Dynasty in China in the ninth century BC, and Krishnamurthy (1998: 464–73) traces the origins of the tradition on the Indian subcontinent back to the fourth century BC. Even the Roman tradition itself predates Cicero, as Kelly (1998: 495–503) points out. It is obviously very likely that translators and scholars from these early times thought about the nature of both the products and the process of translation. But we have no records of the outcomes of their thinking; hence the habit of starting with Cicero and Horace.

Translation in the Roman period was mainly of philosophical and literary texts and almost always from Greek into Latin (see Kelly 1998: 495–6). The audience for these texts was small, and consisted of those who, being educated, were perfectly capable of reading the original Greek texts. Translation, however, was perceived to provide added value to the texts, the target literary system and the target language, a notion that remains alive to this day. Cicero (106 to 43 BC) writes (*De Oratore* I: 35; quoted in Lefevere 1990: 23–4):

> by giving Latin form to the text I had read, I could not only make use of the best expressions in common usage with us, but I could also coin new expressions, analogous to those used in Greek, and they were no less well received by our people, as long as they seemed appropriate.

This quotation raises issues which remain current in contemporary translation theory: Cicero seems to have sought a middle way between two extremes: foreignisation and domestication, to give them their most modern names (see Venuti 1995). The text is given a Latin form, and Cicero chooses expressions common in the vernacular, which will have a domesticating effect. However, the vernacular expressions are intermingled with expressions derived from Greek, and hence novel with respect to Latin, and this seems foreignising; but Cicero stresses that these innovations must seem appropriate to the target audience of educated Romans. They must, at least, be able to slot into the Roman conception of appropriateness to the text, the situation and the language. This issue of audience expectations again remains topical in many current approaches to translation theory.

There is no sense among Roman scholars of resistance to the foreign – quite the opposite. The prevalent Homeric and Hesiodic tradition saw poetry as the product of divine inspiration, and therefore eminently worthy of imitation. In fact, imitation was generally considered preferable to innovation: 'you must give your days and nights to the study of Greek models', Horace (65 to 8 BC) advises the budding Roman poet (*Ars Poetica*, 268–9; Dorsch 1965: 88):

> it is better for you to be putting a Trojan tale into dramatic form than that you should be the first in the field with a theme hitherto unknown and unsung. A theme that is familiar can be made your own property as long as you do not waste your time on hackneyed treatment.

1.3 BIBLE TRANSLATORS

A second tradition that has been extremely influential in shaping Western translation theory is Bible translation. While creativity and the attendant sense of licence with regard to the precise details and meaning of the source text was considered virtuous by the Romans, where Bible translation is concerned, the main consideration tends to be the production of the most authentic, though accessible, guide to the words of the deity. While the quest for authenticity tends to pull Bible translators in the direction of exact rendition of the original, the quest for accessibility tends to make them lean toward a degree of licence, particularly in matters of imagery, and this tension culminates in Nida's (1964) distinction between Formal and Dynamic equivalence (see Chapter 2, section 2.3.i below).

The Bible translator, Eusebius Hieronymus Sophronius, known in English as St Jerome, is perhaps the most famous western translator of all time. He is the Patron Saint of translators and the date of his death, 30 September (the year is thought to be 419 or 420), is celebrated as International Translators' Day. St Jerome is believed to have been born in about 340 in the town of Strido in Dalmatia (later Croatia). In 382 he was commissioned by Pope Damasus to revise the Latin translation of the New Testament, and when Damasus died in 384, Jerome settled in Bethlehem where he translated the Old Testament into Latin directly from Hebrew and the New Testament and the Psalms into Latin from Greek. Jerome's Latin texts form the basis of the Roman Catholic Vulgate in use today (Qvale 1998: 19–20). Jerome's preferred method of translating is documented in his letter to Pammachius, *Liber de optime genere interpretandi* (ed. Bartelink 1980), in which he explains that except when translating sacred texts, he prefers to translate sense for sense: *Non verbum e verbo sed sensum experimere de sensu*, as he puts it in a much quoted passage (see e.g. Qvale 1998: 20; Snell-Hornby 1988: 9; for a translation of the whole letter, by Paul Carroll, see Robinson 1997: 23–30). In the case of Holy Scripture, however, Jerome advocates word-for-word translation. He says (tr. Caroll in Robinson 1997: 25) 'except of course in the case of Holy Scripture, where even the syntax contains a mystery – I render, not word for word, but sense for sense'. For a discussion of this distinction, and attendant exercises, see Chapter 5, section 5.1.ii.

Accuracy remains foremost in the minds of early translators of the Bible into English, though in their case, accessibility and use of the vernacular also comes into play. For example, Richard Rolle (c. 1300–1349), who translated the Psalter into English some time during the 1330s, tries to combine faithfulness and accessibility by exploiting the influence on English of Latin (tr. Rosamund S. Allen in Robinson 1997: 49–50):

> In this work I shall not be using learned expression but the easiest and commonest words in English which approximate most closely to the Latin, so that those who do not know Latin can acquire many Latin words from the English. In the translation I follow the letter as much as I am able to, and where I cannot find an exactly equivalent English word, I follow the sense, so that those who are going to read it need have no fear of not understanding.

The first complete translation of the Bible into English was the Wycliffite Bible, translated from Latin between 1380 and 1384 and named after John Wycliffe (c. 1320–84). Wycliffe believed that everyone should have access to the word of God in a language that they could understand; and for all but the educated elite in England, that meant English. A second edition, believed to have been revised by John Purvey, was complete by 1408 (Bassnett-McGuire [1980] 1991: 46–7). Whereas the first edition, probably mainly the responsibility of Nicholas of Hereford, was strictly literal, Purvey's edition is a sense-for-sense translation; the preface says (Robinson 1997: 54): 'the best translating out of Latin into English is to translate after the sentence, and not only after the words'. But such liberalism vis-à-vis the word of God did not by any means meet with universal approval; and the Archbishop of Canterbury banned the use of all unlicensed Bible translations in 1409. From then on the Wycliffite translators had to operate in secret (Ellis and Oakley-Brown 1998: 336).

The first Bible in German was made by Martin Luther (1483–1546), who published the New Testament in 1522 and the Bible in 1534. He explains his views on Bible translation in *Sendbrief vom Dolmetschen* ('Circular letter about translation', 1530): The Lord's message must be interpreted by the translator and conveyed in language that will appeal to its recipients. This means sacrificing the original's grammar for that of the target language, and Luther also advocates the judicious employment of vernacular imagery when appropriate (Bassnett-McGuire [1980] 1991: 49). According to Robinson (1997: 84), Luther's most important contribution to translation theory lies in his 'reader-orientation'.

The next great English Bible translator was William Tyndale (1494–1536) whose New Testament in English was printed in 1525. It was based on Erasmus's Greek edition,[2] published in Holland, and smuggled in 1526 into England where it was burnt as heretical in the same year. Tyndale himself came to share that fate in 1536; by this time, he had revised his New Testament (1534) and translated parts of the Old Testament from Hebrew (Bassnett-McGuire [1980] 1991: 47; Ellis and Oakley-Brown 1998: 337).

The King James Bible, so called because it was commissioned by King James I/VI (1566–1625), is the work of a team of forty-seven scholars and translators. Work began in 1604, one year after James's accession to the English throne, and was completed in 1611, by which time more than fifty English Bibles had been published. The King James team had been especially encouraged to consult the Bishops'

Bible of 1568 and Tyndale's (1525), Matthew's (Antwerp 1537), Coverdale's (Zurich 1535, England 1537) and Whitchurch's (1539) Bibles, but are known also to have consulted the Middle English Gospels and Psalter and the Wycliffite Bible (Steiner [1975] 1992: 366). The translators allowed all of these older versions to influence their work, and, according to Steiner, this strategy of deliberate archaism (predominantly Tudor rather than Jacobean usage) enabled the 'vitality' and 'logic of a cumulative tradition' to transmute the 'Hebrew, Greek, and Latin sources into English sensibility, where it continues to play a part more immediate than that of Scripture in any other European community, more linguistically central and theologically diffuse' (Steiner [1975] 1992: 367). It is thus a fascinating example of a translation which stands at the end of a long line of translations of the same work, in the role of a text native to its host culture. According to Nida (1998: 25), The King James Bible (also known as the Authorised Version) is regarded as highly by English speaking Protestants as the Vulgate is by Catholics. Notes made by one of the contributors exist in a version edited by Ward Allen (1969), and the preface, written by Miles Smith (d. 1624) in 1611 is reprinted in Robinson (1987: 139–47).

During the period which Nida (1998: 23) designates as 'modern' in Bible translation, namely 1885 till the present, revisions and new translations have been made of the Bible, first into the European languages, and later into the languages of the so-called Third World. Translations into the latter group of languages have been largely the responsibility of a number of missionary societies, most notably the Wycliffe Bible Translators, also known as the Summer Institute of Linguistics. Bible translators often work in teams of three to five full time translators, and generally agree that Bible translation should be based on the most reliable scholarly interpretations of the Greek and Hebrew Bible texts, that the Target Text should be intelligible and acceptable to its intended audience, and that background information must be included in either notes, prefaces or word lists rather than in the text itself (Nida 1998: 27–8).

1.4 THEORISTS

As is evident from the above, thinking translators typically develop principles to guide their practice, and we inherit some of the most firmly established concepts and dichotomies in translation theory from the Romans and from translators of the Bible. These remain in focus for later translators and for translators of other text types and form the basis of further developments in translation theory. These developments fall into two main categories. First, there are lists of requirements for good translation, such as those provided by for example Dolet, Chapman and Batteux. This largely prescriptivist tradition of producing lists of hints, guidelines or rules to be followed in the production of translations has survived tenaciously into the present century, for example in much of Peter Newmark's work.

Secondly, there are advocations of a particular method of translating, which may more properly be called theoretical because they are accompanied by a justification of or reason for preferring one method over another. They include writings by for example Denham, Cowley and Perrot, who argue for free translation, Huet who argues for closer adherence to the source text, Dryden, Pope and Batteux, who argue for a balance between these two extremes, and finally theorists such as Tytler and Herder, for whom the opposition between word-based and sense-based translation seems less straightforward and also perhaps less of a central issue, and who advocate and describe more complex theories and methods of translation.

Of special interest here are theorists within the second category who take an interest in specifically linguistic issues connected to translation. These include Schleiermacher, von Humboldt and Walter Benjamin and before them Gottfried Wilhelm Leibniz (1646–1716), whose essay, *Unvorgreifliche Gedanken, betreffend die Ausübung und Verbesserung der Deutschen Sprache* ('Unexpected thoughts about the use and improvement of the German Language', 1697) advocates translation as a means of coming to a closer understanding of the language being translated into: 'The true test of a language's superfluity or deficiency lies in the translation of good books from another language, for that shows what is lacking and what is available' (in Robinson 1997: 185). This remark foreshadows e.g. Dagut's (1981) notion of semantic voids; and Leibniz's notion that everything *can* be said in any language is repeated by Jakobson ([1959] 1987: 431).

Many scholars of the past, other than those discussed here, have written about translation, and a good selection of their writings on this topic can be found in Robinson (1997).

In his *La manière de bien traduire d'une langue en aultre* (How to translate well from one language to another, 1540), Étienne Dolet (1509–46), 'one of the first writers to formulate a theory of translation' according to Bassnett-McGuire ([1980] 1991: 54), claims that the quality of a translation depends upon five things (see David G. Ross's translation in Robinson 1997: 95–6): (1) the translator's grasp of the author's meaning and motives; (2) the translator's familiarity with the language of the source text and with the language it is being translated into; (3) the translator's ability to free himself from reliance on word-for-word translation; (4) the use of 'normal diction' without any 'extravagant neologisms'; (5) adherence to the principles of rhetorical harmony (Steiner [1975] 1992: 276–7). Dolet's interest in philosophy led to his downfall: he was burnt at the stake in 1546, together with his books, for having translated a passage from Plato's dialogue, *Axiochus*, in a way that could be construed to contradict the Christian doctrine of the survival of the soul after the death of the body.

A list of principles similar to Dolet's can be found in George Chapman's (1559–1634) preface to his translation of Homer's *Iliad* (1611). He says (in Robinson 1997: 137):

It is the part of every knowing and judicial interpreter not to follow the number and order of words but the material things themselves, and sentences to weigh diligently, and to clothe and adorn them with words and such a style and form of oration as are most apt for the language into which they are converted.

However, Chapman also insists that the meaning of the original should be preserved, and considers his own translation of Homer less free than earlier translators'.

The list produced by Charles Batteux (1715–80) in his 'Principles of Translation' (from *Principes de littérature*, 1747–8) is extensive and closer to theorising proper than earlier efforts insofar as Battaux tries to justify his principles with reference to nature, previous authority (for example Cicero) and the alleged universality of patterns of thinking. The list includes for example: That the original's order of events and of ideas should not be altered in the translation; that sentence breaks should not be altered; that conjunction should be preserved, adverbs be kept next to verbs and symmetrical sentences kept symmetrical; and that sentence mood, tropes and proverbs be reproduced faithfully.

Famous in the seventeenth century for poems of his own creation, Sir John Denham (1615–69) remarks in his preface to his translation of Virgil's *The Destruction of Troy* (1656) (from the *Aeneid*) that it is not the business of a poetry translator just to translate language into language, but, rather, to translate poetry into poetry, 'and poesie is of so subtle a spirit, that in pouring out of one language into another, it will all evaporate; and if a new spirit be not added in the transfusion, there will remain nothing but a *caput mortuum*' (head of death; skull; figuratively: useless leftover) (in Robinson 1997: 156). This sentiment is also expressed by Abraham Cowley (1618–67) in his preface to his translation (1656) of Pindar's odes (in Robinson 1997: 161):

> If a man should undertake to translate Pindar word for word, it would be thought that one madman had translated another … And surely rhyme, without the addition of wit and the spirit of poetry … would make it ten times more distracted than it is in prose.

We meet the view that poetry translation is special and more like re-writing again two centuries later with Percy Bysshe Shelley (1792–1822), who expressed one of the most famous metaphors of translation in his *Defence of Poetry* (1821, published 1840; in Robinson 1997: 244–5):

> it were as wise to cast a violet into a crucible that you might discover the formal principle of its colour and odour, as seek to transfuse from one language into another the creations of a poet. The plant must spring again from its seed or it will bear no flower – and this is the burthen of the curse of Babel.

Many later translation theorists have similarly proclaimed the special nature and difficulty of poetry translation and insisted that it can only be carried out successfully, if at all, by someone with a poetic genius of their own.

Cowley justifies free translation – 'I have in these two Odes of Pindar taken, left out, and added what I please' (in Robinson 1997: 162) – with reference to the distance in time, space and culture that may exist between an original and a translation. The two cultures may have different religions, customs, landscapes and peoples, all of which may affect their literatures and make it difficult to translate closely. They may, furthermore, have different types of poetry employing different kinds of metre, which may be far better suited to the original language than to the target language.

The expression, *les belles infidèles*, which has recently received special attention by translation scholars with an interest in gender issues (see Chapter 2, section 2.3.iv), entered translation theory in the writing of Gilles Ménage (1613–92) who used it to describe the free translations of the classics made by Nicolas Perrot (1606–64) (Robinson 1997: 156). According to Robinson (*op. cit.*: 157), Perrot translated so freely that he was once asked why he bothered to translate at all rather than write his own works; his reply has a Roman echo: 'To serve one's country a man ought rather to translate valuable authors than to write new books, which seldom contain anything new'. An interesting variation on this theme, and also in the tradition of thought according to which translating other cultures' literature is considered enriching of the receptor culture's literary system, is Madame de Staël's (Anne-Louise-Germaine Necker, baronne de Staël-Holstein; 1766–1817), declaration, two centuries later, that (from *De l'esprit des traductions*, 'On the spirit of translations', tr. David Ross, in Robinson 1997: 241):

> There is no more distinguished service that can be performed for literature than to transport the masterpieces of human intellect from one language to another. There are so few works of the first rate; genius in any genre whatsoever is so rare a phenomenon that if any modern nation were reduced to its own such treasures, it would be forever poor.

In contrast to the freedom advocated by Perrot and Cowley, Pierre Daniel Huet (1630–1721), whose *De interpretatione* (1661), according to Robinson (1997: 162), was considered by his contemporaries the final word on translation, defines translation as 'Discourse expressed in a better known language offering and reproducing discourse expressed in a less known language' (translated by Edwin Dolin, in Robinson 1997: 167). This, he says, may be done in one of two ways: Either with a focus on reproducing the author accurately, or with a focus on the translator's own or the reader's pleasure, as in the case of the Roman translators. The best method of translation, thinks Huet, is the former (*ibid.*):

> when the translator adheres very closely, first, to the meaning of the author, then also to the actual words themselves, if the capacity of the two languages permit, and finally, when he sketches the innate character of the author, insofar as can be done, and concentrates on one thing only, namely, faithfully to present him diminished in no way and increased in no way, but whole and very like himself in every way.

The reason for this preference is that Huet thinks of translation as imaging the original, which it ought to do truly, even down to mirroring word for word insofar as the languages permit it; but, he ends, 'the conflict and incompatibility of the languages can create many other obstacles preventing the translator from stepping closely and precisely into the footsteps of his author' (in Robinson 1997: 169).

It is also possible to operate with a triadic translation strategy taxonomy, as proposed by John Dryden (1631–1700) in his Preface to *Ovid's Epistles* (1680). Here, Dryden distinguishes between (1) metaphrase, translating word for word; (2) paraphrase, 'or translation with latitude, where the author is kept in view by the translator, so as never to be lost, but his words are not so strictly followed as his sense' and (3) imitation, which may not really deserve the name, 'translation' at all, because in the exercise of this method both words and sense may be altered, leaving only 'some general hints from the original' (in Robinson 1997: 172). Dryden advocates paraphrase, because metaphrase is almost impossible to achieve and the result is typically poor; and imitation misrepresents the author of the original – though Dryden excuses Cowley his latitude in translating Pindar because 'so wild and ungovernable a poet' could be made to speak English only by imitation by 'a genius so elevated and unconfined as Mr Cowley's' (in Robinson 1997: 173).

Alexander Pope (1688–1744), who discusses 'The Chief Characteristics of Translation' in the preface to his translation of Homer's *Iliad* (1715), agrees with Dryden that a middle way between the two extremes, word-for-word and sense-for-sense, is desirable. 'It is certain no literal translation can be just to an excellent original in a superior language; but it is a great mistake to imagine (as many have done) that a rash paraphrase can make amends for this general defect; which is no less in danger to lose the spirit of an ancient by deviating into the modern manners of expression' (in Robinson 1997: 193).

In his *Über die neuere Deutchen Litteratur: Fragmente* (1766–7) ('On Recent German Literature: Fragments'; in Robinson 1997: 207–8), Johan Gottfried von Herder (1744–1803) introduces into theory an early version of the opposition now familiar as that between domestication and foreignisation (Venuti 1995), along with the metaphor of a choice between the author travelling to the readership or the readership being taken to the author's native culture. Herder upbraids the French for making Homer conform absolutely to French tastes: 'Homer must enter France a captive, clad in the French fashion'. Instead, in German, Homer should be seen as he is. This requires annotation and critical commentaries: the translator should 'take us with him to Greece and show us the treasures he has found' (in Robinson 1997: 208).

English language writing on translation theory found a strong advocate of domestication in Alexander Fraser Tytler (1747–1813), who, in his *Principles of Translation* (1791) declares a good translation to be (in Robinson 1997: 209; italics in original):

> *That in which the merit of the original work is so completely transfused into another language as to be as distinctly apprehended, and as strongly felt, by a native of the country to which that language belongs as it is by those who speak the language of the original work*

From this assumption three principles follow: (1) That the translation should give a complete transcript of the ideas of the original, which requires the translator to have perfect knowledge of the language of the original and a good grasp of its subject matter; (2) that the original's style should be retained, which requires the translator to be a competent stylist; and (3) that the translation should read like an original work, and easily, so that if the original is faulty (obscure or ambiguous), then the translator should amend it. This is a highly contentious position and translators who have adopted it often become objects of scorn in later times. A favourite target is Edward Fitzgerald (1809–83) who wrote in the preface to his translation of the *Rubáiyát of Omar Khayyám* (1859) that he had improved as he saw fit on 'these Persians ... who really want a little Art to shape them' (quoted in Bassnett-McGuire [1980] 1991: 3). One reason to question sentiments such as Fitzgerald's and Tytler's is that what is faulty or what is art to one culture at one historical point may not be faulty or may not be art to another at a later date.

A tripartite translation typology with a difference begins to emerge in German romanticism with Novalis (pen name of Friedrich Leopold von Hardenberg, 1772–1801), who writes in his *Blütenstaub* ('Pollen', 1798, in Robinson 1997: 213):

> A translation is either grammatical, or transformative, or mythic. Of these, mythic translations are translations in the noblest style: they reveal the pure and perfect character of the individual work of art. The work of art they give us is not the actual one, but its ideal. ... Grammatical translations ... require a good deal of learning but no more than expository writing skills. ... Transformative translations ... verge constantly on travesty.

'Mythic' translations in this sense of translations that allow us a glimpse of the ideal work behind the actual written one resurface later in the writings of Walter Benjamin.

With Johann Wolfgang von Goethe (1749–1832), we meet again the metaphor of travel encountered in the writings of Herder. Goethe writes, in *The Two Maxims* from *Rede zum Andenken des edlen Dichters, Bruders und Freundes Wieland* ('Speech in memory of the noble poet, brother and friend, Wieland', 1813; in Robinson 1997: 222):

> There are two maxims for translation: the one requires that the foreign author be brought over to us so that we can look upon him as our own; the other that we cross over to the foreign and find ourselves inside its circumstances, its modes of speech, its uniqueness.

In *West-Östlicher Divan* (1819), however, he refines the domestication/foreignisation and travel metaphors with the introduction of a tripartite translation typology which is unique so far in translation theory. The judgement of which type of translation is to be preferred is here made not on the basis of aesthetic and ethical considerations of beauty and loyalty, but on the grounds of different degrees of 'cultural readiness' for translation from particular languages and of particular genres. He writes (in Robinson 1997: 222–3):

> There are three kinds of translation. The first familiarises us with the foreign country on our own terms. For this, a simple prose translation is best ... because it startles us with the wonder of the foreign right in the midst of our ordinary lives ... This approach is followed by a second epoch in which one seeks to project

oneself into the circumstances of the foreign country, but in fact only appropriates the foreign meaning and then replaces it with one's own. I want to call this kind of era the parodistic. ... This second epoch brought us to a third, the last and highest of all. Here one seeks to make the translation identical with the original, so that the one would no longer be in the stead but in the place of the other.

The epochs may be repeated and reversed and occur simultaneously, but the third epoch is nevertheless called the last because it 'leads us onward, drives us towards the source text, and so finally closes the circle in which the alien and the familiar, the known and the unknown move towards each other' (in Robinson 1997: 224).

The metaphor of travel and the call for foreignisation are both repeated by Friedrich Schleirmacher (1768–1834), in *Über die verschiedenen Methoden des Übersetzens* ('On the different methods of translation', 1813, in Robinson 1997: 225–38); Schleiermacher says (*op. cit.*: 229):

The translator either (1) disturbs the writer as little as possible and moves the reader in his direction, or (2) disturbs the reader as little as possible and moves the writer in his direction. The two approaches are so absolutely different that no mixture of the two is to be trusted, as that would increase the likelihood that the writer and reader would miss each other entirely.

To follow the first method, the translator needs to convey to the reader that the text is foreign, but this has to be done, obviously, in the reader's native language, and without alienating the reader completely from the text. It can only be undertaken successfully when people recognise the desirability of understanding the foreign and when they allow for a certain flexibility in the use of their native language. A famous example of the exploitation of the flexibility of language in translation is the translational activity of William Morris (1834–96), whose translations of the Icelandic sagas, classical Greek literature, and Old French romances are characterised by the use of special vocabulary and by the mirroring of the grammatical structure and metre of the originals.

Schleiermacher was wary of the approach that would attempt to convey in the Target Language what had been said in the original in such a way that the translation read like an original. This was because he doubted whether the expressed could be divorced from the medium of expression, given what he saw as the intimate connection between, on the one hand, a language and a culture and, on the other, a writer's thoughts and the language units used to express them. In the writings of Wilhelm von Humboldt (1767–1835) these intimacies are further elaborated in a theory of linguistic relativity which is the precursor of the linguistic relativity thesis of Sapir and Whorf (see Chapter 3) and the theory of cognitive linguistics as propounded by, e.g., Langacker (1987 and 1991; 1991; 1999).

According to Humboldt (and, later, to Roman Jakobson and Roman Ingarden, among many others), all works of great originality are untranslatable. Humboldt presents this thesis in the introduction to his translation (1816) of Aeschylus' *Agamemnon*, and relates it to the differences between languages, which, in turn, arise because of the different ways in which stretches in different languages relate to and differentiate concepts from one another (in Robinson 1997: 238):

> with the exception of expressions denoting material objects, no word in one language is ever entirely like its counterpart in another. Different languages are in this sense only synonymous: each one puts a slightly different spin on a concept, charges it with this or that connotation, sets it one rung higher or lower on the ladder of affective response.

The notion that it is possible to separate expression from content is again questioned by Matthew Arnold (1822–88) in his *On Translating Homer* (1861): It is a mistake to 'suppose that it is *fidelity* to an original to give its matter, unless you at the same time give its manner; or, rather, to suppose that you can really give its matter at all, unless you can give its manner'. In order to ensure good translation, the translator ought to be guided neither by assumptions about how the Greeks would have understood Homer, because these are impossible to prove, nor by the general tastes of the present day, because these are unlikely to allow for a reproduction of Homer and 'the translator is to reproduce Homer'. The only proper advisor for the translator, therefore, is the scholar, who 'alone has the means of knowing that Homer who is to be reproduced. He knows him but imperfectly, for he is separated from him by time, race, and language; but he alone knows him at all'. So the effect the translator ought to aim to achieve with the translation is the effect which the original text now has on those most carefully trained in literary appreciation, namely literary scholars (like Arnold). In the next century, Nabokov (1955) was similarly to argue for heavily annotated, literal translation aimed at an academic readership.

Clearly, it may often be the case that a scholarly translation which aims to affect scholars in the same way that the original affects them will not seem particularly approachable to the general reading public, and Arnold's contemporary, Francis William Newman (1805–97), declares it to be his 'sole object … to bring Homer before the unlearned public' (*Homeric Translation in Theory and Practice* 1861; in Robinson 1997: 257). The debate between Arnold and Newman can be found in its entirety in Arnold's *On Translating Homer* (1862). On the other hand, it would be a mistake to think that a translation informed by scholarship must necessarily appear forbidding (nor is this Newman's argument – he is clear that it is necessary for a translator to be well versed in his subject): A translation such as the immensely popular, bestselling *Beowulf* by Seamus Heaney is far from forbidding, in spite of the scholarly influences Heaney acknowledges (1999: 105).

The idea that the audience should be a primary consideration for a translator falls away altogether in the writings on translation of Walter Bendix Schoenfliess Benjamin (1892–1940). Benjamin argues in *Die Aufgabe des Übersetzers* ('The task of the translator', 1921) that a work of art is not made for a reader, and 'if the original does not exist for the reader's sake, how could the translation be understood on the basis of this premise?' (tr. Harry Zohn; in Venuti 2000: 16). For Benjamin, the importance of translation lies in the fact that it takes us closer to the pure work in a pure language which we saw hinted at in the writings of Novalis. 'Certain works' (*op.*

cit.: 16) are inherently translatable, according to Benjamin, and this translatability connects them intimately to their (successive) translations, which issue from the original's afterlife. The ultimate purpose of translation is to express 'the central reciprocal relationship between languages ... the kinship between languages is brought out by a translation far more profoundly and clearly than in the superficial and indefinable similarity of two works of literature' (*op. cit.*: 17). Because languages change continually, a final literalness in translation cannot be its ultimate goal; instead, each translation reveals a little of the 'intention underlying each language as a whole – an intention, however, which no single language can attain by itself but which is realized only by the totality of their intentions supplementing each other: pure language' (*op. cit.*: 18).

Some later linguists (e.g. Sapir 1921; Jakobson 1959) have agreed that translation is an excellent way of discovering relationships between languages, particularly to demonstrate their similarities or to suggest a common semantic base underlying their surface differences (see Chapter 3).

The 'certain texts' which Benjamin considers inherently translatable are works of what he calls a high level, including literary works of art. In this, Benjamin differs radically from most other writers on translation in the first half of the twentieth century, who tend, on the whole, to consider that translatability decreases as the literary value of a text increases. Many arguments to this effect derive from structuralist principles. For example, Ingarden ([1931] 1973) considers that all literary works of art are formed of four strata, the phonetic, the semantic, the aspectual and the representational, of which the semantic stratum of meaning units provides the structural framework for the whole, while the phonetic 'forms the external, fixed shell ... in which all of the remaining strata find their external point of support' ([1931] 1973: 59). Obviously, this stratum will be replaced in translation, with the result that 'no genuine, really valuable lyric poem can be translated into a foreign language, precisely because the phonetic stratum is then replaced by a completely different verbal material, which cannot ever perform all those functions which were performed effortlessly in the original' ([1937] 1973: 266). In fact, Ingarden's pessimism is not confined to lyric poetry; he believes that 'A faithful translation of truly great literary works of art hardly seems possible' ([1937] 1973: 156), because in them form and content are just as interdependent as in the lyric.

Jakobson argues similarly, from a more overtly functional perspective, that 'poetry by definition is untranslatable' (1959: 238). According to Jakobson, there are three types of translation ([1959: 233] 1987: 429): (1) Intralingual translation or *rewording* is an interpretation of verbal signs by means of other signs of the same language; (2) interlingual translation or *translation proper* is an interpretation of verbal signs by means of some other language; (3) intersemiotic translation or *transmutation* is an interpretation of verbal signs by means of signs of nonverbal sign systems.

Intralingual translation (rewording/rephrasing) does not always produce complete synonymy, that is, complete sameness of meaning at word level, but it is possible, usually, to produce equivalent messages. This is also true of interlingual translation

([1959] 1987: 430): 'translation involves two equivalent messages in two different codes'. The problem, as far as the translation of literature is concerned, is that there is a specific focus in literary texts on the code itself: Aspects of the code become part of the message so that the message cannot be equivalent because the codes differ. This comes about in the following way:

Any act of verbal communication involves six factors (Jakobson [1960] 1987: 66): (1) The addresser, who sends a message to (2) the addressee, who receives it; (3) the context, which makes the message operative, that is, which makes the expressions involved into a message about something; (4) the message itself; (5) the contact, which is the 'physical channel and psychological connection between the addresser and the addressee, enabling both of them to enter and stay in communication'; and (6) the code, which is the language shared more or less fully by the participants.

Each of these factors 'determines a different function of language' ([1960] 1987: 66). Almost all messages perform each of the functions, but different types of message impose different hierarchical orders of importance on the functions. The functions are: (1) the expressive/emotive function, which enables the addresser to express attitudes and emotions by means of interjections, emphasis, tone, and so on; (2) the conative function which represents an orientation towards the addressee, and is most obviously expressed in the vocative and imperative moods; and (3) the referential/denotative/cognitive function (determined by the context) which enables the interactants to talk about things in the environment, and which is expressed by means of lexical words (nouns, verbs, adjectives, adverbs, some prepositions).

These three functions derive from Bühler's (1933) account of language; attention was first strongly drawn to the next, phatic, function by Malinowski (1953).

The phatic function is determined by the contact factor of the speech situation; it is the function which supports people's efforts to get along with one another and which facilitates sociability; it is expressed by means of ritualistic, formulaic language. In addition, there is a function which enables interactants to focus on the code itself, for example to check the extent to which it is shared between them. This function is the metalinguistic function expressed by means of 'language about language'.

When the orientation [*Einstellung*] of a linguistic act is primarily towards the message itself, then the final, *poetic* function of language predominates. This function enables people to play with language, persuade with language and make art with language. It is expressed by means of equivalences, repetition and other forms of patterning, including rhyme, rhythm, and alliteration.

Any given text or text part will be oriented primarily towards one of the six functions that correspond to the six factors involved in linguistic interaction; and in the case of literary texts, the predominant function is typically the poetic ([1959] 1987: 434):

In poetry, verbal equations become a constructive principle of the text. Syntactic and morphological categories, roots, and affixes, phonemes and their components (distinctive features) – in short, any constituent of the verbal code – are confronted, juxtaposed, brought into contiguous relation according to the principle of similarity and contrast and carry their own autonomous signification. Phonemic similarity is sensed as semantic relationship. The pun, or to use a more erudite and perhaps more precise term – paranomasia, reigns over poetic art, and whether its rule is absolute or limited, poetry by definition is untranslatable. Only creative transposition is possible.

1.5 THE TARGET TEXT TURN

Such defining away of the very possibility of translation is characteristic of a good deal of work in the field of literary translation, where, as Toury (1980a) points out, it leaves a vast, embarrassing gap between theory and the reality of existing translations, and strongly militates against any systematic study of these translations. To counteract this situation, Toury (1978; 1980a: 35–50; 1981) proposes a shift away from an exclusive orientation towards the source text as the measure of translation adequacy, towards a primary concentration on the translation as an empirical fact. From such a point of view, scholars are freed from the need constantly to deliberate about the degree of equivalence – never the total equivalence required of course – which a given translation segment displays with a given source text segment. Instead, it becomes possible to view equivalence as the relationship which actually obtains between the translation and the source text: an empirical rather than an ideal phenomenon, open to description. The data derived from such a description are then, in turn, available for theory construction.

It is no exaggeration to say that with the turning away from an exclusive pre-occupation with equivalence as defined from the point of view of the source text, Toury radically altered the course of much theorising about both literary and other types of translation, and opened the way for progress in modern translation theory. In Chapter 2, we shall consider the scope of this relatively new discipline, including Toury's own descriptive approach. It is worth pointing out, however, that many theorists and critics, especially of literary translation, still maintain a primarily source text oriented point of view of translation, and that this is also true of many practising translators, for example all those whose views on the translation process are expressed in Schulte and Biguenet (1992).

1.6 PRACTICE AND DISCUSSION

Practice

Erik Haugaard's translation of Hans Christian Andersen's story *Suppe paa en Pølsepind* ('Soup on a sausage-pin'; 1858) begins as follows (in Haugaard 1974: 516):

How to Cook Soup upon a Sausage Pin
In all countries there are old sayings that everyone knows, even the school children, and it is hard to understand that the rest of the world does not know

them too. Such a familiar expression in Danish is 'to cook soup upon a sausage pin.' It means to make a lot out of nothing; gossips and journalists are expert at preparing this dish. But what is a sausage pin? It is a small wooden peg used for closing the sausage skin after the meat has been stuffed into it; you can imagine how strong a soup one could cook on that. Well, that was the introduction; it contained information and that is always useful. Now I can begin the story.

'It was a delightful dinner last night!' exclaimed an old female mouse to an acquaintance, who had not been invited to the party ...

Andersen's text begins as follows:

SUPPE PAA EN PØLSEPIND

I

'Suppe paa en Pølsepind'

'Det var en udmærket Middag igaar!' sagde en gammel Hun-Muus til En, der ikke havde været med ved det Gilde ...

The original's opening sentence corresponds to the last one in the extract from Haugaard, whose entire opening paragraph is an addition.

DISCUSSION

Why do you think that Haugaard has made this extensive addition? Do you approve of his strategy? Do you think that a critic's reaction to it would be influenced by whether the critic was adopting a source text oriented approach or a translation oriented approach to translation?

NOTES

1. A splendid array of writings on different traditions is available in Baker (1998) and an anthology of early Chinese translation theory is in progress (Cheung and Lin, forthcoming).

2. Desiderius Erasmus (1467–1536) published a New Testament in Greek in 1516, based on several early Greek manuscript versions. Along with the Greek text, Erasmus also published his own Latin translation of it, together with annotations, a critical commentary, apologias and an introduction. He began revising this work immediately, and by 1535 had produced what he considered the definitive, fifth edition (Hermans 1998: 399).

Chapter 2

Mapping and approaching translation studies

2.1 INTRODUCTION

In Chapter 1, a number of high points in the development of the European tradition of translation studies were charted, starting with Roman writings on translation and ending with the emergence of translation studies as an academic discipline with an identifiable body of data ready to be described and researched. This Chapter introduces the mapping of this revitalised field of study carried out by Holmes ([1972] 1988) and discusses some of the approaches scholars have taken to it since around the mid-twentieth century.

2.2 MAPPING OUT A DISCIPLINE

James Stratton Holmes (1924–86) was an American poet, translator and translation scholar who spent most of his working life in the Netherlands. Holmes is widely credited with having mapped out the discipline of Translation Studies, initially with his presentation to the Third International Congress of Applied Linguistics (Copenhagen, 21–26 August 1972). What has become the standard version of his paper, the article, 'The name and nature of translation studies' (Holmes [1972] 1988), achieved its initial wider impact indirectly through the work of other scholars such as Gideon Toury, André Lefevere, Anton Popovic, Itamar Even-Zohar and Raymond van den Broeck, because it was not made widely available until 1988 when it was included in a collection of Holmes' papers edited by van den Broeck.

Holmes begins with the distinction, standardly drawn in science, between description and theory, followed by a discussion of the relationship between them: The point of translation theory is to use ([1972] 1988: 73)

> the results of descriptive translation studies, in combination with the information available from related fields and disciplines, to evolve principles, theories, and models which will serve to explain and predict what translating and translations are and will be.

Of Descriptive Translation Studies, Holmes ([1971] 1988: 72–3) says that it can be product oriented, function oriented, or process oriented.[1]

Product oriented Descriptive Translation Studies describes existing translations, and may compare existing translations of one text in one or more languages, from one or from different periods. It can contribute to a general history of translations, and it produces corpora of texts and text commentaries which can be of use to translators looking for guidance from others' solutions to translation difficulties. Scholars interested in a variety of aspects of translated texts and in various relationships between translated texts and source texts will also be helped by these corpora. Descriptions may be made ranging from what we might consider the most 'externally oriented' listings of what has been translated within a particular domain or at a particular time, to the most 'intimate' descriptions of the finest linguistic detail of the texts. Between these extremes fall for example descriptions of the treatment of various themes in translations, or of how translators have dealt with aspects of texts such as illustrations, use of foreign words (relative to the language of the source text), quotations from other texts, and so on.

Function oriented Descriptive Translation Studies is concerned with the functions of translations in their recipient cultures, and therefore incorporate a good deal of description of context. From a function oriented point of view, listings of what has been translated at various times would not culminate in a history of translation, but would focus on the effects the translations had in their contexts, on, for example, genres of original writing in the recipient culture, reading habits, the general intellectual climate, the education system, medical practice, leisure pursuits, religious practice and belief, cooking, and so on.

In Holmes' exposition, Process oriented Descriptive Translation Studies is concerned solely with what goes on in the translator's mind during the process of translation, so its outcome is translation psychology. A broader view might, however, embrace both mental processes at the subliminal and at the conscious level as well as more clearly delineated translator strategies, and also the organisational processes and procedures employed by translation service providers in the interests of quality control.

Beyond these initial divisions, Holmes draws further distinctions, presented by Toury (1995: 10) in a figure similar to Figure 2.1.

Holmes points out that any *general* translation theory, that is, a theory capable of covering all translational phenomena, would 'necessarily be highly formalized and, however the scholar may strive for economy, also highly complex' ([1972] 1988: 73). In reality, scholars tend to produce *partial* theories that focus on just one or a few of the following aspects of translation:

- the translation *medium*, that is, the medium through which a source text is processed and the translation produced. This may be simply a human translator, but it may also be a machine translation programme; or a human translator may work with a translation memory system or with a machine translation programme or terminology extraction system, or any other technical translation aid.
- the translation *area*, that is, translation between a particular language-pair or between groups of language, or between particular pairs or groups of cultures.

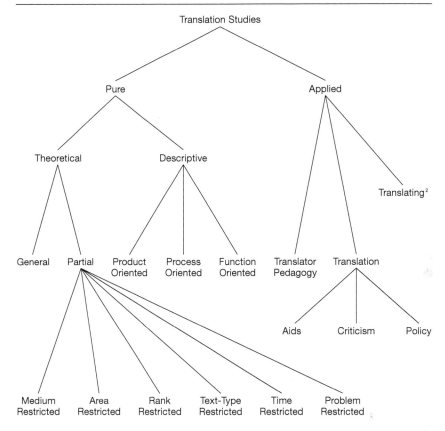

Figure 2.1   Based on Toury's (1995: 10) representation of Holmes' basic map of translation studies.

- **the ranks** at which translation may take place. For example, much discussion has centred on whether it is preferable to translate word for word (see Chapter 1 and Chapter 5, section 5.1.ii) or whether some higher linguistic rank (clause, sentence, discourse, text, sub-corpus or corpus) is the only place at which translation can truly be said to succeed.
- **translation of particular text-types** such as literary texts, sacred texts, scientific texts, and so on.
- **translation at a particular historical time**, for example, translation in the Middle Ages, translations of contemporary texts, and so on.
- **a particular problem**, for example, the issue of equivalence, or the translation of metaphor, how to deal with punctuation in translation, what to do about rhyme and alliteration, and so on.

In addition to the two main branches of translation studies, descriptive and theoretical studies, Holmes identifies the area of Applied Translation Studies (1988:

77–8), which draws on the findings of descriptive and theoretical translation studies, as well as on other disciplines, to further some practical purpose such as Translation Pedagogy (teaching about and training in translation),[3] the development of Translation Tools[4] (electronic and book-form dictionaries, grammars, word processors, translation memories, machine translation programmes, etc.), and Translation Criticism. To these, I have added *translating*, which is curiously absent from Toury's map. According to Toury (1995: 17), 'it is no concern of a scientific discipline ... to effect changes in the world of our experience' and the only practitioners who need apply translation theory are translation critics, teachers and planners. Practising translators are excluded, unless, Toury says (1995: 17–18) they 'wish to train themselves for the profession in a fully conscious way'. He argues that it is not the concern of translation theory to determine appropriate ways of translating any more than it is the concern of linguistics 'to determine appropriate ways of language use'. However, one may as well argue that a text writer may draw consciously on an understanding of linguistic effects which he or she has gained from, for example, text, discourse and genre analysis, and this seems to be a way of applying linguistics; similarly, a translator might very well base a number of translational decisions on understanding gained from translation studies of, for example, the concept and importance of translational norms, translational purposes and translational contexts, and this seems to be a way of applying translation studies.

Finally, the applied branch of the discipline has a subdivision concerned with Translation Policy, the remit of which is (1988: 78):

> defining the place and role of translators, translating and translations in society at large: such questions, for instance, as determining what works need to be translated in a given socio-cultural situation, what the social and economic position of the translator is and should be, or ... what part translating should play in the teaching and learning of foreign languages.

All of these issues and areas of translation studies may be discussed from the point of view of any of the diverse approaches to translation studies which scholars have adopted in modern times. In section 2.3 below, four particularly influential approaches will be introduced.

2.3   APPROACHES TO TRANSLATION

In this section, we shall cover four more or less distinct approaches to translation which have a direct bearing on major issues in translation studies: linguistic, descriptive, functional and cultural approaches.

To adopt an approach to a topic can mean one of at least three rather different things. It is possible to approach translation studies with a particular theory belonging to another field of study in mind, and trying to widen that theory to encompass translational phenomena within its sphere of explanation. This can benefit a theory because it is commonly accepted that the strength of a theory is partly measured in terms of the number of phenomena it can account for. Procedures of this type often (though not always) lead to the claim that translations and translational phenomena are special cases of whatever is the subject matter of the other discipline (see for example Gutt 1991). This sense of 'approach' will not be used in this book.

Secondly, it is possible to try to develop a theory of translation by applying to it a theory drawn from another discipline. This can lead to translation studies being seen as a sub-branch of the informing discipline (see for example Catford 1965), particularly when the informing discipline is linguistics. It is particularly tempting for linguists to classify translation studies as a branch of (applied) linguistics, because translations are linguistic phenomena, which look to linguists like those text-objects which are one of the standard foci of their attention. Some of the approaches discussed in this chapter are approaches in this sense: writings on translation which approach the topic with theories drawn from other disciplines in mind. It is interesting and instructive to study this type of work because it shows the multifaceted nature of translational phenomena and highlights the extent to which a theory, in this case a theory of translation, can be shaped by the background assumptions of the theorist.

Thirdly, it is possible to apply knowledge gained in another discipline to translational phenomena while still considering translational phenomena to be subject specific, and while acknowledging that translation studies has a central theoretical, conceptual and notional core of its own. When this is done, insights from the other disciplines feed into translation studies in order that its own scope may be widened and phenomena inherent in it may become better understood. This may go hand in hand with a specific interest in those aspects of translations and translational activity and phenomena which are closest in type to the foci of the informing theory; and it may be done in the hope that insights from translation theory might in turn be fed back into the informing theory. In this book, the main focus is on the language of translations, and linguistics and philosophy are viewed as sources of insights that can be used in its study; but we keep in mind the special nature of translating and translations.

2.3.i. Linguistic approaches

Catford

Among attempts at drawing on linguistic theory in setting up a theory of translation, Catford's (1965) is one of the most thorough, systematic and well informed, and it is not fortuitous that one of the major developments in translation theory in the twentieth century, Toury's (1980) re-conceptualisation of the notion of equivalence, is formulated against the background provided by Catford. Catford's theory has been the target for some of the most acerbic criticism levelled at linguistic approaches to translation from within translation studies itself, primarily because of Catford's insistence that 'the theory of translation is essentially a theory of applied linguistics' (1965: 19) but also because of Catford's foregrounding of the notion of equivalence and his advocacy of a bilingual's or translator's introspective powers as suitable sources of information about instances of equivalence (see for example Snell-Hornby 1988: 22).

The book's opening paragraph provides a rationale for subsuming translation theory under linguistic theory (1965: 1):

> Translation is an operation performed on languages: a process of substituting a text in one language for a text in another. Clearly, then, any theory of translation must draw upon a theory of language – a general linguistic theory.

The linguistic theory Catford draws on is that of Halliday (1961) – an early version of systemic functional grammar. This theory was influenced by the work of J. R. Firth (see Firth 1957), and Catford's definition of meaning derives directly from Firth. Meaning, says Catford (1965: 35), is 'the total network of relations entered into by any linguistic form'.

The relations that a linguistic form can enter into may be of two kinds (1) formal relationships (with other forms as classified by linguistic theory) and (2) contextual relationships (between the linguistic form and aspects of the context defined by linguistic theory as relevant to it). A linguistic form, therefore, has both formal and contextual meaning, though it is contextual meaning that is 'most usually understood by "meaning"' (1965: 5).

To understand what Catford means by 'formal meaning', it is necessary to consider certain aspects of the linguistic theory he is working with. This theory makes a number of abstractions from language-involving events in order to explain how meaning arises in situations. It abstracts, first, a number of 'levels' of two types: Levels of substance and levels of form. Secondly, it draws finer distinctions within these level types.

There are two levels of substance: (1) the level of medium-substance – the phonic (audible) and graphic (visible) manifestations of language, and (2) the level of situation-substance, which consists of those aspects of the situation of linguistic interaction which are relevant to what is said, for example things and events being referred to, the relationships between the interactants and the nature of the event (lecture, fax transmission, e-mail exchange ...). These substantial levels are extralinguistic: The sounds made in speaking, the marks made when writing and the environment in which the linguistic interaction takes place.

The formal levels are properly linguistic. From a linguistic point of view, phonic and graphic substance are categorised into levels of medium-*form*, namely phonology and graphology, grammar and lexis. Each form at these levels has a formal meaning (value, function, role) which arises from its relationship to all of the other forms in its relevant system or set (see below). In addition, they have contextual meaning which arises from the relationship between lexis and grammar (the lexico-grammar) on the one hand and situation substance on the other. In other words, any linguistic form has meaning derived from (1) its relationships with other linguistic forms and (2) its relationships with the non-linguistic context.

Grammar consists of closed systems while lexis consists of open sets (see further Chapter 5, section 5.2.i). A system contains a finite number of terms which are mutually exclusive; and if a new term is introduced, or if one term is discarded, then the formal meaning of each of the others will be altered. For example, the grammatical number system in English contains singular and plural. Singular has the formal meaning 'one as opposed to more than one' and plural has the formal meaning 'more than one as opposed to one'. But if a new term, 'dual', were introduced to the English number system, it would have the formal meaning 'two as opposed to one and as opposed to more than two'; singular would come to formally mean 'one as opposed to two and as opposed to more than two' and plural would come to formally mean 'three or more as opposed to two and as opposed to one'. So singular has a different formal meaning in a system that only contains singular and plural, than it has in a system that contains singular, dual and plural.

A system such as the grammatical number system is a subsystem of the entire language system and no two language systems are exactly identically organised: 'every language is ultimately *sui generis* – its categories being defined in terms of relations holding within the language itself' (Catford 1965: 27). Therefore no two languages can realise the same formal meanings; only approximate formal correspondence can be established. Formal correspondence occurs when a category in one language occupies as nearly as possible the same place in the 'economy' of its language as a category in another language occupies in the economy of its language .

The open sets of the vocabulary are the words traditionally classed as nouns, adjectives, verbs and adverbs. It is possible to add new words to these sets when required, though in fact brand new words are rarely 'manufactured' (suggested manufactured words include 'kodak' and 'gazump'; see e.g. McCarthy 1991: 320). Instead, old words often get new uses, e.g. *hardware* for computers, or combine in new ways, e.g. *software*). Formally, lexical items are dealt with in terms of collocation and lexical sets (see Chapter 6).

Collocation, a notion also derived from Firth (1957), is 'the company words keep'. For example, according to Firth (1957: 196), it is part of the meaning of 'night' that it collocates with 'dark'. The words that a term collocates with are its collocational range, and it is as unlikely that terms in two languages will have identical collocational ranges as it is that the systems of the languages will correspond exactly. So from this point of view, as well as from the point of view of formal, systemic meaning, any correspondence between terms from two languages will be approximate.

Contextual meaning is similarly language bound, since the grouping of relevant situational features that a linguistic item is related to is 'rarely the same in any two languages' and is, in any case, 'related to formal meaning' (Catford 1965: 36). Catford provides an example from the deictic systems of North East Scottish dialect and Standard English. In the Scottish dialect, a three-term system operates (*this, that, yon*), while in English there are four terms (*this, these, that, those*). Then (Catford 1965: 37; italics in the original):

if we assume that both systems cover approximately the same total contextual field we can represent the contextual meanings of the constituent terms diagrammatically as follows:

	S	P		
			this	1
I	this	these	that	2
II	that	those	yon	3
	ST. E.		N.E. Sco.	

The Standard English system is represented here as contextually two-dimensional: it embodies two degrees of deixis (I, II) and two numbers (Singular, Plural). The N.E. Scots system is unidimensional, embodying only deixis – 3 degrees this time (1, 2, 3). Numerosity is a contextually irrelevant feature of situations for the N.E. Scots system.

It is clear that if we translate from Standard English to Scots we cannot 'transfer meaning'. There is no way in which, for example, Scots *that* can be said to 'mean the same' as English *that* or *this* or *these* or *those*. On a given occasion it may refer to, or be relatable to, the same feature of the situation as one of the English deictics – but its formal and contextual *meaning* is clearly different.

In view of this, it is clear that when Catford defines translation as '*the replacement of textual material in one language (SL) by equivalent textual material in another language (TL)*' (1965: 20, italics in original), he cannot mean by 'equivalent' 'equivalent in meaning', and it is well worth bearing this in mind when attempting to evaluate criticisms of Catford's preoccupation with the notion of equivalence. Once meaning is defined as 'the total network of relations entered into by any linguistic form', it follows that meaning: 'is a property of a language. An SL text has an SL meaning, and a TL text has a TL meaning' (1965: 35).

What Catford in fact wishes to establish is what he calls 'translation equivalence': 'A central task of translation theory is that of defining the nature and conditions of translation equivalence' (1965: 21). He begins by defining 'some broad types or categories of translation in terms of the *extent*, *levels*, and *ranks* of translation'.

The extent of translation can be described as either full or partial. In a full translation 'every part of the SL text is replaced by TL material'. In a partial translation 'some parts of the SL text are left untranslated: they are simply transferred to and incorporated in the TL text' (*ibid.*). For example, the Danish SL text *Hun gav mig to kroner* might be fully translated into English as 'She gave me two crowns'; it might be partially translated into English as 'She gave me two *kroner*'. In the first case, there is a danger that an English reader would be misled into believing that what is at issue is two splendid ornaments for the head, when what is overwhelmingly likely to be meant in the Danish is two coins. This suggests that it might be best to transfer the Danish term to the translation, even though the transferred term would be unfamiliar in English and perhaps difficult to understand.[5] The resultant translation would be partial, since part of the original text appears in the translation.

The level of a translation depends on the levels of language at which translation takes place. In what is normally called 'translation' – 'total translation' in Catford's terms – each of the linguistic levels (phonology/graphology, grammar and lexis) of the Source Language are replaced by Target Language material. Then total translation can be defined as '*replacement of SL grammar and lexis by equivalent TL grammar and lexis with consequential replacement of SL phonology/graphology by (non-equivalent) TL phonology/graphology*' (1965: 22; italics in the original). It is obviously rarely the case that words which are deemed to be translation equivalents will sound the same, or be written in the same way, in two languages, and it is this necessary replacement of medium form in translation that leads to Ingarden's and Jakobson's pessimism about the possibility of translating valuable works of art, poetry in particular (see Chapter 1, section 1.4 above).

In restricted translation, replacement of Source Language textual material by equivalent Target Language textual material is carried out at only one linguistic level. For example, Catford views speaking with a foreign accent as a form of translation at the level of phonology alone and the matching of related letters of different alphabets as graphological translation (see Catford 1965: 48).

Finally, a translation may be either unbounded or rank-bound. The ranks are those of the Hallidayan (1961) rank-scale for grammar, going from the lowest rank, morpheme, through the ranks of word, group and clause up to the highest rank, sentence. In normal total translation, which is what Catford terms 'unbounded translation', equivalences shift freely up and down the rank-scale. In a rank-bound translation, equivalents are deliberately confined to one rank only, as when a word-for-word or literal (word-for-word as far as possible but conforming to the grammar of the language being translated into) translation of a Source Text is presented as an aid to understanding the difficulties involved in arriving at a Target Text, for example, or to illustrate differences between the ways in which different languages convey the same information. For example, the German expression, *Ich muss nach Hause gehen* is arguably equivalent to the English expression, 'I must go home'; but in a word-rank bound translation it might be conveyed as 'I must to house (or home) go'.

Translation equivalence, when it exists, obviously has to exist between items in texts. It is therefore an empirical, observable phenomenon. It is possible to establish which items in texts translation equivalence is likely to hold between by asking a competent bilingual which parts of a translation are altered when the Source Text is altered. For example, for the Source Text, *Er ist nach Hause gegangen*, the translation might be 'He has gone home'; if we alter the Source Text to *Sie ist nach Hause gegangen*, the translation might become 'She has gone home'. We can then hypothesise that *er* and 'he'; and *sie* and 'she' are translation equivalents in these texts. If this experiment is repeated in sufficient numbers of text instances, it is possible to establish the statistical likelihood of these pairs functioning as translation equivalents in texts of a certain type. So extensive textual observation can lead to the formulation of statements of the statistical probability that item x in the Source Language will be appropriately translated by item y in the Target Language. Rules derived from such probabilities can be fed into machine translation programmes and given as guidance for human translators and lexicographers. With the advent of large, machine readable corpora of texts and their translations, statements of this form have become far more precise and far sounder, empirically, than they could be when Catford wrote, and corpora of source texts and translations are used extensively in translation pedagogy (see for example Zanettin, Bernardini and Stewart (eds) 2003) and in bilingual lexicography (see for example Viberg 1996).

The condition for the occurrence of translation equivalence is, according to Catford (1965: 49), that the relevant Source and Target Language items must be '*interchangeable in a given situation*' (italics in the original); and since 'the sentence is the grammatical unit most directly related to speech-function within a situation', 'translation equivalence can nearly always be established at sentence-rank'. However, even if a pair of textual items are interchangeable in a given situation, it is rarely the case that both pair members will be relatable to all of the same features of the situation. In light of this, Catford assumes that (1965: 49):

> the greater the number of situational features common to the contextual meanings of both SL and TL text, the 'better' the translation. The aim in total translation must therefore be to select TL equivalents not with 'the same meaning' as the SL items, but with the greatest possible overlap of situational range.

Situation substance may be shared between two languages, even if the cultures in which the languages operate are different: People, events and things, and aspects of these, can be found in all cultures. So in spite of cultural differences, it is likely that some common ground will exist, and textual translation equivalents can be established in virtue of such common ground. On the other hand, it is unlikely that all of the ground will be common, so to speak.

For each language and each culture, certain situational features are relevant to the selection of a particular textual item in text making. Some of these features will be 'linguistically relevant' in the sense that the language system demands that they be taken into account. For example, in Russian, the sex of a speaker is relevant to the choice of past tense verb form in the first person; in English it is not. The Russian translation equivalent of 'I've arrived' will depend on the sex of the speaker, simply because the language system makes this feature relevant. Because the English language system does not make the speaker's sex relevant, however, 'I've arrived' will be functionally equivalent of both the feminine and the masculine Russian expression. In principle, this might cause problems for a translator translating from English into Russian, if faced with the sentence 'I've arrived'. In practice, however, the co-text or context will almost always make it clear whether the speaker is male or female.

Functionally relevant features of the situation are features 'relevant to the communicative function of the text in that situation' and (1965: 94):

> For translation equivalence to occur ... both SL and TL text must be relatable to the functionally relevant features of the situation. A decision, in any particular case, as to what is *functionally* relevant in this sense must in our present state of knowledge remain to some extent a matter of opinion. The total co-text will

supply information which the translator will use in coming to a decision, but it is difficult to define functional relevance in general terms.

What is possible, however, is to discuss untranslatability in terms of functional relevance: 'Translation fails – or untranslatability occurs – when it is impossible to build functionally relevant features of the situation into the contextual meaning of the TL text' (1965: 94). Such untranslatability may, apparently, be of two kinds: (i) *linguistic untranslatability* and (ii) *cultural untranslatability*. But Catford argues toward a position according to which untranslatability, even when apparently cultural, can be seen to be always linguistic: He reduces cultural factors to linguistic factors (see below).

Linguistic untranslatability occurs when a formal feature of the Source Language is functionally relevant in the Source Text, and the Target Language has no formally corresponding feature. Catford singles out puns which rely on ambiguity, but the difficulty might be thought to pertain to any text which foregrounds its language, as Jakobson and Ingarden insist (see Chapter 1, section 4). In addition, translation difficulties arise when the Target Language demands that a selection, such as that for sex of speaker, be made in the Target Text, but the Source Text does not contain the required information, as mentioned above in connection with the example of a translation into Russian of 'I've arrived'.

The apparently different problem of cultural untranslatability arises 'when a situational feature, functionally relevant for the SL text, is completely *absent* from the culture of which the TL is a part' (1965: 99). Dagut (1981: 64) refers to such cases as 'extralinguistic voids'. For example, there is in Japanese a word, *yukata*, which denotes a 'loose robe bound by a sash, worn by either men or women, supplied to guests in a Japanese inn or hotel, worn in the evening indoors or out of doors in street or café, or in bed ...' (1965: 100). Clearly there is no identical phenomenon in mainstream British or American society; although English words such as 'dressing gown', 'bath robe' and 'house-coat' cover part of the total range of situational features covered by *yukata*, no single term covers them all. However, Catford argues that such apparent cultural untranslatability can always be reduced to linguistic untranslatability, via the notion of collocation, and that it is therefore unnecessary to draw the distinction between it and linguistic untranslatability. For the item, *yukata*, for example, it can be argued that whichever approximate English translation equivalent we might choose would produce some unusual collocational patterns in an English text (1965: 101):

> Thus, in the Japanese text *hoteru-no yukata*, the item *hoteru-no* has the straight-forward English translation equivalent *hotel's* or *hotel* (as modifier); but any possible English near-equivalent of *yukata* would collocate strangely with *hotel* – i.e. *hotel dressing-gown, hotel bath-robe, hotel nightgown*, etc. are all low probability collocations in English – though the original Japanese collocation is a normal, or high-probability one.

Clearly, a text like 'After his bath he enveloped his still-glowing body in the simple hotel *bath-robe* and went out to join his friends in the café down the street' (Catford

1965: 102) would read strangely, and Catford's suggestion is that we can describe its strange effect as collocational shock rather than as cultural shock. We are simply not used to seeing items like *hotel, bath-robe, went out to*, and *café* in co-occurrence. Catford thinks that it is desirable to limit untranslatability to linguistic untranslatability since this would increase the power of translation theory and enlarge the horizon of machine translation. A language is more easily and precisely describable than a culture is, and it is easier to provide a machine with information about collocations than about the totality of items available in a culture.

Nida

For Catford, then, translation equivalence occurs when a Source Text and a Target Text or item both relate to those features of the situation in which the texts are used which are relevant to the communicative function of the text in that situation. Catford deals in detail mainly with translation at ranks up to sentence, which is where the rank scale for grammar ends. He does not provide extensive discussion of larger texts, or of reader reactions to texts, and when he does, it happens after the initial chapters dealing with definitions and the outline of the scope of translation theory. This is of course in accord with his belief that translation equivalence can almost always be established at sentence rank because the sentence is the linguistic unit most directly related to a speech action in a situation, even if shifts between the grammatical ranks below sentence may occur in the process. Catford's starting point is relationships between languages and his units of measure remain essentially linguistic units throughout.

In contrast, Nida's fundamental measure of translation equivalence is reader response. As his (1964) subtitle, 'With Special Reference to Principles and Procedures Involved in Bible Translating' implies, his main concern is with texts in the case of which the reader's response may be of paramount importance. In Bible translation, the over-riding aim often is to create conditions favourable for the conversion of the reader to Christianity, and this requires the reader to be able to respond to the text in a very deep, emotional, personal way. One of the few other text types that may elicit this type of response is the literary text, and Nida's point of departure is in fact adverse reactions to literary translations. The problem for the translator, according to Nida, is that (1964: 2): 'the translator is under constant pressure from the conflict between form and meaning. If he attempts to approximate the stylistic qualities of the original, he is likely to sacrifice much of the meaning, while strict adherence to the literal content usually results in considerable loss of the stylistic flavour'.

Nida adopts Jakobson's (1959: 233) tripartite division of translation into intralingual, intersemiotic and interlingual translation. By intralingual translation is meant (Nida 1964: 3–4) 'rewording something within the same language', that is, paraphrase. By intersemiotic translation is meant 'the transference of a message from one kind of symbolic system to another', as in the case of messages sent by flag in the army. But it is interlingual translation which is normally meant by 'translation': 'the interpretation of the verbal signs of one language by means of the verbal signs of another'. Nida takes very seriously, in this definition, the idea of interpretation, the art of which, he agrees with Isenberg (1953: 234; Nida 1964: 5), 'has by far outstripped the theory'. It is Nida's hope that theory might be helped to catch up if account is taken of (1964: 5) 'numerous insights which have become increasingly significant in a number of related fields'. He mentions anthropological, structuralist and generative linguistics, anthropology, semantics, the philosophy of language, psychology, psychiatry, philology and the theory of Biblical interpretation, and is obviously vastly more interdisciplinary that Catford. The reason his work is nevertheless discussed here under the heading, Linguistic Approaches, is that, his interdisciplinary awareness and interests notwithstanding, he declares his 'fundamental thrust' to be (1964: 8) 'linguistic, as it must be in any descriptive analysis of the relationship between corresponding messages in different languages'.

Whereas, as we saw above, Catford (1965) bases his theory of translation firmly on an early version of Halliday's systemic grammar (Halliday 1961), Nida takes as his own starting point Chomsky's generative view of language which he considers (1964: 9):

> particularly important for a translator, for in translating from one language into another he must go beyond mere comparison of corresponding structures and attempt to describe the mechanisms by which the total message is decoded, transferred, and transformed into the structures of another language.

Nida also operates with a different theory of meaning than Catford's, who, as we saw above, uses Firth's definition of meaning as the total set of relationships entered into by any linguistic item, including formal and functional relationships. Instead, Nida divides meaning into linguistic, referential and emotive meaning. Of these, linguistic meaning 'structurally precedes referential and emotive meanings, which may be said to "begin where linguistic meaning leaves off"' (1964: 57). By linguistic meaning Nida means essentially what Catford means by formal meaning. By referential meaning he means essentially what Catford covers by the notion of functional meaning: 'Referential meanings refer primarily to the cultural context identified in the utterance'. Emotive meaning, which Nida discusses explicitly whereas Catford leaves it implicit, concerns 'the responses of the participants in the communicative act' (Nida 1964: 70).

Nida's list of components of the communicative act is strongly reminiscent of Jakobson's enumeration of the factors involved in verbal communication (1960/ 1987: 66 see section Chapter 1, Section 1.4 above). According to Nida (1964: 120), the communicative act consists of (1) the subject matter, (2) the participants, (3) the linguistic act, (4) the code used and (5) the message, that is 'the particular way in which the subject matter is encoded into specific symbols and arrangements', and the participants and the message are especially important, since the many different types of translation that exist 'can generally be accounted for by three basic factors in translating: (1) the nature of the message, (2) the purpose or purposes of the author and, by proxy, of the translator, and (3) the type of audience' (1964: 156).

Messages 'differ primarily in the degree to which content or form is the dominant consideration' (1964: 156), although content and form can never be completely divorced from one another.

The translator's purpose may be the same as the source text author's, but not necessarily so: the translator may want to give the audience an insight into an alien society; may want to provide information purely and simply about the subject matter of the source text, or information about the form of the source text, or both; may want to accomplish these purposes with the further aim of eliciting a particular kind of response in the audience; may want the audience to wish to behave in a certain way after reading the target text, and so on (1964: 157–8). In emphasising these potential purposes on the part of the translator and the possibility (or even probability) that these may differ radically from the purposes the author hoped the target text would fulfil, or that it did in fact fulfil in its own cultural context, Nida foreshadows later developments in translation theory, in particular in Germany, which we shall cover in the section below on functional approaches to translation.

Whatever the translator's aim – ranging from mere intelligibility to full equivalence with the source text – they have to consider the intended audience, for 'audiences differ both in decoding abilities and in potential interest' (1964: 158). At this point, Nida draws his famous distinction between formal and dynamic equivalence: Total equivalence, he asserts, is never possible in translation, so 'one must seek to find the closest possible equivalent. However, there are fundamentally two different types of equivalence: one which may be called formal and another which is primarily dynamic' (1964: 159). Of these, he has the following to say (*ibid.*):

> Formal equivalence focuses attention on the message itself, in both form and content. In such a translation one is concerned with such correspondences as poetry to poetry, sentence to sentence, and concept to concept.
>
> Viewed from this formal orientation one is concerned that the message in the receptor language should match as closely as possible the different elements in the source language. This means, for example, that the message in the receptor culture is constantly compared with the message in the source culture to determine standards of accuracy and correctness …
>
> In contrast, a translation that attempts to produce a dynamic rather than a formal equivalence is based upon 'the principle of equivalent effect' (Rieu and Phillips 1954). In such a translation one is not so concerned with matching the receptor-language message with the source-language message, but with the dynamic relationship … that the relationship between receptor and message should be substantially the same as that which existed between the original receptors and the message.
>
> A translation of dynamic equivalence aims at complete naturalness of expression, and tries to relate the receptor to modes of behavior relevant within the context of his own culture; it does not insist that he understand the cultural patterns of the source-language context in order to comprehend the message.

However, 'if a translation is to meet the four basic requirements of (1) making sense,

(2) conveying the spirit and manner of the original, (3) having a natural and easy form of expression, and (4) producing a similar response, it is obvious that at certain points the conflict between content and form (or meaning and manner) will be acute, and that one or the other must give way' (1964: 164).

Nida (1964: 182; cf. Gutt 1991) claims that 'Other things being equal, the efficiency of a translation can be judged in terms of the maximal reception for the minimal effort of decoding'. Since linguistic forms and cultural backgrounds are diverse, a translation very easily becomes overloaded and thus inefficient in terms of decoding effort. The general efficiency of the communication process is one of three criteria which Nida considers basic to the evaluation of all translating. The other two are comprehension of intent and equivalence of response.

Comprehension of intent depends on 'the accuracy with which the meaning of the source-language message is represented in the translation'. This criterion can be applied either with the source culture in mind, in a formal-equivalence translation, or with the receptor culture in mind, in a dynamic-equivalence translation. Then (1964: 182–3):

> In a F-E translation, the comprehension of intent must be judged essentially in terms of the context in which the communication was first uttered; in a D-E translation this intent must be understood in terms of the receptor culture. The extent to which intent can be interpreted in a cultural context other than the one in which the message was first given is directly proportional to the universality of the message.

To a translator who believes in the universality of the Biblical message, this reads like good news, since, from this perspective, Bible translation stands a good chance of success.

The third criterion of translation quality assessment, equivalence of response, is also either source culture oriented, 'in which case the receptor must understand the basis of the original response' or receptor culture oriented, 'in which case the receptor makes a corresponding response within a different cultural context'; and 'the extent to which the responses are similar depends upon the cultural distance between the two communication contexts' (1964: 183). The distinctions between intent and response, and source and receptor contexts are not absolute and relate principally to focus of attention.

The three criteria interact, since 'a translation which is exceedingly literal [a Formal Equivalence or F-E translation] contains numerous awkward expressions, and is hence 'overloaded' as far as the prospective receptors are concerned' (1964: 183–4). On the other hand, 'a D-E translation may likewise fail to come up to a valid standard, if in the translator's concern for the response of the receptors he has been unfaithful to the content of the original message'. On the whole, though, Nida favours Dynamic Equivalence translation since the overload which results from Formal Equivalence translation easily becomes so great that the translation becomes quite incomprehensible. The worst that can happen in Dynamic Equivalence translating is that translators may conceal their 'slanting' (1964: 184). In Nida and

Taber (1969), dynamic equivalence is renamed 'functional equivalence', but its characteristics remain fundamentally the same.

2.3.ii Descriptive approaches

Descriptive approaches to translation emphasise the mutual dependence in a research programme of its descriptive and its theoretical branch – on the one hand, the need to test any theory against data and, on the other, the need for theory to inform our approach to data and to explain them (see Chapter 1, Sections 1 and 5 and Toury 1995: 1). Above (section 1), we saw a mapping of the various branches of descriptive translation studies. Here, we shall look at Toury's arguments in favour of a target text oriented descriptive approach to translation studies, and at its relationship to the notion of norms. We shall begin by relating Toury's approach to the work of Catford and Nida.

As we saw, for Catford, translation equivalence occurs when a source text (item) and a target text (item) relate to the same functionally relevant features of situation, so justifying a claim for equivalence between an item in the source text and an item in the target text would involve testing whether it is possible to relate both the source text and the target text to the same features. But Catford also points out that, as Toury formulates it (1981: 27):

> We have to distinguish between, on the one hand, translation equivalence as an empirical phenomenon, discovered by comparing SL and TL texts; and, on the other hand, the underlying conditions, or justification, of translation equivalence.

In Toury's work, this distinction is taken especially seriously and translation equivalence as an empirical phenomenon is the primary focus of attention.

For Nida, the underlying conditions for translation equivalence are not described as functionally relevant features of the situation surrounding the texts, but rather in terms of the projected function and reception of the texts, determined at least in part by features of the recipients' socio-psychological make-up. Nida insists that a translator may be oriented more towards either the source culture, where the text to be translated originates, or more towards the target culture, which is to be the home of the translation.

In Toury's work, a related, though certainly not identical, distinction is drawn between description which is source text oriented and description which is oriented towards the target text. In addition, Toury points out that not all features of texts are necessarily equally relevant and that their place in the 'hierarchy of relevance' (1980: 38) may not be the same from the points of view of both the target text and the source text. He maintains that most translation theories to date 'are ST-oriented and, more often than not, even SL-oriented' (1980: 35), which makes them:

> directive and normative in nature. They consider translation from the point of view of its being a reconstruction – in general a maximal (or at least optimal) reconstruction – of ST (i.e., the formalization of ST's systemic relationships),

or even of SL, in TL, in such a way and to such an extent that TT and ST are interchangeable according to some preconceived definition of this inter-changeability.

This primary concentration on the source text and source language, he argues, makes such theories 'unable to supply a sound starting point and framework for a descriptive study of actual translations'. In source text oriented theories of translation equivalence, a postulate is made regarding the conditions which an item must fulfil in order to be equivalent to another. These conditions can never be completely complied with by any item. Therefore no pairs of items can be proper translation equivalents, and therefore no translation can be adequate, that is, no translation is a proper translation as defined by the theory. It is difficult to see how such an approach can deal satisfactorily with those existing texts which are in fact *regarded* as translations and which in practice *function* as such. The theory becomes a theory without any objects and a huge gulf comes to exist between theory and actuality.

According to Toury, the way out of this dilemma is to regard translations as empirical phenomena which occupy a certain position in the literary polysystem[6] of the culture in which they exist. Put simply, what a culture regards as a translation ought in principle and at least initially in any enquiry[7] to be accepted as such. Description can then get under way. It will begin at the target text end of the translational relationship, but will work its way from there to the source text to establish translation equivalence by means of a mapping of target text segments onto source text segments (Toury 1995: 37). The relationships of translation equivalence thus established are no longer ideal, unobtainable relationships: 'from TT's point of view, equivalence is not a postulated requirement, but an empirical fact, like TT itself: the *actual* relationships obtaining between TT and ST' (Toury 1980a: 39; italics in the original).

For every (sanctionable) TT-ST item pair there will, then, be one instantiation of translation equivalence. But for every such pair, other possible equivalence relation-ships exist, given the languages involved, the text typologies available in the cultures involved, the relationships between the cultures, and so on (1980: 46). Therefore, it is necessary to explain the selection of one or other of these potential equivalence relationships rather than another, and in the course of arriving at this explanation, Toury moves from Catford's (1965: 50) general definition of translation equivalence:

> *translation equivalence occurs when an SL and a TL text or item are relatable to (at least some of) the same features of substance* (italics in the original)

to a relativised definition (Toury 1980a: 37):

> Translation equivalence occurs when a SL and a TL text (or item) are relatable to (at least some of) the same relevant features.

Here, the added notion of relevance is to be understood as always 'relevant *for* something' or 'relevant *from* a certain point of view'; and it should be born in mind that not every feature is as relevant as every other: There are '*hierarchies of relevance*, rather than ... absolute relevance' (1980: 38). The question to be asked of a pair of TT-ST texts is then not whether they are equivalent, but '*what type* and *degree* of translation equivalence they reveal' (1980: 47).

Descriptions of these relationships have as one important aim the formulation, within the theoretical branch of the discipline, of 'a series of coherent *laws* which would state the inherent relations between all the variables found to be relevant to translation' (Toury 1995: 16). These 'laws' are not, of course, to be understood as legislative, prescriptive statements about how to translate; rather, they are like those explanations which scientists posit for phenomena which they observe in the physical or psychological worlds we inhabit: The 'laws of nature', physical 'laws', and so on. And, like those, the 'laws' of translation studies are subject to regular scrutiny and re-writing in light of further observation (description). The laws differ from the observable pairs of translation equivalents in being non-observable phenomena posited as explanations for the observables (Toury 1995: 36), and the most famous name given to them by Toury is 'norms'. Translation norms, in turn, derive from another unobservable, namely the concept of translation which operates in a given culture (Toury 1995: 37). These unobservables are (re)-constructable only on the basis of observation of the empirical phenomena which are translations and their source texts. Just as the laws of nature receive formulations by physicists, translational norms can also become verbalised. However (Toury 1999: 15):

> it is important to bear in mind that there is no identity between the norms as the guidelines, as which they act, and any formulation given to them in language. Verbalisations obviously reflect awareness of the existence of norms and their significance. However, they always embody other interests too, particularly a desire to control behaviour – i.e. dictate norms ... or account for them in a conscious, systematic way (e.g. by scholars). Normative formulations may, therefore, serve as a source of data on norm-governed behaviour, and hence on underlying norms as such, but they may do so only indirectly: if one wishes to expose the bare norms, any given formulation will have to be stripped of the alien interests it has accumulated.

The concept of norms in translation studies has a great deal in common with the concept of maxims in Grice's theory of conversational implicature (Grice 1975): they guide behaviour implicitly and may be identified and described by scholars only on the basis of analyses of (the products of) behaviour (cf. Toury 1999: 16). They are subject to change over time, and because they exist within a larger system of cultural norms and conventions, establishing a set of translation norms for a given period, and perhaps comparing them with others, can be instructive of other aspects of the culture surrounding the translations in question. There may be different sets of norms within one culture at a given time and sometimes these compete with one another. Such competing sets may be representative of the current mainstream, or remnants of an older set and an emergent set (Toury 1999: 27–8), or they may represent the *status quo* acceptable to the relevant establishment, on the one hand,

and a rebellious group on the other: Like all textual production in a culture, translation may be used in the service of ideology.

2.3.iii Functional approaches

At around the same time as Toury was formulating his target oriented approach to the *description* of translations, a number of scholars working mainly in German speaking countries, but including also Justa Holz-Mänttäri (1984) in Finland, began to formulate an approach to the *production* of translations which has become known as 'Skopos theory' (Vermeer 1978/1983). *Skopos* is Greek for 'purpose', and Skopos theory roots itself in a theory of human action which holds that it, including the action of translating, is determined by its purpose (see Schäffner, 1998: 236). However, scholars working in the tradition are also in the habit of citing linguistic functionalists among their theoretical forebears, so the term 'functional' is frequently used of their work. For example Reiss (2000 [1971]: 25–6) quotes Bühler's (1933) representative, expressive and appellative functions and suggests that texts can be classified into types according to which of these functions they prioritise: Informative, content-focused texts prioritise the representative function; expressive, form-fucussed texts prioritise the expressive function and appeal-focused, operative texts prioritise the appellative function. Nord (1995), similarly, makes use of Bühler's functions, though she adds a few identified during the course of her analysis of a corpus of titles. One of these is Malinowski's phatic function and the others are a distinctive function and a metatextual function. Similarly Reiss and Vermeer (1984/1991: 45) employ Bühler's notion of language functions to derive a typology of text genres, and they use the German terms *Funktionskonstanz* and *Funktionsänderung* ('constancy of function' and 'change of function', respectively) to refer to cases where the function of the target text and source text are the same or different, respectively. According to Schäffner (1998: 236–7) they use the terms 'skopos', 'function' and 'purpose' interchangeably.

The main tenet of Skopos theory is that the purpose which the initiator of the translation act (for example the translator's client) specifies for the target text (sometimes referred to in this approach as the 'translatum' (Vermeer 1979: 174) or 'translat' (Reiss and Vermeer 1984/1991: 2)) should be the overriding determinant of it. This purpose is more important in shaping the target text than the form and content of the source text. If, for example, in the case of the translation of advertising material, the purpose of the target text is to sell the goods being advertised, then it is obviously more important to produce a text which is likely to make the product seem appealing to the projected audience than it is to produce a text which replicates the source text as closely as the target language allows. For this to be possible, the target text must 'cohere' (see further Chapter 7, section 7.2.iii on coherence) with the background knowledge and situation of the projected audience, which may be somewhat different from that of the audience for the source text. In order to remain a translation, however (as opposed to an original creation based loosely on the source text), some relationship must also remain between it and the source text (though this relationship is somewhat loosely defined).

In the development of this approach by Reiss and Vermeer (1984/1991), a text is considered to be its author's offer of information (*Informationsangebot* in German) to its projected recipient. A translation, then, is a second order offer of information: It offers information to its recipient about the offer of information made by the source text author to the intended recipient of the source text. It may do this selectively, however, depending on its skopos, and the skopos is typically determined by the perceived needs and expectations of the target text recipients (cf. Nida 1964 discussed in section 2.3.i above). Obviously, the skopos may be to inform the target text recipient exactly what the source text was like, so optimal content-equivalence between source and target texts is not ruled out by this approach, only relegated to one among a gamut of possible purposes a translator may have in mind for his or her translation.

2.3.iv   Cultural approaches

Susan Bassnett (1998: 110) identifies the mid-1980s as the time when translation studies took a particularly 'cultural turn' (Bassnett and Lefevere 1991/1995). It is a commonplace in translation studies that translators need to be well versed not only in their languages but also in the cultures within which the languages are spoken; that is, almost everybody acknowledges the importance of cultural understanding to translators' activities, because almost everybody agrees that aspects of culture *shape* aspects of texts, are *reflected* in aspects of texts and are also in turn *affected* by texts. By a cultural approach to translation studies, however, is meant an approach which especially foregrounds these aspects of translational activity. Typically informed by post-structuralist theories of discourse which emphasise the role of language in making and maintaining meanings, these approaches often highlight the relationship between translation and ideology, i.e. the role played by translation in maintaining, questioning or altering, through specific translation practices, relationships of domination of certain cultural groups by others. So although it is possible to define culture very broadly, as the entire way of life of a people, including their patterns of thinking and behaving, their values and beliefs, their codes of conduct, the political, economical and commercial arrangements under which they live, etc. (Hatch 1985: 178), culturally oriented debates within translation studies have tended to fall mainly within two major, carefully defined areas, Post-colonial Translation Studies (as represented by e.g. Bassnett and Trivedi 1999) and gender oriented Translation Studies (as represented by e.g. Simon 1996). In addition, there are more loosely composed, general areas of interest in questions of translation and minorities and translation and politics including for example translating for children, translating gay literature (see e.g. Harvey 1998; Keenaghan 1998) translation and political censorship (see e.g. Craig 1998) and translation into and out of minority languages (see e.g. Millán-Varela 1997). However, many writers on translation studies also focus on specific difficulties involved in translating highly culture specific aspects of texts such as references to, for example, festivals and practices, and in the translation of culturally loaded terms, metaphors and proverbs (see for example Leppihalme 1997).

2.4 PRACTICE AND DISCUSSION

Practice: which approach?

Below is a collection of pairs of translations of extracts from Hans Christian Andersen's stories. In the case of each pair, the first pair part is a translation intended to stay as close to the original as possible; the second pair part is Mary Howitt's translation, which was the first translation made into English (Howitt 1846). Compare the pairs carefully and see if you can categorise the differences between them.

Pair 1
From *Ole Lukøie* (1842):
… and they all talked about themselves, except the spittoon, which stood silent, cross that they could be so vain as to only talk about themselves and only think about themselves and have no thought for it, even though it stood so humbly in the corner and let itself be spat on.

Howitt (1846), *Olé Luckoiè* (4–5):
Everything talked except the old door mat, which lay silent, and was vexed that they should be all so full of vanity as to talk of nothing but themselves, and think only about themselves, and never have one thought for it which lay so modestly in a corner and let itself be trodden upon.

Pair 2
From *Paradisets Have* (1838):
Half thawed snow with moss, sharp stones and skeletons of walruses and polar bears lay there, they looked like giants' arms and legs, with mouldy greenness … I blew at the fog a little so you could see the shed: it was a house made of a wreck and covered with walrus-skin; the meaty side was turned outwards, it was full of red and green … Furthest down the walruses were writhing about like live intestines or gigantic maggots with swines' heads and ell-long teeth!

Howitt (1846), 'The Garden of Paradise' (69–70):
Half covered with dwarfish mosses, sharp stones and leg-bones of walruses and ice-bears lie scattered about, looking like the arms and legs of giants … I blew the mist aside a little, that one might see the erection there; it was a house, built of pieces of wrecks, covered with the skin of the walrus, the fleshy side turned outwards … Down below tumbled about the walruses, like gigantic ascarides, with pigs' heads and teeth an ell long!'

Pair 3

From *Storkene* (1839):

'Now we'll be revenged!' they said.

'To be sure' said the mother stork. 'My plan is just right! I know where the pond is, where all the little human children lie until the stork comes to take them to their parents. The pretty little children sleep and dream more wonderfully than they'll ever dream again. All parents would like to have such a little child, and all children would like a sister or brother. Now we'll fly to the pond, fetch one for each of the children who haven't sung the nasty song and made fun of the storks, for those children will have none at all!'

But the one who started the singing, the nasty horrible boy!' the young storks screeched, 'what shall we do with him?'

'In the pond lies a little dead child, it has dreamt itself to death, we will take it to him, then he'll cry because we have brought him a dead little brother; but the good boy, I'm sure you haven't forgotten him, the one who said: it is a shame to make fun of the animals! We'll take him both a brother and a sister, and as that boy was called Peter, you'll all be called Peter too!'

And it happened as she said, so all the storks were called Peter, and they still are.

Howitt (1846), 'The storks' (126–7):

'Now let's have revenge,' said they.

'Leave off talking of revenge,' said the mother. 'Listen to me, which is a great deal better. Do not you remember the good little boy who said, when the others sung, "that it was a sin to make fun of the storks"; let us reward him, that is better than having revenge.'

'Yes, let us reward him,' said the storks.

'He shall have, next summer, a nice little sister, such a beautiful little sister as never was seen! Will not that be a reward for him?' said the mother.

'It will;' said the young ones, 'a sweet little sister he shall have!'

'And as he is called Peter,' continued the mother, 'so shall you also be called Peter altogether.'

And that which she said was done. The little boy had the loveliest of little sisters next year; and, from that time, all the storks in Denmark were called Peter; and so are they to this day.

Pair 4

From *Tommelise* (1835):

There was once a woman who would like to have a little tiny child, but she had no idea where she could get one from; then she went to see an old witch and said to her: 'I would so very much like to have a little child, won't you please tell me where I can get one from?'

'Yes, we'll get around that all right!' said the witch. 'There's a corn of barley, it is not at all the kind that grows on the farmer's field or that the chickens are given to eat, put it in a flower pot, and wait and see what'll happen!'

Howitt (1846), 'Tommelise' (33):
Once upon a time, a beggar woman went to the house of a poor peasant, and asked for something to eat. The peasant's wife gave her some bread and milk. When she had eaten it, she took a barley-corn out of her pocket, and said – 'This will I give thee; set it in a flower pot, and see what will come out of it.'

Pair 5
From *Paradisets Have* (1838):
The most beautiful girls, floating and slender, dressed in waving gauze so you could see their lovely limbs, floated in dances

Howitt (1846), 'The Garden of Paradise' (86):
The most beautiful maidens floated in the dance

Pair 6
From *Paradisets Have* (1838):
Then the fairy beckoned and called lovingly: 'follow me! follow me!' and he rushed towards her, forgot his promise, forgot it already on the first evening, and she beckoned and smiled. The scent, the spicy scent all around, grew stronger, the harps intoned far more beautifully, and it was as if the millions of smiling faces in the hall where the tree grew nodded, singing: 'Everything ought to be known to us! Humanity is master of the earth.' And they were no longer tears of blood that were dripping from the leaves of the tree of knowledge, they were red, fiery stars, it seemed to him. 'Follow me, follow me!' sounded the quivering notes, and with every step the prince's cheeks burned hotter, his blood moved more strongly. 'I must!' he said, 'it isn't a sin after all, it cannot be! why not follow beauty and happiness! I want to see her sleeping! Nothing is thereby lost, as long as I don't kiss her, and I'm not going to do that, I am strong, my will is firm!'
And the fairy cast off her brilliant clothes, and a moment later she was hidden within.
'I haven't sinned yet!' said the prince, 'and I won't;' and then he drew back the branches; there she was, already asleep, lovely as only the fairy in the garden of Paradise can be; she smiled in her dream, he bent down over her and saw the tears quiver between her eye lashes!
'Are you crying for me?' he whispered, 'don't cry beautiful woman! Only now do I comprehend the happiness of paradise, it is streaming through my blood, through my thoughts, I feel the cherub's power and eternal life within my earthly body, let eternal night fall upon me, a minute like this brings riches enough!' and he kissed the tear away from her eye, his mouth touched hers.

Howitt (1846), 'The Garden of Paradise' (87–8):
Then beckoned the Fairy, and said, 'Follow, follow me!'
He started towards her – he forgot his promise – forgot it all the first evening!

'Follow, follow me!' alone sounded in his heart. He paused not – he hastened after her.

'I will,' said he; 'there is really no sin in it! Why should I not do so? I will see her! There is nothing lost if I only do not kiss her, and that I will not do – for I have a firm will!'

The Fairy put aside the green depending branches of the Tree of Knowledge, and the next moment was hidden from sight.

'I have not sinned,' said the prince, 'and I will not!' He also put aside the green, depending branches of the Tree of Knowledge, and there sat the Fairy with her hands clasped, and the tears on her dark eyelashes!

'Weep not for me!' said he passionately. 'There can be no sin in what I have done; weep not!' and he kissed away her tears, and his lips touched hers!

DISCUSSION

In discovering the differences between the translations, you were approaching them descriptively. Which of the approaches discussed in Section 2 might best explain the differences between the source text (which the first pair parts reproduces closely) and Mary Howitt's target texts?

NOTES

1. My exposition of Holmes is not wholly faithful in what follows because some of his lower-level divisions and categories do not seem to me to be as helpful as they might be. Compare, therefore, the account given here to Holmes' own or to Toury's (1995).

2. Curiously, neither Holmes nor Toury appear to consider that translating as such can be an application of translation studies. Of course, one might argue that indeed it is not, anymore than text creation is applied linguistics. However, just as a first-writer may draw consciously on an understanding of linguistic effects gained from, for example, text, discourse and genre analysis, a translator might very well base a number of translational decisions on understanding gained from translation studies – of, for example, the concept and importance of translational norms, translational purposes and translational context.

3. Holmes wants to restrict the pedagogical branch of the subject to the training of translators; but there is no reason why the many postgraduate courses aimed less at training people *to do* than at teaching people *about* translation (some courses, of course, do both) should not be included.

4. Holmes mentions lexicographical and terminological aids and grammars. Latterly, the average translator's tool-box has grown vastly to include computers, modems, machine translation programmes, translation memories, corpora, the internet, etc.

5. Another possibility would obviously be to calculate the value of the coinage and convert it into an English coin of equivalent value, though the success of this strategy would depend heavily on the setting for the text or text part: If the setting is clearly Danish, it might be odd to be reading about British money.

6. Toury's discussion is focused on literary texts, but what he says is true of any text genre. Polysystem theory was developed by the Russian Formalists, and entered translation studies in the work of Itamar Even-Zohar (1971; 1978; 1990). The theory views the entire pool of texts that exists in a culture as a system in which numerous subsystems (genres) exist, interrelate and derive value and status from their relationships with one another. So the value and status of a given genre derives from its position within the polysystem. Similarly, any given text within one of these systems achieves its value and status from its interrelationships with the other texts in its system.

7. The inquiry will then sometimes reveal that the text has no source text, but has been passed off as a translation by a writer for his or her own purposes – for example to lend the text a certain aura, mystique, authority or status of e.g. antiquity, a lost people, or an admired foreign culture. Such texts are known as 'pseudotranslations' (Toury 1980a: 48), and a particularly famous example is James Macpherson's (1783) *Ossian*.

Chapter 3

Translation and language

3.1 INTRODUCTION

In Chapters 1 and 2, the scope of translation theory and of translation studies was outlined in rather broad terms. This chapter concerns two issues that affect individual theorists' more detailed understanding of the nature of translation. The first is the issue of linguistic, cultural or ontological relativism, which has a strong bearing on how meaning might most helpfully be conceived of within translation theory. The second is the issue of the relationship between linguistic theory – the science of language – and translation theory. Once these issues have been discussed, the way is prepared to move on to the more practical, applied chapters of the book.

3.2 LANGUAGE, CULTURE AND UNDERSTANDING

Most linguists, philosophers and social scientists agree that there are close links between the language a person speaks, the person's culture and the person's understanding of the world around them. Language is one of the most important carriers of information during a person's socialisation and maturation process; a great deal of our practical, historical, cultural and social knowledge is acquired by means of language, and the world around us is to a very large extent categorised and labelled for us in the course of our language acquisition and learning processes. But it is obvious that not all languages reflect exactly the same categorisation systems; we have already seen, in Chapter 2, section 2.3.i, how the space between a speaker and an object referred to may be divided differently by different deictic systems, and examples of lexical incompatibilities between languages also abound. The diagram on page 43 is taken from Palmer (1981: 68–9), who draws on Hjelmslev (1953: 33). This example illustrates that even with reference to something as apparently objectively available (to persons with normal vision) as the colour spectrum, languages differ in the distinctions they make and the high points they isolate. Similarly, apparently straightforward spatial relationships may not correspond to prepositions that match those of other languages. In Figure 3.1 Bowerman (1996: 151–3) provides an example from Korean and English.

From an English-speaking perspective, it seems clear that Figure 3.1 illustrates that

English	Welsh
	gwyrdd
green	
	glas
blue	
grey	
brown	llwyd

the apple is being put INto the bowl and the cup is being put ONto the table; and that by analogy these cases can be used to model the relationships between, on the one hand, the video-tape and its case and, on the other, the lid and the bowl: The video-tape is to be contained by its case so it is going INto it; and the lid is going to be supported by the bowl so it is going ONto it. In Korean, however (Bowerman 1996: 151):

> your reliance on 'containment' and 'support' would lead you astray. In this language, putting a video cassette into its case and a fitted lid on a container are typically distinguished from putting an apple in a bowl and a cup on the table, respectively, and grouped together into the SAME spatial category on the grounds that they both involve bringing an object together with another object in a relationship of three-dimentional meshing or fit.

Partly on the basis of classification differences of these kinds, scholars have formulated a number of versions of *relativism*, the idea that people growing up in different cultures and different languages may have more or less radically different world views.

The antithesis to relativism is *universalism*, and although it is, as Gumperz and Levinson (1996: 3) point out, apparently possible to adopt 'an intermediate position, in which ... attention is paid to linguistic and cultural difference, such diversity being viewed within the context of what we have learned about universals (features shared by all languages and cultures)', a staunch relativist would not accept an intermediate position that acknowledged the existence of universals. The relativist either denies the existence of deep-seated universals or maintains that their existence has no effect at the level of consciousness. To a true relativist, the 'intermediate' position is universalist and therefore untenable.

The primary focus of versions of relativism may be cultural, linguistic or ontological, and we shall discuss each in turn. However, as the discussion will show, they are closely connected.

ENGLISH

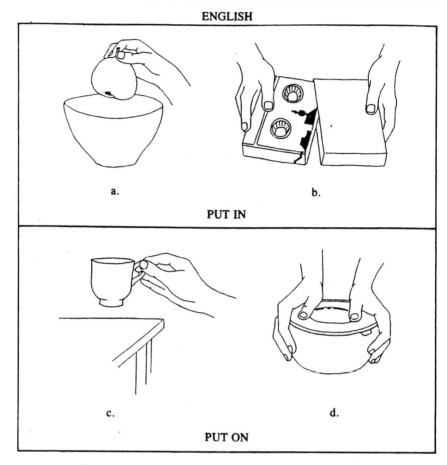

Figure 3.1a   Semantic classification of four actions in English.

3.3 CULTURAL RELATIVISM

Cultural relativism finds expression in a number of statements made by the anthropologist Bronislaw Malinowski (1884–1942), well known for his fieldwork in the Trobriand Islands. He claims (1923) that a translation of a Trobriand utterance would not enable someone who did not know Trobriand culture, but who knew the language of the translation, to understand the utterance, because no utterance is comprehensible except in the context of the whole way of life of its speaker (see Sampson 1980: 225). Malinowski thought that this was so for two reasons (1923): A language evolves in response to the specific demands of the society in which it is used; and language use is entirely context dependent so that no utterance can be understood unless the situation in which it is used is available to the interpreter of the utterance.

KOREAN

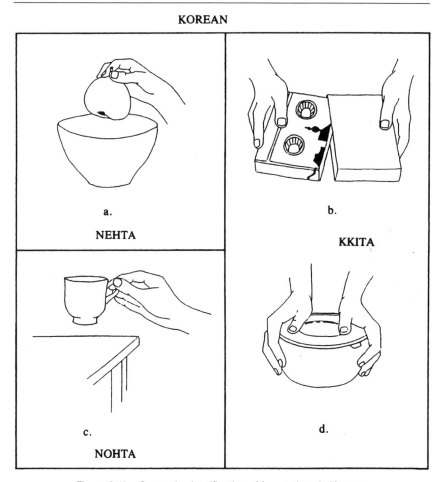

Figure 3.1b Semantic classification of four actions in Korean.

By situation, Malinowski means on the one hand the actual situation in which a given speech event occurs, and, on the other hand, a more generalisable and abstract situation context which can be partly defined in terms of the functions performed by language within the situation. Malinowski shared his functionalist view of language – though not, as we shall see, his fundamental relativism – with a number of contemporaries including Roman Jakobson (1896–1982), and functionalism has remained influential in British linguistics, predominantly in the person of Michael Halliday. In translation studies, versions of functionalism find expression in the work of Katarina Reiss and Christiane Nord among others.

3.3.i Cultural universalism: Halliday's functions and the notion of register

Halliday expresses a universalist position directly relatable to Malinowski's relativist position. He writes (1970: 141):

> The nature of language is closely related to ... the functions it has to serve. In the most concrete terms, these functions are specific to a culture: the use of language to organize fishing expeditions in the Trobriand Islands, described half a century ago by Malinowski, has no parallel in our own society. But underlying such specific instances of language use, are more general functions which are common to all cultures. We do not all go on fishing expeditions; however, we all use language as a means of organizing other people, and directing their behaviour.

According to Halliday (see especially 1978 and 1985), language enables people to organise other people and direct their behaviour through one of three so-called metafunctions of the semantic system of language, common to all speakers and to all languages, namely the *interpersonal function*. By means of a second metafunction, the *ideational function*, speakers are able to reflect on the world around and within them, and by means of a third function, the *textual function* of language, speakers are able to order the text into units of information which are connected to each other (see Chapter 7, sections 7.2.i and 7.2.iii). This function enables speakers to highlight some units as thematic and also to indicate which units of information speakers are treating as already within the hearer's consciousness, and which they consider to be new information for the hearer (see Chapter 8, section 8.1.ii).

The context of situation, in turn, is theorised into the abstract categories of field, tenor and mode. Field covers what is taking place, in the sense of a particular situation type; tenor covers who is taking part, in the sense of both personal and more institutional role relationships between the participants in the speech event; and mode covers the part that the language is playing in the interaction. Finally, language functions and situational aspects are related to each other through the notion of register: speakers of a language develop expectations about the kinds of linguistic item which may appropriately be selected for use, given certain configurations of field, tenor and mode on the one hand, and, on the other hand, certain configurations of ideational, interpersonal and textual functions.

The field (what is going on) will influence choices among verbs, nouns, adjectives, adverbs and prepositions, choices of tense and aspect, and choices in the transitivity or theta role system (see Chapter 8). The tenor (who is taking part) will influence choices among personal pronouns and in mood and modality; the mode (the part the language is playing) will influence choices of style (formal, informal, conversational, interview-style), choices of thematic structure, and choices that create textual cohesion and coherence (see Chapter 8).

According to Halliday, whereas it is possible to say the same in different dialects and, presumably, in different languages, it is not possible to say the same in different registers (1978: 185). Consider the expression, 'nice ball'. Clearly, a speaker using this expression as part of a televised football match commentary would 'say' something quite different by means of it (namely that a given player had kicked the ball particularly skilfully) than a speaker using the expression to comment on a colourful ball while playing with a small child. The translation of the expression into different languages might be different depending on which of the two situations obtained and depending on the kinds of fine distinction speakers of the other languages draw among situation types. For example, in German,[1] a probable expression when playing with a small child would be *Das ist aber ein schöner Ball!* ('that is but a nice ball'), whereas several possibilities exist for the football commentary situation: If a player has passed a ball exceptionally skilfully, the commentator might say, *Ein schöner Pass* ('a nice pass'); *Ein schöner Ball* ('a nice ball') is possible in this context, but rare. If the ball has been crossed in, the most likely comment would be *Eine schöne Flanke in den Strafraum* ('a nice cross into the penalty box'); again, *Ein schöner Ball in den Strafraum* is possible in this context, but rare. If someone has shot skillfully at the goal, the commentator might say *Ein schöner Schuss* ('a nice shot').

In Italian,[2] the situation is complicated by the fact that there are two terms for 'ball' depending on the size of the ball in question; a football may be referred to using either of the two terms, *palla* (feminine) ('(small) ball') or *pallone* (masculine) '(large) ball'), but a football match commentator is more likely to say *un bel pallone* than *una bella palla*, partly to avoid confusion with the idiomatic expression *è una palla*, which means 'It's a bore'. In the case of playing with a small child with a colourful ball, the expression of the ball-appreciation sentiment could either take the form, *una bella palla*, if the ball was not very large, or, *un bel pallone* if the ball was large.

In Chilean Spanish,[3] the most likely expression used by a football commentator would be *buena jugada* ('a dexterous move with the ball'), whereas a person playing with a small child would probably say *hermosa pelota* ('a beautiful ball').

It is generally not possible to predict this type of interlinguistic variation according to contextual features with reference to the language typological closeness or distance between the languages involved: As we see above, European languages, both Germanic and Romance, differ from English in the case at issue in demanding different expressions depending on the context. In contrast, Chinese[4] resembles English in allowing the same expression, *hao qiu*, to be used in both contexts.

3.3.ii Practice and discussion

Practice

The following newspaper report concerns two boys' rugby matches. Although a typically English sport, rugby is played in many countries throughout the world and terminology has accordingly developed in the relevant languages. Translate the text into your other language. If necessary, make use of reports on rugby matches originally written in that language.

From *The Reporter*, 30 April 1998, p. 54:

Shelford's best yet

EIGHTEEN months ago **Shelford's** under-14 side were totally overwhelmed by **Diss**. But the boot was on the other foot on Sunday when Shelford wrapped up their season with their best performance yet and came away from Norfolk with an emphatic 62–12 success under their belts.

Neil Hayden converted tries from Dean, Jackson, Conlon and Worthington to give Shelford a 28–7 lead at half-time and Shelford ran in five more tries after the break through Worthington (2), Hayden, Poulter and Raine.

Douglas Finlayson took the honours by running in seven tries in **Shelford** under-7s 40–30 success over previously unbeaten **West Norfolk**.

Nils Downes went over for Shelford's other try.

Discussion

In your translation, you may have used different figurative expressions than those found in the English text, whether these are figurative in common use ('the boot was on the other foot'; 'wrapped up'; 'under their belts'; 'took the honours'), or whether they are used with specific meanings in this genre ('season'; 'converted'; 'tries/try'; 'ran in/running in'; went over'). To what extent do you think that your choices, and those in the English original, are culturally influenced?

3.4 LINGUISTIC RELATIVITY

The linguistically oriented version of the relativist claim is often know as the *Sapir-Whorf Hypothesis*, because of the particularly clear and widely popularised thoughts about how language and world view might be linked, formulated by, respectively, Edward Sapir (1884–1939) and Benjamin Lee Whorf (1897–1941). This hypothesis does not arise for functionalist reasons, but rather for reasons related to variations between the grammatical categories found in different languages. A selection of Whorf's writings is available in Carroll (1956) and a selection of Sapir's in Mandelbaum (1949).

Sapir and Whorf wrote at a time when many linguists educated in the American/European tradition of descriptive linguistics were engaged in recording the languages spoken by Amerindians – an urgent task, because these languages were under threat of extinction as a result of the growing dominance of English in the USA. These linguists' preferred descriptive strategy was to apply to the Amerindian languages descriptive categories appropriate to Indo-European languages; but in his extraordinarily influential *Handbook of American Indian Languages* (1911), Boas (1858–1942) strongly criticises this strategy (see the preface). According to Boas, a linguist's task is to discover the grammatical structure peculiar to each language under investigation and to develop descriptive categories appropriate to it.

Taking Boas's advice to heart, linguists began to notice a number of apparently radical differences between Amerindian grammatical categories and the categories familiar from European languages (see for example Hockett 1958). Whorf, who carried out fieldwork among the Hopi Indians, came to believe that the grammatical categories found in Hopi reflected a conception of the universe which differed radically from the Western model. He writes (in 'An American Indian model of the universe', written ca. 1936 and discovered among Whorf's papers after his death) that whereas Western metaphysics imposes two cosmic forms, time and space, on the universe, Hopi imposes on the universe a rather different pair of cosmic forms, namely 'manifested' and 'manifesting'/'unmanifest'. The space of Western languages is thought of as static, three dimensional and infinite, while time is seen as divided into past, present and future, and these conceptualisations are reflected in grammar, for example in spatial deixis (here-there; this-that) and in the tense system. In contrast, the Hopi 'manifested' comprises all that is or has been accessible to the senses; there is no attempt to distinguish past from present, but future is excluded. Future and everything mental fall within the manifesting/unmanifest category, which includes all that appears in the minds of people, animals, plants and things.

The notion that different languages reflect different forms that are imposed on the universe by different metaphysics was one that, if true, would have radical consequences for the preferred Western tradition of analytical philosophy. In his *Critique of Pure Reason*, Kant (1781 and 1787; see Kemp Smith 1933) had explained and justified what he believed to be universal, human ways of experiencing by showing that there are categories, namely time and space, which are not mere concepts which we operate with and about which we might be mistaken, but which are, rather, the very conditions of our having any experience whatsoever: Time and space are the fundamental categories, the very form of human experience and understanding: Whereas it is possible to imagine space as empty and time as infinite, it is not possible for humans to imagine the absence of time and space; and the most basic, human conscious experience has the form 'sensation here now'. On the basis that it makes no sense to inquire about our 'right' to employ these categories – since, given the human cognitive apparatus, human experience is conditional upon them – Kant goes on to justify our use of concepts such as cause and effect, and objects versus processes, by demonstrating that they are derived logically from the distinctions and relationships between time and space.

Sapir and Whorf themselves were far from blind to the potential consequences of their views. In Sapir's formulation (1929/Mandelbaum 1949: 69):

Human beings do not live in the objective world alone, nor alone in the world of social activity as ordinarily understood, but are very much at the mercy of the particular language which has become the medium of expression for their society. It is quite an illusion to imagine that one adjusts to reality essentially without the use of language and that language is merely an incidental means of solving specific problems of communication or reflection. The fact of the matter is that the 'real world' is to a large extent built up on the language habits of the group. No two languages are ever sufficiently similar to be considered as representing the same social reality. The worlds in which different societies live are distinct worlds, not merely the same world with different labels attached.

Of course, Sapir may be understood to be speaking here of the *social* world alone, rather than of the physical world, and the view he expresses in his earlier work, *Language*, 1921, is certainly universalist (see below, section 3.6.i). However the possibility of radical relativism remains in the minds of a number of scholars of a relativist persuasion. For example Lakoff and Johnson (1980: 181) maintain that:

> people with very different conceptual systems than our own may understand the world in a very different way than we do. Thus they may have a very different body of truths than we have and even different criteria for truth and reality.

3.4.i Linguistic universalism

Whorf himself was led to formulate a somewhat weaker version of what he terms (1940/Carroll, 1956: 214) 'a new principle of relativity', namely that

> No individual is free to describe nature with absolute impartiality, but is constrained to certain modes of interpretation ... All observers are not led by the same physical evidence to the same picture of the universe, unless their linguistic backgrounds are similar, or can in some way be calibrated.

Of course, Whorf writes in English about the very different language systems that interest him, and he manages to explain fairly successfully how these differ from English. To that extent, therefore, he must have believed that the languages could, in fact, be 'calibrated'. And although it might be very difficult to translate between distant languages such as English and Hopi, translation, at some level, would be possible. A similar position is expressed in Jakobson's famous passage (1959/1987: 431–2):

> All cognitive experience and its classification is conveyable in any existing language. Whenever there is a deficiency, terminology can be qualified and amplified by loanwords or loan translations, by neologisms or semantic shifts, and, finally, by circumlocutions. ... No lack of grammatical devices in the language translated into makes impossible a literal translation of the entire conceptual information contained in the original.

Optimism grew, too, about the commonality of the colour spectrum on the basis of work done by Berlin and Kay (1969), who examine the colour terminology of around one hundred languages. They find that even though the colour terminology differs between languages, it differs in a principled way. Each language contains a subset of terms corresponding to a selection from a set of eleven colour categories, but there is not free variation among subsets selected.

Schematically, the relationship between the basic colour terms can be depicted like this (see Palmer 1981: 73):

$$
\begin{bmatrix} \text{white} \\ \\ \text{black} \end{bmatrix} < [\text{red}] < \begin{bmatrix} \text{green} \\ \\ \text{yellow} \end{bmatrix} < [\text{blue}] < [\text{brown}] < \begin{bmatrix} \text{purple} \\ \text{pink} \\ \text{orange} \\ \text{grey} \end{bmatrix}
$$

If a language has a term to the right in this figure, then it will have all the terms to the left. So if a language has any colour terminology – and according to Berlin and Kay, all languages do – the fewest number of terms it can have is two. These will be used to distinguish basically dark/cool (black/green/blue ...) from light/warm (white/red/yellow...). If a language has three colour terms, then the third will stand for red. If a language has more than three colour terms, then the fourth will be either green or yellow. Any language that has one of the terms to the far right of the figure will have brown, blue, either green or yellow or both, and red, white and black.

As Levinson (1996: 195) points out, Berlin and Kay's (1969) study provided a model which was followed by many other researchers interested in establishing universal semantic constraints on variation, 'cultural selection from a small, finite inventory of possible percepts/concepts'. Some studies identify categories claimed to be present in all languages. These range from studies that posit sharedness of several, specific concepts to studies that posit communality only at a more abstract conceptual level. Wierzbicka's studies of 'semantic primitives' or 'semantic primes' (1972: 3; 1996: 9 and *passim*) fall into the first category, while Bowerman's (1996) study referred to in section 3.2 above falls into the second: Wierzbicka claims to have identified a fixed set of meaning components, which cannot be broken down into smaller meaning components, and which are universal in the sense that every language has terms for them. These include, among others, components that express what is expressed in English by means of the terms, 'I', 'you', 'someone', 'something', 'where', 'when', 'big', 'small', 'good', 'bad', 'do', 'happen' (Wierzbicka 1996: 14). Bowerman (1996: 149–50), on the other hand, concedes merely that although the boundaries between spatial relationships, and therefore what counts as any one particular spatial relationship, vary between languages, it is the case that 'all languages make categorical distinctions among spatial configurations for the purpose of referring to them with relatively few expressions, such as the spatial prepositions'.

These arguments or sets of evidence will cut no ice with a determined relativist, however. As we shall see in the following section, empirical evidence can simply not be used in the face of a stance such as that expressed by Lakoff and Johnson (see above) to the effect that people may have such radically different conceptual systems that they do not merely have different sets of truths and different views of reality, but may actually differ in terms of what they think of as truth and what counts for them as reality. This argument cannot be convincingly tested against any 'evidence' provided by reality, because, according to the relativist, 'reality' is not objectively available, but always tainted by its perceiver's subjective view of it.

3.5 ONTOLOGICAL RELATIVITY

The philosophical version of the relativist argument is often known as ontological relativism. This is a belief that no evidence of any type could ever be produced which would settle the relativism/universalism debate. Our beliefs are not amenable to testing against the facts because our belief about what 'the facts' are is obviously among our beliefs. The universalist, neo-Kantian reply to this scepticism is that the relativist argument is internally inconsistent and that without an assumption of universalism at some, admittedly rather deep level of language and thinking, communication with others, let alone linguistic communication, would simply not take place. Interestingly, both parties to this argument employ the example of translation (strictly speaking, interpreting) between languages for illustrative purposes.

3.5.i Quine's pessimism

The philosophical logician, Willard van Orman Quine, makes one of his earliest statements of the relativist position in an article published in a volume on translation (in Brower 1959). Here (1959: 171), he remarks that 'it is only relative to an in large part arbitrary manual of translation that most foreign sentences may be said to share the meaning of English sentences'. Quine is a strict empiricist, so he believes that all our knowledge is acquired through the senses (1960: 26): 'Surface irritations generate, through language, one's knowledge of the world. One is taught so to associate words with words and other stimulations that there emerges something recognizable as talk of things, and not to be distinguished from truth about the world'. However, given that no two people's language/world learning experiences are exactly identical, and given that we continue learning our language and our world throughout our lives (1960: 13), the resultant idiolects may be assumed to differ widely, even though the differences will not be perceptible (1960: 8): 'Different persons growing up in the same language are like different bushes trimmed and trained to take the shape of identical elephants. The anatomical details of twigs and branches will fulfill the elephantine form differently from bush to bush, but the overall outward results are alike'. In other words (1960: 26): 'Two men could be just alike in all their dispositions to verbal behavior under all possible sensory stimulations, and yet the meanings or ideas expressed in their identically triggered and identically sounded utterances could diverge radically, for the two men, in a wide range of cases.' This means that as far as correlations between language and what it is about are concerned, there is simply no fact of the matter: even for each *individual's* language (1960: 27):

> the infinite totality of sentences ... can be so permuted, or mapped onto itself, that (*a*) the totality of the speaker's dispositions to verbal behavior remains invariant, and yet (*b*) the mapping is no mere correlation of sentences with *equivalent* sentences, in any plausible sense of equivalence however loose. Sentences without number can diverge drastically from their respective correlates, yet the divergences

can systematically so offset one another that the overall pattern of associations of sentences with one another and with non-verbal stimulation is preserved.

It is in the course of clarifying his relativism vis-à-vis a single individual's language that Quine resorts to the example of translation – radical translation, as Quine terms it.

By 'radical translation', Quine means the type of translation that a field linguist might carry out of a hitherto quite unknown language (1960: 28). Such a linguist would begin by trying to establish the meanings of utterances triggered by events in the informant's environment. For example (1960: 29) 'A rabbit scurries by, the native says "*Gavagai*", and the linguist notes down the sentence "Rabbit ..." as tentative translation, subject to testing in further cases'. The testing involves trying to eliminate competitor understandings of the rabbit-event, such as the presence of a white thing or of an animal (of any colour), which might give the translations, 'White' or 'Animal' as competitors to 'Rabbit'. So the field linguist tries to establish what counts as assent and dissent in the alien language and tries out the utterance, *gavagai* in situations involving rabbits, white things and other animals. If assent is only triggered from informants when rabbits are involved, the linguist feels justified in confirming for him or herself that *gavagai* does, indeed, mean 'rabbit'.

But it is important to remember that 'what prompts the native's assent to "*Gavagai*?" [is] stimulations and not rabbits' (1960: 31) and that, therefore, in matching the two utterances, '*Gavagai*' and 'Rabbit', 'it is stimulations that must be made to match, not animals' (*ibid.*). The question to be answered then becomes the question, what kind of evidence, available to an interpreter, might support his or her belief that the stimulations for the two utterances are identical?

According to Quine, no such evidence is available. In the case of the term, *gavagai* (1960: 51–2):

> Who knows but that the objects to which this terms applies are not rabbits after all, but mere stages, or brief temporal segments, of rabbits. In either event, the stimulus situations that prompt assent to 'Gavagai' would be the same as for 'Rabbit'. Or perhaps the objects to which 'gavagai' applies are all and sundry undetached parts of rabbits; again the stimulus meaning would register no difference. When from the sameness of stimulus meanings of 'Gavagai' and 'Rabbit' the linguist leaps to the conclusion that a gavagai is a whole enduring rabbit, he is just taking for granted that the native is enough like us to have a brief general term for rabbits and no brief general term for rabbit stages or parts.

The stimulus meaning for 'There is a rabbit' is the same as for (Hookway 1988: 134) 'An undetached part of a rabbit is over there', or 'Rabbithood is instantiated over there' or 'A stage in the history of a rabbit is over there', or 'That spot is one mile to the left of an area of space one mile to the right of a rabbit', or some other sentence, because what the person 'sees' or understands as stimulus meaning is not unmediated reality, but depends on what they are 'ontologically committed' to: to rabbit parts, to rabbithood, to stages in the history of rabbits, or to areas of space, for example. The hearer attaches a stimulus meaning to the utterance that the speaker uses, but has no way of checking whether the speaker's ontological commitment, and therefore the stimulus meaning he or she perceives, is the same as the hearer's own. A speaker may only predicate 'rabbit' of his or her experience when what the hearer perceives as whole rabbits are present; but what the speaker thinks of as present may be entities of radically different kinds, such as collections of rabbit parts, rabbithood, historical rabbit stages, or areas of space. So the translation of terms cannot be supported by stimulus synonymy of sentences, and stimulus meaning is all the impact that physical facts have on us.

Of course, we have ways of living with the resultant indeterminacy of translation. We prefer to count speakers right by our own standards as often as possible, that is, we employ a 'principle of charity' (1960: 59). We also tend to think it more likely that speakers have one term for whole, enduring, middle sized objects like rabbits than for rabbit stages or parts. But such beliefs are not substantive laws of speech behaviour; they are mere supplementary canons which we employ to keep ourselves sane. We proceed pragmatically, but the fact that this is useful does not guarantee that it is true that others share our ontological commitment. Our ontological commitment is encapsulated in the language as a whole and cannot be read off individual sentences, and as no evidence could ever show what an individual's ontological commitment is, there can be no justification for the assumption that it is the same as the observer's: Relationships between utterances, whether in the same or in different languages, are simply not within the realm of theorisation, which means that there cannot be a theory of meaning.

The consequences of this pessimism for a theory of translation are obviously not encouraging, and in the following section, we shall examine a more optimistic view. This view embodies a conception of meaning that is particularly helpful for the theory of translation because it absolves theorists from any commitment to the troublesome notion of equivalence of meaning.

3.5.ii Davidson's optimism

According to Donald Davidson, Quine is right to insist on the indeterminacy of translation and on the inscrutability of reference. But he does not agree that a theory of meaning is a theory of the mutual translatability of terms or individual sentences. Such a theory tells you what a term or expression means the same as, but it does not tell you what the term means. Davidson speaks of radical interpretation in order to emphasise this difference between his own view and Quine's (Davidson [1973] 1984: 126, note 1). Another difference between the two is that Davidson does not share Quine's strict empiricism and is therefore able to afford cognitive processing a more central place in his theory than Quine.

Since Quine's work has shown that the notion of meaning appears an unhelpful starting point in setting up a theory of meaning, Davidson (1967: 307–9) advocates a different starting point, with another concept that has traditionally played an important role in theories of meaning, namely the concept of truth. This has the clear advantage that truth is (1984 [1973]: 134) 'a single property which attaches, or fails to attach, to utterances, while each utterance has its own interpretation', so that we might be justified in declaring some utterances true without claiming to understand them. Of course, taking truth as the starting point for a theory of meaning commits us to justifying the assignment of truth to utterances, but since the attitude of holding their own utterances true is an attitude which it is not unreasonable to suppose that speakers adopt towards their own utterances most of the time, this, again, is not a major problem. The question is how this evidence can be used to support a theory of meaning.

Perhaps we could proceed as follows: We observe that a speaker, Kurt, who belongs to a speech community which we call German, has a tendency to utter *Es regnet* when it is raining near him at the time. We could take this, together with evidence provided by a mass of other German speakers in similar circumstances, as evidence for the statement ([1973] 1984: 135): '"Es regnet" is true-in-German when spoken by x at time t if and only if it is raining near x at t', where x stands for any speaker and t for any time. The notion of truth is thus not absolute, but relativised to times, speakers, languages, utterances and sets of circumstances. Similarly, we could take the case of informants and the passing rabbits as evidence for the statement (Hookway 1988: 168), '"Gavagai" is true-in-L when uttered ... if and only if there is a rabbit near x at t'. These statements are not about what the sentences, 'Es regnet' or 'Gavagai' mean, as such; they are about the circumstances in which utterances tend to be held true. This seems to promise a theory of translation equivalence similar to Catford's which measures translation equivalence against equivalence between aspects of situation substance (see Chapter 2 section 2.3.i) and we may also be reminded of the Hallidayan notion of register (see section 3.3.i above), which attaches importance to the influence of situational features on what is 'said' by means of utterances. In Davidson's view, the relationship between utterance and circumstances is not couched in terms of statements about relationships of meaning equivalence between utterances, such as '"es regnet" means "it is raining"'. Rather, we get statements about the circumstances in which a speaker of a given language holds true a given utterance.

To make this theory function as a theory of translation requires us to assume enough similarity between speakers to make it likely that the utterer of the sentence in quotation (in this case '*es regnet*') would agree with the description of the circumstances in which the utterance is held true *whether or not* the language of description is the same as the language of the sentence in quotation. In other words, regardless of the languages involved, utterer and interpreter must be able to agree, for any utterance U that '"U" is true if and only if C', where C is a statement of the circumstances in which 'U' is held true.

Quine's suggestion is that this assumption is fundamentally and fatally (as far as the theory of meaning is concerned) unjustified. But perhaps it is not (Davidson 1984 [1973]: 137):

The methodological advice to interpret in a way that optimizes agreement should not be conceived as resting on a charitable assumption about human intelligence that might turn out to be false. If we cannot find a way to interpret the utterances and other behaviour of a creature as revealing a set of beliefs largely consistent and true by our own standards, we have no reason to count that creature as rational, as having beliefs or as saying anything.

Whereas the principle of charity was for Quine an optional extra, or, at least, a principle we just might decide to adopt for pragmatic reasons, according to Davidson, it is a principle we could not do without. By assuming that someone is making noises that are part of rational speech behaviour, we are already assuming that they are enough like us to have beliefs which are consistent and true by our own standards. The formulation of this assumption is an inherent part of any attempt at interpreting the behaviour, including the linguistic behaviour, of another being (Davidson 1974): To hold that a creature is making meaningful noises is to hold that the creature has beliefs. But having beliefs is the same as holding something true. So any creature whose noises we bother to interpret is thereby credited with a notion of holding something true. If we were to deny the attitude of holding true to the creature, we would at the same time be denying that it had beliefs. But the cultural relativist certainly does not want to do that; s/he just wants to deny that the creature has any beliefs which we could gain access to. According to the cultural relativist, the reason why we cannot gain access to the creature's beliefs is that we cannot translate its language into our own; the creature has beliefs, that is, it has a notion of holding something true, but it is impossible to translate from its language into ours. In other words, the creature's language is true (for it), but not translatable.

The trouble with this theory is that there does not seem to be any way in which the truth predicate can be explicated without reference to the notion of translation. As Tarski (1956) points out, the predicate, 'is true' functions in such a way that for any sentence S of a language there is a statement of the form, 'S is true iff p', where p is the translation of S into the language of the theory. This explicitation of the truth predicate assumes translation. Davidson reverses the direction of explicitation; taking the attitude of holding true as given, the possibility of interpretation/ translation follows. Either way, the notion of truth is inseparable from the notion of translation, and any theory that seeks to separate the two, as the theory of cultural relativism does in order to retain the idea that speakers have beliefs while maintaining the untranslatability of their language, is internally inconsistent.

The theory Davidson advocates provides a method and a conception of what meaning is which allows us to make sense of the linguistic and other behaviour of other persons, and to see how their use of certain sentences relates to their use of certain other sentences. References for parts of utterances are worked out on the basis, in principle, of an understanding of the language as a whole, but it is not our point of entry into the language; it is the notion of holding utterances true that provides this entry point. The theory supports a view of meaning as a relation between (at least) a speaker, a hearer (each with their background knowledge), a time, a more extensive set of circumstances and an utterance, or more formally, of meaning as a function from a speaker, a hearer, a time, a more extensive set of circumstances and an utterance to an interpretation (Lewis 1983). It is not, then, replicable.

What seems to happen whenever people communicate, according to Davidson (1986), can be modelled as follows (see Malmkjær 1993):

	Prior theory	Passing theory
Speaker	What the speaker believes the Hearer's Prior Theory to be	The theory the Speaker intends the Hearer to use to interpret the Speaker
Hearer	How the Hearer is prepared in advance to interpret the Speaker	The theory the Hearer actually ends up using to interpret the Speaker

Whenever we approach another person (or a reading public) linguistically, we have some ideas about how they are prepared to interpret what we say (or write). This is called 'the speaker's prior theory'. It is called a theory because it is arrived at by relating people's uses of utterances to each other relatively systematically, as every language-using person is forced to do throughout their never-ending language learning process. So the theory is constantly, though systematically, updated. But in many cases (perhaps always), we want our interlocutors to interpret us slightly differently than we believe they are prepared in advance to interpret us. The theory we wish them to use is called 'the speaker's passing theory'.

The audience for our remark also has a theory, in advance of hearing our utterance, about how we are to be interpreted, and this is called 'the hearer's prior theory'. But when we actually say something, the hearer may understand that a slightly different theory is required, because the one they came armed with will not allow them to make sense of the utterance. The theory they end up employing is called 'the hearer's passing theory'. Communication succeeds to the degree that speaker's and hearer's passing theories converge, and the degree of convergence is dependent on the past histories of the two parties, including their familiarity with each other and with each other's backgrounds, cultures, past history, practice in using the language in question, etc. In this account, nothing is fixed except the human inability to fail to perceive relationships of various kinds, including relationships between utterances.

In this view, meaning is used deferentially to future users, not to past users, and past usage becomes a background against which linguistic items participate in meaning relationships formed by the momentary fusion of speaker, hearer and situation. Since these are ever new, language use is ever and inherently forward looking and meaning is inherently unrepeatable.

The implications of this for the concept of translation equivalence are fairly clear. Most obviously, if each instance of meaning is unique because it results from the combination of all of the features of the momentary speech situation, then it cannot be replicated, whether in the same or in another language. So when we speak of translation equivalence, we cannot mean the kind of ideal notion which we saw Toury (1980a) dismiss in Chapter 1, section 1.5 above. Instead, it must be seen as something like his alternative notion of the actual relationship between translation (item) and source text (item). Toury argues for the target text oriented approach on pragmatic grounds: We need a target text oriented view – at least we need to dismiss the then prevalent source text oriented view – if translation theory is to have any objects to describe and theorise. But we now see that the ideal view of translation equivalence gives way on theoretical grounds also. In section 3.6 below, we shall work through some of the implications of the theory for the relationships between translation theory and linguistics.

3.6 THE RELATIONSHIP BETWEEN LINGUISTIC THEORY AND TRANSLATION THEORY

It may be helpful, when considering the kinds of interaction that may take place between translation studies and linguistics, to consider what has happened in the past.

In addition to the common practice of using a linguistic theory as the theory of translation discussed in Chapter 2, section 2.3.i above, the following have been common practice in the past: the use of translation studies as a source of data for linguistics, and the use of linguistics as a source of data for translation studies. Both practices still hold sway, having renewed themselves with advances engendered in linguistics. They will be discussed in section 3.6.i, 3.6.ii and 3.6.iii below, while section 3.6.iv will introduce the way in which linguistics will be used to inform the study of translation in the remainder of this book.

3.6.i Translation studies as a source of data for linguistics

A number of linguists of the past have advocated the use of translational data in linguistic theorising and description. Among the English-speaking linguists of this persuasion we find for instance Edward Sapir (1921: Ch. 5). Sapir provides an analysis of the concepts and relations expressed in a number of sentences, such as 'The farmer kills the duckling', and in translations of them into languages such as German, Yana, Chinese, French, Latin, Greek, Cambodian, Nootka, Tibetan, Bantu, Russian and Chinook to establish what the 'absolutely essential concepts' are 'that must be expressed if language is to be a satisfactory means of communication' ([1921] 1926: 98). He considers that these are, first, the 'basic or radical concepts' of objects, actions and qualities, of which at least two must be expressed or be retrievable from the context for a proposition to be intelligible; and, secondly, those relational concepts that fix the radical concepts to each other and give the proposition what Sapir calls its 'definite, fundamental form'. These essential concepts are universally expressed, whereas dispensable concepts are 'but sparsely developed in some languages, elaborated with a bewildering exuberance in others' ([1921] 1926: 99). He concludes that ([1921] 1926): 'No language wholly fails to distinguish noun and verb, though in particular cases the nature of the distinction may be an elusive one. It is different with the other parts of speech. Not one of them is imperatively required for the life of language.' Notice that this is basically a universalist position, rather than the relativist position Sapir (1929) seems to adopt less than ten years later. It is a universalist position shared by Roman Jakobson, who is with Sapir in advocating translations as providing important information for linguistics (1959: 233–4):

> Equivalence in difference is the cardinal problem of language and the pivotal concern of linguistics … No linguistic specimen may be interpreted by the science of language without a translation of its signs into other signs of the same system or into signs of another system. Any comparison of two languages implies an examination of their mutual translatability; the widespread practice of interlingual communication, particularly translating activities, must be kept under constant scrutiny by linguistic science. It is difficult to overestimate the urgent need for, and the theoretical and practical significance of, differential bilingual dictionaries with careful comparative definition of all the corresponding units in their intention and extension. Likewise differential bilingual grammars should define what unifies and what differentiates the two languages in their selection and delimitation of grammatical concepts.

Jakobson was, however, unusual among his contemporaries in arguing for the use in linguistics of translational data derived from situations of actual communication. From today's perspective, it is remarkable that Sapir makes no use at all, or at least no mention, of examples quoted from actually occurring speech or writing. As far as we can tell, all of his examples are made up on the basis of his own or informants' introspection. It is Jakobson's method that has prevailed. From the 1980s onwards a number of studies in contrastive linguistics, as well as many projects in descriptive translation studies, are carried out on corpora of language in use, either parallel or translational or both (see for example Johansson and Oksefjell, 1998 and *Meta* 43(4)). Such corpora are used for both lexicographical and pedagogical purposes (see for example Zanettin, Bernardini, and Stewart (eds) 2003 and Viberg 1996), and as the basis for new, descriptive grammars.

Studies based on corpora have the advantage over earlier studies of having masses of textual data to draw on, and of showing relationships between languages in use as opposed to relationships between languages as static systems. Translational corpora – corpora of translations with their source texts – are not thereby freed from reliance on introspection, because before a translation corpus can be searched, it has to be aligned, that is, the two sets of text have to be matched up clause for clause or sentence for sentence, insofar as this is possible. To get the process of alignment under way, it is necessary to focus on so-called 'anchor words' (Hofland and Johansson 1998: 87), reasonably frequent words which 'have fairly straightforward equivalents in the two languages' and which are identified (Hofland and Johansson 1998: 88) 'partly based on intuition, and partly on (manual) matching of original and translated texts' – the latter being of course the result of the translators' introspections about equivalence relationships. Given the insights derived from the philosophical approaches to translation discussed in section 3.5 above, we can see that this is less of a problem than it seems to be to, for example, Mary Snell-Hornby (1988: 22) who castigates Catford for his reliance on the introspection of bilinguals. But the philosophical approach should also serve to remind us that however large a corpus is and however carefully it has been analysed, the analysis is always of past usage, and there is no guarantee that future usage will mirror it exactly (in fact, as we have seen, there is a guarantee that it will not). The contribution to linguistics and to translation studies made by corpora has been and is likely to continue to be invaluable, and we shall use them regularly in this book. Nevertheless it is important to think carefully about the nature of the evidence that corpora and other resources for translators provide, and in the following section, we shall begin to do so.

3.6.ii Linguistics as a source of data for translation studies

By their very nature, bilingual dictionaries tend to be used as sources of advice for translators about relationships of translation equivalence. Equally, many grammars of foreign languages, that is grammars written in their native language for learners of another language, do not hesitate to offer translational advice or to use translational examples. For example, Allan *et al.*'s English language grammar of Danish (1995: 366–7) offers a number of translational examples in their section on the Danish discourse particles.

For the discourse particle, *jo*, they suggest '(as) you know' as a possible translation equivalent. The sentence 'Tom er *jo* en flink fyr' is translated as 'Tom's a nice chap, *you know*', and 'Han er *jo* i London' as 'He's in London, *you know*'. Axelsen's Danish–English dictionary (1984: 239) concurs. *Jo* is translated as 'you know' or 'you see' in contexts of explanation, while for other types of context the following equivalents are suggested:

> Protesting: 'why': 'I cannot betray him; why he is my best friend'
> *Der er han jo*: 'Why there he is'
> *Vi vidste jo godt at ...*: 'Of course we knew that ...'
> *Du har jo været der?*: 'You have been there, haven't you?'

According to Davidsen-Nielsen (1992: 8), *jo* is a hearer-oriented discourse particle, which expresses the speaker's or writer's presupposition that information being conveyed is shared by the hearer, and in English, this presupposition is, of course, suggested by each of the apparent recommendations for establishing translation equivalence provided by the grammar and the dictionary, with the possible exception of 'why!', which is in any case somewhat stilted. However, actual translation practice displays a degree of variation from the advice provided.

In Barbara Haveland's (1994) translation of Høeg (1993), for example, of fifty identified occurrences of *jo* in the source text, almost half (21 occurrences, 42 per cent) do not have an overt equivalent in the translation at all, and the same number of occurrences are translated in ways not mentioned in the dictionary and grammar, as follows: Eight occurrences are translated with 'after all'; seven with 'well'; five with intensifiers; and one occurrence is translated with 'but then'. Five occurrences are translated with the form 'of course', as suggested by the dictionary, one with a tag question, 'isn't it'; one with 'you see'; and one with 'you know'. In other words, the translation equivalents suggested in grammar and dictionary account for 16 per cent of the data, and the 'preferred' equivalent, 'you know', accounts for 2 per cent.

It would be difficult to argue that most of the translator's choices of translation equivalents for *jo* must be inappropriate, since she works closely with the author (personal communication) whose own English is good. But it would be equally problematic to suggest that grammars and dictionaries produced by experienced linguists and lexicographers are as unhelpful as the data reported above might indicate. A more likely explanation for the apparent discrepancy between advice and reality might be that grammars and dictionaries should not be understood to provide translation equivalents. Instead, perhaps they can be viewed as a source of information that is essential to an understanding of lexical and grammatical items. Translations, on the other hand, provide evidence of the linguistic lengths to which such an understanding has enabled a language user to go, and, therefore, encouragement of future creativity. In section 3.6.iii below, we will consider whether the study of translations may also help to show limits to these creative lengths. But first, to support the suggested explanation of the discrepancies between the translational data and the information given in the grammar and in the dictionary, it will be helpful to discuss the translator's selection of translation equivalents for *jo* a little further. The examples are presented as follows: The source text segment (D) is presented first, with the published translation of the segment (E) below. Numbers refer to the pages of the novels from which the examples are taken. The examples are followed by a schematic illustration of the logical structure or the argumentation within them, where this may prove helpful. Only a few, clear examples of the major categories are provided; for a full analysis of all the examples, see Malmkjær (1999b).

JO – AFTER ALL

D182: Det må De have set, det skrev han jo flere steder.
E163: You must have seen that, **after all** it turns up several times in his writing.

D218: En dag påpegede hun at det ikke var for sent, de var jo alle i live
E198: One day she pointed out that it was not too late. **After all**, they were all still alive

In these examples, the clause with 'after all' introduces a premise for a conclusion presented in the previous clause:

Exp	Premise (clause 2)	Conclusion (clause 1)
D182/E163	It turns up several times in his writings	You must have seen that
D218/E198	They were still alive	It was not too late

JO – WELL

D 81: Hendes stemme var hæs af søvn, jeg havde jo vækket hende.
E 69: Her voice was husky with sleep. **Well**, I had woken her up.

D 181: Jeg har afklapset dem, sagde han. Det gør man jo.
E 163: "I've spanked them," he said. "**Well**, one does."

Here, the clause with 'well' presents a cause for the consequence presented in the preceding clause:

Example	Cause	Consequence
D81E69	I had woken her up	Her voice was husky with sleep
D181/E163	one does (spank them)	I have spanked them

JO – OF COURSE

There are, as mentioned above, five instances in which *jo* is translated with 'of course' – one of the choices offered by Axelsen's Danish-English dictionary (1984: 239). Below are two of these:

D 226: Men man så ingen udvej. Indtil jeg traf Katarina. Men derefter brød alt jo sammen.
E 204: But you saw no way out. Until I met Katarina. But then, **of course**, everything fell apart.

D 227: Undertiden, de nætter jeg ligger vågen … da frygter jeg, at det måske ikke skulle have forandret sig, ude i verden, at tidens greb skulle være usvækket.
Jeg håber, jeg tager fejl. Dette er mit højest ønske. At have taget fuldstændig fejl.

Der var jo også skoler andre steder, det véd jeg. Men vel ingen steder med en vision som Biehls.

E 205: Now and then – those nights when I lie awake … I fear that things may not have changed, out in the world; that time's grip will not have slackened.
I hope I am wrong. This is my greatest wish. To be utterly wrong.

Of course there were schools elsewhere too, this I know. But surely no place with a vision such as Biehl's.

Here, the clause carrying 'of course' in some way runs counter to the train of thought under way, but this clause is then itself countered by the clause following, so that the original train of through is reinstated.

Example	First state	Counter state 1	Reinstatement
D226/E204	I saw no way out	I met Katarina	But then everything fell apart
D227/205	I hope it is not the case that time still rules the world as in Biehl's school	But there were schools elsewhere so it might	But surely those schools were not like Biehl's

JO – INTENSIFIER

Cases in which clauses *jo* is translated with intensifiers resemble premise–conclusion cases, except that the evidence that leads to the conclusion tends to be presented either at some distance from the clause containing *jo* or has to be inferred from large stretches of text. In the example below, the reader has to infer from the entirety of previous discourse on the topic of Oscar Humlum that he was not considered good enough:

> D90: Oscar Humlum for eksempel var jo ikke god nok
> E77: Oscar Humlum, for example, was **just** not good enough.

It is possible that the reason that intensification is preferred in such examples is that English adverbials have more limited scope than the Danish discourse particles, so that it is difficult to use them to signal evidentiality that stretches far back or far ahead from their own locus. Ip (in progress) finds a similar discrepancy in scope between English and Chinese clause connectives. The alternative translational equivalent – intensification – seems appropriate in view of the mass of evidence surrounding the assertion.

JO – NO OBVIOUS EQUIVALENT

To explain the instances in which *jo* seems not to have been translated at all, we might remind ourselves of the function which Davidsen-Nielsen (1992: 8) assigns to *jo*: it is a hearer-oriented particle which expresses the speaker's presupposition that the information conveyed is shared by the hearer, and it is, as Davidsen-Nielsen also remarks (1992: 32) extensively used in both speech and writing in Danish. Furthermore, discourse particles in Danish tend to be unstressed and monosyllabic and therefore unobtrusive in the flow of discourse. So we might surmise that in Danish, where the use of the common ground marker *jo* is pervasive though discreet, it would seem abrupt, not to say impolite, to simply state the information which is shared, without using the marker. To do so would suggest that the speaker assumed that the information was *new* to the interlocutor, and this would threaten their face. But in English, which does not have the discourse particles, it is acceptable to state information which can be assumed shared without marking it explicitly as shared; in fact, marking it as such would suggest that the hearer needs reminding of the obvious fact that the information is already in their domain, and *that* would threaten their face. The following are typical examples:

> D42: Desværre kommer dette år jo ikke igen,
> E34: Unfortunately that year will never come round again.

> D122–3: de meddelte at de havde indberettet mig til Overpræsidiet og til Børne- og ungdomsværnet, da jeg jo havde friplads
> E109: They advised me that I had been reported to the Children's Panel and to the child welfare services, since I was on a scholarship.

> D153: Jeg ventede på dig, sagde hun. – Jeg har jo skemaet, jeg vidste du ville komme.

E137: 'I was waiting for you,' she said, 'I have the timetable, I knew you would come.'

To insert 'you know' in such examples might seem to imply that the addressee needed reminding of information which he or she ought to be very well aware of.

In just about every case where *jo* has been translated, it seems to have helped to signal an aspect of argument structure in the source text. In contrast, in the instances in which *jo* has not been translated, it seems to have *only* the function which Davidsen-Nielsen outlines for it and which the grammar echoes in its examples with 'you know'. When *jo* has this function only, it need not be translated and translating it may give the misleading impression that the speaker/writer is adopting an overbearing or even insulting attitude towards the hearer/reader. But when *jo* has the additional function of signalling an argument structure, it is safe to translate it into English and an element may be lost if it is not translated. In light of this, we might argue that dictionaries and grammars should be seen, as suggested above, as providing essential information which a language user needs to know in order to be able to use the item in question correctly; but they should not be considered sources of translation equivalents, because contexts of use, which grammars and dictionaries cannot cater for comprehensively, may include features which make other translation equivalents more acceptable.

If this is so, it clearly supports Jakobson's advocacy of the use of translational data in linguistics (see above, section 3.6.i). Such data can bring to linguistics evidence, not only about contextualised translation equivalents, but also about the uses and functions of linguistic items in the source language beyond what is easily discovered by introspection or by looking at source language corpora alone. Relationships of translation equivalence between one source text term and target text terms that vary systematically with variation in the contexts in which the terms are used, can reveal aspects of the source text term not readily identifiable from its use in the source language alone. However, there are two obvious problems with this approach: translators sometimes make mistakes; and translators often make choices that are determined not only by what the source texts says, but also by what kind of translation they wish to create, given what they believe about their target audience's tastes and needs and about the boundaries of acceptability in the receiving culture. In the following section, we shall look at potential ways of determining whether translators' choices may be erroneous or whether they are affected by extra-textual considerations.

3.6.iii Equivalence, error and manipulation

It is often said that if several translators are asked to translate the same text, it is most unlikely that any two will produce exactly the same translation. It is easy to find examples to support this assertion. Consider, for example, the following thirteen translations of the last line of Hans Christian Andersen's story, 'The Princess on the Pea' (1835):

Source Text	*See, det var en rigtig Historie!*
De Chatelain (1852: 232):	And this, mind you, is a real story.
Dulcken (1866: 36):	Look you, this is a true story.
Wehnert (1869: 44):	Now, this is a true story.
Hersholt (1942: 20):	There, that's a true story.
Keigwin (1950/1976: 28):	There, that's something like a story, isn't it?
Kingsland (1959: 29):	And that's a true story!
Spink (1960: 25):	There, now that was a real story!
Peulevé (196?: 62):	Now, this is my idea of a good story!
Haugaard (1974: 21):	Now that was a real story!
Corrin (1978: 66):	How about that for a true story!
Lewis (1981: 12):	There's a fine story for you!
Corrin and Corrin (1988: 60):	How about that for a real story!
Blegvad (1993: 29):	Now, what did you think of that for a story!

No two translators produce identical translations; even (Sarah) Corrin and (Stephen) Corrin (1988) produce a different version from that of (Stephen) Corrin (1978), from ten years before. And yet, the variations seem somehow constrained within the parameters of what we might term 'semantic fields': The story is constant in all the translations; descriptions of it cluster within the sense 'a good example of its kind' ('real', 'true', 'good', 'something like' and 'fine'); there is generally an attention-summoning summing up device ('look you', 'Now', 'There', 'And', 'How about'); there is a discourse deictic expression pointing back to what has been told ('this', 'that', 'There'); and there is tense, in most cases ('is', 'was'). However, it is not difficult to find other translations of this text extract which seem to illustrate a different type of choice. For example, as Hjørnager Pedersen (2004: 97) points out, von Jenssen (1839) 'translates' the final line of the story in question as *'War das nicht eine Dame von wirklich feinem Gefühl?'*, a rhetorical question which, in Boner's (1846) and Peachey's (1846) English translations, which are probably based on von Jenssen's German, becomes, respectively 'Now was not that a lady of exquisite feeling' and 'Was not this a lady of real delicacy?'.

Common sense tells us that this choice is not the result of error or misunderstanding of the source text; yet we cannot without stretching the notion of a 'semantic field' further than we might wish include a lady of exquisite feeling/real delicacy in the same semantic field as a good/real/true story. These three translators (or von Jenssen, at least) seem to have exercised a degree of poetic licence beyond any indulged in by the translators in the group of thirteen examples referred to earlier, and if translations are to serve the purpose that Jakobson outlines for them (see 3.6.ii above), it is necessary to find a way of distinguishing between this strategy (which we might term manipulation), error, and non-manipulative translation. Otherwise, any information gained from examinations of translations about translation equivalence might be considered too unreliable.

Fortunately, there is reason to suppose that a distinction between source text translation, manipulation and error may be drawn on the basis of a distinction between semantic patterning that can be explained in terms of translator motivation in the case of manipulation, and formal patterning in the case of error (Malmkjær 2004). This leaves the notion of the semantic field free to hold together those choices that we may want to refer to as translation equivalents proper. A distinction of this type will also help to delimit the apparently boundless freedom to engage in new language usage and novel translation selections which the Davidsonian approach to meaning and Toury's (1980a) approach to translation equivalence may appear to offer.

To illustrate the distinction between errors and manipulation, it is helpful to concentrate on a corpus of translations made by a translator about whom enough is known for it to be possible to argue on extra-textual grounds that he or she has a particular objective in mind in translating, beyond the production of a translation that represents the original closely. Mary Howitt's (1846) translations of a selection of Hans Christian Andersen's stories constitute such a corpus. Howitt (1846) includes translations of nine individual stories and of one story taken from within the longer story, 'The Flying Trunk'. These were published under the title, *Wonderful Stories for Children. By Hans Christian Anderson* [sic], *Author of 'The Improvisatore' etc.* and contain a helpful selection of obvious errors as well as plentiful examples of manipulation which Bredsdorff (1954: 492–4) puts down to Howitt's puritan morals. Hjørnager Pedersen (2004: 80–7) concurs: Mary Howitt grew up a devout Quaker who subsequently converted to Roman Catholicism and she is, as Hjørnager Pedersen (2004: 83) puts it, 'among those mid-nineteenth century female translators who tried to check what they saw as Andersen's masculine frivolity to underline and enlarge on the moral and religious qualities already present in many of the stories'.

Howitt manipulates the stories by means of omissions, additions and substitutions in order to avoid mention of anything repulsive or blasphemous or suggestive of sexuality or other improper sentiments or emotions, such as, for example, pride or vengeance.

The repulsive, and Howitt's way of managing it, may be illustrated in the following examples, which are from the same story and mutually dependent (original text marked as 'A', with a gloss below, Howitt's translation marked as 'H' with a page reference to Howitt's collection):

A   *skar hans Hoved af og   begravede det med Kroppen i den bløde Jord*
GLOSS   cut his head off and buried   it with the body in the soft earth
H   and then buried him in the bloody earth (58)

A   *saa tog hun det blege Hoved med de lukkede Øine, kyssede den*
GLOSS   then took she the pale head with the closed eyes kissed the
A   *kolde Mund og rystede Jorden af hans deilige Haar*
GLOSS   cold mouth and shook the earth off his lovely hair
H   so she cut away a beautiful lock of his hair, and laid it near her heart (60)

A   *tog hun Hovedet med sig hjem*
GLOSS   took she the head with her home
H   she went home (60)

There are thirteen instances of this type in the translation corpus.

Patterning in examples of blasphemy avoidance is especially clear because it regularly involves omission of vocabulary that refers to the inhabitants of the metaphysical spheres evoked in the texts, or replacement of it by vocabulary with more secular connotations. The following examples are typical of nine identified in the corpus:

A	*Gud, hvor den stakkels Tommelise blev forskrækket,*
GLOSS	God how the poor Thumbelina became frightened
H	'Poor Tommelise! How frightened she was' (38)

A	*Tak Du Gud for ham!*
GLOSS	Thank you God for him
H	'Be thankful that thou canst get such a one!' (49)

A	*at de aldrig vilde døe, og at Paradisets Have skulde evig blomstre*
GLOSS	that they never would die and that Paradise's garden should ever bloom
H	that they who were purified by trial should never die, and that the Garden of Paradise for them should bloom for ever! (86)

Avoidance of sexual connotations is equally clearly patterned semantically because it regularly involves omission of words and phrases denoting body parts, acts of intimacy, or actions that might provoke sexually-charged thinking. Below is one of eleven examples, many of considerable length:

A	*De skjønneste Piger, svævende og slanke, klædte i bølgende Flor,*
GLOSS	The most beautiful girls, floating and slim, dressed in waving gauze,
A	*saa man saae de deilige Lemmer, svævede i Dandse,*
GLOSS	so one saw the lovely limbs floated in dances
H	'The most beautiful maidens floated in the dance' (86)

Avoidance of improper sentiments or emotions is entertainingly illustrated by the following extracts from a story which consists in the original in large part of the plotting of revenge, instigated by young storks but supported and indeed executed by their mother, on some boys who have teased them; in Howitt's translation, the young storks meekly comply with their mother's advice to let revenge give way to forgiveness:

A	*og altsom de blev større, vilde de mindre taale det; Moderen*
GLOSS	and as they grew bigger would they less bear it the mother
A	*maatte tilsidst love dem, at de nok skulde faa Hævn*
GLOSS	must finally promise them that they PART should get revenge
H	'and the more they were determined on revenge, the less they said of it to their mother. Their mother, they thought, would at last grant their wishes' (125–6)

A   *'Nu   skulle vi   hævnes!'*   *sagde de.*
GLOSS   Now shall we be revenged said   they
A   *'Ja vist!'*   *sagde Storkemoderen.*   *'Hvad jeg have udtænkt,*
GLOSS   Yes certainly said the stork mother What I   have planned
A   *det er just det rigtige!'*
GLOSS   that is just the right.(thing)
H   'Now let's have revenge,' said they.
           'Leave off talking of revenge,' said the mother. 'Listen to me, which is a
           great deal better' (126)

It seems clear that these additions, omissions and substitutions can be explained with
reference to Howitt's wish to produce a set of stories suitable for the Victorian child.
Regularities in the kinds of item added, taken out or exchanged are regularities of
theme and they can be explained with reference to probable translator intention and
motivation.

In contrast, Howitt's errors seem either inexplicable on any grounds, or explicable
with reference to formal patterns. An example of inexplicability is the following:

A   *Bajonetten   nede   imellem Brostenene*
GLOSS   The bayonet down between the cobble stones
H   'His bayonet down among the stones of a sink' (114)

Formal patterning in other examples is of the kind that produces what is often
known as 'false friends', in Howitt's case not only false English friends of Danish, but
also of Swedish and German:

A   *han vil bare have at   de   skulle være rolige*
GLOSS   he will only have that they shall be   still
H   'he only wants to amuse them' (1)

(In Swedish, *rolig* means, roughly, amusing; in Danish it means, roughly, still/
quiet/peaceful.)

A   *over   Isen*
GLOSS   across the ice
H   'over the iron' (70)

(In German, *Eisen* means 'iron'; in Danish, *isen* means 'the ice'.)

ST   *det kan man saa rart*
GLOSS   that can one so nicely
TT   'people can do that so seldom' (93)

(The Danish word *rart* means, roughly, 'nicely', but Howitt seems to have associated
the word with the English word 'rarely'.)

Howitt also produces erroneous calques such as the following:

A   *'Sommetider, om Natten,'*
GLOSS   sometimes   at (the) night

H   'In the summer season at night' (99)

and she regularly selects the wrong sense of a homonym even though the context should have told her otherwise:

A   *'det skal være saadan en deilig Leilighed!'*
GLOSS   it   shall be   such   a lovely flat (can also mean opportunity)
H   'it will be such a nice opportunity' (10)

These examples suggest that one aspect of error identification may involve noticing formal relationships between expressions in the original and surprising expressions in the translation. A second aspect of error identification may be inexplicability on motivational grounds (for further examples and discussion see Malmkjær 2004). Where neither manipulation nor error seems likely, we may assume that a translator has simply sought for the translation equivalent he or she considers most suitable, given the context in which the original term is used and the context in which the translation equivalent will occur, and these translation equivalents can then be safely used to the ends outlined in the previous section of this chapter.

All that remains to do in this chapter, now, is to explain how linguistics will be used in the remainder, more applied chapters of this book.

3.6.iv Drawing on linguistics to inform descriptive translation studies

In addition to, or rather than, applying a linguistic theory wholesale to translation studies, it is perfectly possible and often extremely helpful to use linguistics as a source of information about the types of linguistic phenomenon that make up a text. Arguably, texts, including translations, stand to linguistics as paintings stand to the study of colour and perspective and as dance and athletics stand to human anatomy, and these more statically oriented disciplines can often illuminate the more performance oriented arts. In translation studies, in particular, it seems that attending to the language of a translation is one way, among others, of adopting the so-called aesthetic attitude to translation: approaching translation with a wish to describe it in order to clarify one's reactions to it (Scruton 1974: 145). This is clearly something very different from applying linguistics to translation as Catford did: Catford paid attention to linguistic theory and applied its categories in setting up a particular theory of translation. In the remainder of this book, we shall apply insights from linguistics in order to become clearer about the nature of the relationships between translations and their source texts.

NOTES

1. I am indebted for the German examples to my colleague, Edgar Schröder.
2. I am indebted for the Italian examples to my colleague, Abele Longo.
3. I am indebted for the Chilean Spanish examples to my colleague, Francisco Dominguez.
4. I am indebted for the Chinese examples to my colleague, Hu Wei.

Chapter 4

Sounds and rhythms in translation

4.1 INTRODUCTION

People who regularly come into contact with others from countries whose languages they do not speak may become so familiar with the sounds of those languages that they can recognise each and distinguish it from other foreign languages. This can happen because every language has its own particular patterns of sounds and rhythms. These are the objects of study of phonetics and phonology. Articulatory phonetics explicates how different vowels and consonants are produced by the speech organs. These are described accordingly (see section 4.2 below) and given a symbolic representation in the International Phonetic Alphabet (IPA), which contains a symbol for every speech sound that is distinctive in languages, in the sense that if it replaces another sound in a word, the meaning of the word will change. A copy if the IPA can be found on the IPA website at http://www2.arts.gla.ac.uk/IPA/ipa.html. Although it is not necessary for a translator to master these symbols, it is important for translators to be able to distinguish clearly between sound representation in standard writing systems and the actual sounds used in speech. The IPA represents the latter.

The sounds symbolised in the IPA are combined in different languages into syllables, words and phrases according to patterns which are described in phonology (see section 4.3 below). These are the patterns that in their language-specific combinations cause each language to sound different from every other language. Sound is obviously primarily a feature of speech, while translation takes place through the written medium. However, alphabetic writing systems are phonographic, that is, they are designed with sound representation in mind, so that at least some patterns of sounds are mirrored in the patterns of graphs (the units of the writing system) that represent the sounds.[1] Writers of advertising copy, newspaper headline writers and poets are among those who frequently exploit this feature of alphabetic writing systems. Poetry, in particular, in virtue of both its layout and other visible patterning, explicitly invites attention to virtual sound, and poetry is in any case often written with a special eye to the sound effects that may be achieved at readings. However, silent reading of any text may effect an impression of the sound of the text if read aloud, and, like all linguistic patterning, sound patterns may be important elements in the process of meaning construction. It is therefore important that translators keep an eye on this type of patterning, all the more so in light of the possibilities for interaction between spoken and written text offered by electronic media, which means that it can no longer be assumed that translated texts will remain objects of silent reading only.

4.2 SOUND IN LANGUAGE AND IN TRANSLATION

Few facts are more obvious than that a translated text will sound differently than the text that is its source text. The degree to which this may matter obviously depends on the degree to which sound representation is relevant to the text's meaning-engendering potential and to the function that it is intended to perform. Generally speaking, different text genres differ in the degree to which this applies to them; for example, sound representation tends to play a significant part in poetry and some prose, and a much smaller part in academic and scientific writing. Between these extremes, however, are a number of text types in which the significance of sound representation is less predictable and, like so much in translation, dependent on the purpose the translation is intended to serve. Consider, for example, song translation. It might be thought that how the text sounds is extremely important in this genre; but as Low (2003: 103–6) points out, songs are translated for a number of different purposes, for each of which a different kind of translation is appropriate. For a performer's crib, a translation has to provide all relevant information about phenomena mentioned in the original so that the singer can understand fully what the song is about, and perform accordingly. For a recording insert, Low recommends what Newmark (1988: 46–7) calls 'semantic' translation, usually represented along-side the original and therefore observing at least its line-order and as far as possible also its remaining structural features. It will not, however, strive to retain rhymes and rhythm. For a programme text, Low suggests Newmark's (1988: 46–7) 'communicative' translation type, which renders what the original says in an approachable, reader-friendly way. In cases where a singer needs to provide a précis of the song before singing it, Low suggests using a 'gist' translation, which simply provides the main points of the song's narrative. Finally for a text to be sung, what is required is obviously a singable translation, and in producing these, translators are, indeed, constrained by considerations of how the text will sound – and the fact of the music imposes added constraints (Low 2003: 105):

> Translators ... cannot ignore the rhythms, the note-values, the phrasings or the stresses of the music ... Those working into English must also seek to reduce the number of short vowel-sounds and the clustering of consonants.

Low (2003: 106–7) provides the following ilustrations of the different kinds of translation applied to the first quatrain of a poem by Charles Baudelaire, 'La vie antérieure' (1857), which was set to music by Henri Duparc in 1884:

Baudelaire

J'ai longtemps habité sous de vastes portiques
Que les soleils marins teignaient de mille feux,
Et que leur grands piliers, droits et majestueux
Rendaient pareils, le soir, aux grottes basaltiques

Low: Performer's crib

For a long time I lived under vast porticoes
which the suns of the sea coloured with a thousand fires;
and the great pillars [of these porticoes], straight and majestic,
made them look similar, at evening, to caves of basalt.

Low: recording insert

For a long time I lived under vast porticoes
which the ocean sunshine coloured with a thousand fires;
their great columns, which were straight and majestic,
made them look similar, in the evenings, to basalt caves.

Low: programme text

For a long time I lived by the sea in a palace
which was lit up in fiery colours by the ocean sunshine.
Its vast porticoes had tall, majestic pillars,
which, in the evenings, made them look like basalt caves.

Low: spoken text

In a previous life I lived by the ocean in a tall palace from which I could see tropical sunsets reflected in the surging waves.

Low: sung text

For a long time I dwelt under porticoed halls
which ocean sunshine tinged with light of many flames
and whose majestic pillars standing straight and tall
made them appear, at dusk, like vast palatial basalt caves.

He compares his own translation, made to fit Duparc's melody, with the following translation by James McGowan (1993: 31), who treats the poem as a literary work of art alone, and not like a song. McGowan chooses, instead, to place himself under the constraints of the iambic pentameter (each line contains five stresses, and the metre is iambic – see below):

I once lived under vast and columned vaults
Tinged with a thousand fires by ocean suns,
So that their grand, straight pillars would become,
In the evening light, like grottoes of basalt.

In what follows, we shall develop familiarity with some of the terminology and concepts used in the description of language sound.

The major distinction between individual speech sounds in all languages is between consonants and vowels (or consonantal types and vowel types; see Gimson 1980: 32), and many languages also use tones to create meaning distinctions (see below). Alphabetic writing systems have graphs to represent either consonants and vowels independently, or consonants alone, or whole syllables. Chinese logographic script, which represents units of meaning (morphemes or words) rather than sound, may nevertheless include a phonetic, which indicates pronunciation, and Japanese is a mixed, partly logographic, partly phonographic script. But whatever script is employed to write a language down, the spoken form of that language will contain consonantal sounds, vowel sounds and often also tones.

A vowel is produced when air passes unobstructed from the lungs out through the mouth while the vocal folds are vibrating. If an obstruction is formed by the speech organs of the sound at any stage of its journey, then a consonantal sound is produced. Consonants are further subdivided as follows (see Gimson 1980: 34–5):

- Plosives are made when the airstream moving to or from the lungs is stopped by firm contact between two speech organs e.g. [p, b, t, d, k, g, ʔ]
- Fricatives are made when the airstream moving to or from the lungs passes between two speech organs which are close enough together to cause audible friction e.g. [f, v, θ, ð, s, z, ʃ, ʒ, ç, x, h].
- Affricates are made by slowly and partially releasing the closure made by two speech organs. They include the consonants at the beginning and end of the English words 'church' and 'judge', [tʃ, dʒ].
- Nasal sounds [m, n, ŋ] are produced when, although there is complete closure somewhere in the mouth, air is able to escape through the nose because the palate is lowered.

For further details see Gimson (1980).

Vowel sounds differ from each other depending on the shape of the lips and the position of the tongue in the mouth when the sound is made. The major distinctions are between lip rounding and lip spreading (or unrounding), and between placing the front of the tongue as close to the palate as possible without producing friction, and placing the whole of the tongue as low as possible in the mouth. These distinctions provide the following list, with tongue-high vowel sounds leftmost and tongue-low vowel sounds toward the right. (from Gimson 1980: 41):

Unrounded [i, e, ɛ, a, ɑ, ʌ, ɣ, ɯ, ɨ]
Rounded [y, ø, œ, ɶ, ɐ, ɔ, o, u, ʉ]

The vowel sounds listed above are known as monophthongs, as opposed to diphthongs, which are produced when the tongue and mouth move while a vowel sound is being produced; they include for example the vowels in 'low' and 'high' (see further Gimson 1980: 93 ff.).

The movements and shapes of the mouth and tongue which produce different vowel-consonant combinations need to be taken into consideration in dubbing (the replacement of original speech by speech in another language in films and other visual media) because the replacing expressions must be credible utterances given the vocal posture of the actor who is seen speaking.

The IPA also lists the tones of tone languages. These include a number of African and Amerindian languages and the dialects of spoken Chinese. Different tones are formed by changing the position of the vibrating vocal folds within the larynx, which affects their tautness. This, in turn, affects the frequency of vibration of the vocal folds and creates variation in perceived pitch. In non-tone languages, pitch variation can be used for emphasis or to produce for example a questioning intonation. But in tone languages, specific patterns of pitch variation create meaning distinctions between words which share the same vowel and consonant sounds. For example, in Putonghua Chinese, the four tones, falling, rising, level and dipping will determine whether the consonant-vowel combination /ma/ will mean 'to scold', 'hemp', 'mother' or 'horse' (Wang 1982: 58; 2002: 553).

The major distinction between sound patterns within syllables is between the alliterative type and the rhyming type. Rhyme occurs between two or more stretches of speech when all of the sounds present from the *end* of the stretches up to and including their last fully accented vowel are the same. Leech (1969: 92) gives the examples, 'save' – 'gave', and 'save you' – 'gave you'. The rhyme-type illustrated in the latter pair, in which the last syllable of the rhyming stretch is unstressed, is sometimes known as 'feminine rhyme' while the rhyme-type illustrated by the 'save'–'gave' pair, where the final (and in this case only) rhyming syllable is stressed, is sometimes known as 'masculine rhyme'. Identity of final, unstressed syllables only is known as 'homoioteleuton'. Leech (1969: 83) quotes from Wordsworth's *Ode: Intimations of Immortality*:

> ...
> But for those obstinate question*ings*
> Of sense and outward things,
> Fall*ings* from us, vanish*ings*,
> Blank misgiv*ings* of a creature
> ...

While true rhyme is a matter of pronunciation alone, written text can carry what is known as 'eye-rhyme', which occurs when identical letters represent different sounds. Leech (1969: 92–3) illustrates with 'great' and 'meat', but points out that because pronunciation changes over time, 'it must be continually borne in mind, when reading poetry of past centuries, that what is only an eye-rhyme to us may have been a "true rhyme" to the poet'. Of course, there are also identical sound sequences that are represented with different sequences of graphs, such as, for example, the final vowel-consonant combination in both 'red' and 'dead'. Sometimes, rhymes that are not directly visible in writing may be made so by advertisers to provide an extra, eye-catching dimension to a campaign. For example, in the slogan used in the 1980s to promote milk consumption in the UK, 'Drinka pinta milka day', a speech sound rhyme was represented graphically by closing up the gaps between 'drink' and 'a' and between 'milk' and 'a', and converting 'of' to 'a' and closing it up to 'pint'.

Alliteration is usually carried by the main stressed syllable (see section 4.2 below) of words. Leech (1969: 92) gives the following example from Tennyson's *In Memoriam*, vii: 'Here in the *l*ong un*l*ovely street'. Repetition of vowel sounds is often referred to as assonance, and it, too, features in '*lo*ng' and 'un*lo*vely'. In alphabetic scripts, particularly those which indicate both consonant and vowel sounds, alliteration is especially visible, and greatly favoured by journalists and headline writers because it makes for catchy headlines, which help to capture the attention of readers. For example, 'The Man, the Myth, the Millions – and Marty' (about Martin Scorsese) (*Time*, 29 September 2003: 73); 'The Roots Reinvent The Rock-Rap Sound' (about a band of musicians, The Roots) (*Time*, 29 September 2003: 76).

These examples illustrate the phenomenon of 'chiming', which Empson (1947: 12; quoted by Leech 1969: 95) describes as the connection between 'two words by similarity of sound so that you are made to think of their possible connections'. Advertisers often play with rhyme, eye-rhyme and alliteration to achieve this effect. For example, the well known advertising slogan for Heinz baked beans, 'Beanz Meanz Heinz' combines what we may term eye-alliteration between the 'z' graphemes present in all three written words with the rhyme between 'beans' and 'means' in normal speech, presumably to reinforce, both visually and by means of allusion to the rhyme that would be present in speech, consumers' belief in a close connection between (baked) beans and one of the companies that produce them, namely Heinz. Chiming is regularly employed by brand namers. For example Begley (2002) reports 'an in-house analysis' by the firm Lexicon Branding Inc according to which:

> The name 'Viagra' rhymes with Niagara,[2] the most famous waterfall in this hemisphere … Water is psychologically linked to both sexuality and life. And Niagara Falls, home of thousands of heart-shaped beds, connotes honeymoons. This initial 'vi-' is a homonym of 'vie', meaning to fight or compete, and echoes the beginning of 'vitality' and 'vigor,' while 'agra' evokes 'aggression.' On the basis of semantics alone 'Viagra' is a winner. But the sound symbolism of the name also works. V, says Dr. Leben, 'is one of the fastest, biggest and most energetic sounds in language …'

Of course, questions of meaning are usually considered the province of higher linguistic levels than the level of individual sounds or sound sequences. Apart from occasional onomatopoeia – the phenomenon of mirroring natural sounds in human languages, as in, for example, 'buzzing (bees)', 'cuckoo' and 'woof woof' in English – the relationship between linguistic sound and what it stands for is taken to be on the whole arbitrary. If it were not arbitrary, then, as Locke (1977 [1690]: book 3, chapter 2) points out, 'there would be but one language amongst all men'. Nevertheless, it is, as Robins (1989 [1964]: 17) remarks, possible to perceive a 'general association' between some sounds and certain types of thing or event, 'as in many English words ending in *-ump*, such as *thump clump, stump, dump*, which tend to have associations of heaviness, thickness, and dullness'.

This idea has remained current in linguistics and psychology for a considerable time; it was present in Jespersen (1922), Firth (1930) and Köhler (1947), and occupies a good deal of virtual, internet space. Hard copy publications also exist, for example Hinton, Nichols and Ohala (1994). Robins himself reports, further, that if speakers are presented with made up words, they tend to be able to group them under categories such as 'rounded' or 'spiky', depending on the type of sound contained in the words. For example, *maluma* and *oomboolu* are round whereas *takete* and *kikeriki* are spiky. This distinction may correspond to the lip-rounding and tongue lowering associated with producing the two former words, and the lip-spreading associated with producing the two latter words. Similarly, Denofsky (http://www.conknet.com/~mmagnus/SSArticles/Denofcl.html, visited on 23 May 2004) relates the manner of production of the consonant cluster /kl/, as well as the closeness of the two symbols that represent the sounds in the alphabet, to the meaning he claims for it of togetherness, and which he thinks is illustrated by words such as 'clap', 'clip', 'clop', 'close', and so on. This kind of sound-meaning association is known as phonaesthesia, and the sound elements that are thought to carry meaning are known as phonaesthemes. Commonly cited phonaesthemes include /gl/ in English which seems to connote shining and light: 'glass', 'gleam', 'glisten', 'glow', 'glare', glint' (Shisler 1997: 2). This association obtains for Swedish too, according to Abelin (http://www.ling.gu.se/~abelin/phonest.html visited 23/05/04: 5).

Whatever we think about the wider claims made by some proponents of a phonaesthetic view of language (visit one or two web sites devoted to the topic), the notion, along with other types of sound symbolism, plays a significant role in brand naming decisions and advertising, and may therefore clearly be of significance to translators. It is true that advertisements are rarely translated directly; nevertheless, translators may be charged with producing copy which is as catchy, chiming, or appealing in the new language as the original was in its language. There is a growing literature on brand name translation which emphasises the importance of awareness in such translation of sound symbolism, perhaps especially between European languages and Chinese, because sound symbolism and naming are especially important in the latter language. Ho (2003: 11–12) reports that when Coca-Cola initially entered the Chinese market in the 1920s, the Chinese characters chosen to represent the product because they would produce pronunciation close to the original, 'ke ke ken la', were the logographs for 'tadpole tadpole nibble candle'. About ten years later, a slightly different transliteration (using the western alphabet to represent the closest equivalent of sounds of words in one language – in this case American English – in another language – in this case Chinese), namely 'ke kou ke le', was used as the basis for selection of two characters that mean 'delicious enjoyable'. Success for Coca-Cola in China followed, and now several Chinese domestic drinks manufacturers employ the second character in their own brands to produce for example 'tian fu ke le', which means 'Sichuan Enjoyable'.

The kind of adjustments that need to be made to brand names and advertising materials is often known as localisation. Localisation generally refers to the need to make advertising copy or brand names suitable for a given culture, but the underlying need to appeal to a projected audience of consumers is of course as keenly felt in campaigns intended to attract a given consumer group in a company's home country. Consider the speed with which Marks and Spencer removed its disastrous television advert that ran in the UK in which an unremarkable woman was seen to proclaim delightedly, 'I'm normal'. Being one of the crowd is manifestly not what most twenty first-century women aspire to.

4.2.i Practice and discussion

Practice

Consider the opening paragraph of Vladimir Nabokov's novel, *Lolita* (1955):

> Lolita, light of my life, fire of my loins. My sin, my soul. Lo-lee-ta: the tip of the tongue taking a trip of three steps down the palate to tap, at three, on the teeth. Lo. Lee. Ta.

Look at the IPA and see whether you can identify the symbol standing for the sound that must be represented by 'Ta' in the passage, if the narrator's description of the final step in the trip his tongue takes is accurate.[3]

Copy out the passage and devise colour coding for marking out the patterns of alliteration in the passage.

Now compare with the French translation by Maurice Couturier (2001):

> Lolita, lumière de ma vie, feu de mes reins. Mon péché, mon âme. Lo-lii-ta : le bout de la langue fait trois petits pas le long du palais pour taper, à trois, contre les dents. Lo. Lii. Ta.

Colour code it for alliteration, as you did for the English language version, and compare the patterns obtained.

Discussion

It is remarkable that although the patterns of alliteration in the two passages obviously differ, they are just about equally noticeable. While some of the noun initial sounds represented by 'l' in the English passage, and which clearly alliterate with the name 'Lolita', are not reproduced in the translation, the fact that the French article *le/la/les* begins with the same sound provides opportunities to include several instances of it in the French passage. The sound represented by 't' in several words in the source text, either alliterates or, if pronounced as the narrator describes, 't' itself eye-alliterates with the final syllable-initial consonant in the name 'Lolita'. This is less clearly the case in the translation; however, by using the adjective *petits* ('small') to modify *pas* ('steps'), the French translator achieves very noticeable alliteration between these words and *palais pour taper* ('palate to tap'), which in a sense fills the gap between and thus links the 't' of *trois* with that of *taper* and that of *trois* immediately following. This passage, though brief, is an excellent illustration of the possibility of producing a translation that offers very similar opportunities for poetic attention and interpretation as the original using similar means to those employed in the original text, though in somewhat different realisations.

Compare Couturier's translation with translations into other languages of the opening paragraph of *Lolita* or with the earlier translation into French (by Eric Kahane, 1959, Olympia Press) and discuss the differences and similarities between the translations and between the translations and the original.

4.3   RHYTHM IN LANGUAGE AND IN TRANSLATION

Each language has its own rhythm or regular beat. As Leech puts it (1969: 103), it is possible to split utterances in every language 'into segments that are *in some sense* of equal duration' (Leech 1969: 103). In French, which is a syllable timed language, it is syllables that are of roughly equal duration; in English, which is a stress timed language, the unit of the beat of the language centres on one stressed syllable plus up to four unstressed syllables.

By stress is meant the force of breath used in uttering a syllable relative to the force of breath used in uttering the syllables immediately surrounding it. Stress tends to fall on so-called content words (nouns, verbs, adjectives) while so-called grammatical words tend not to be stressed, except that prepositions tend to be stressed in news reportage.

The kind of rhythm or beat discussed above is found in ordinary, everyday speech; it can be used together with metre in poetic language to contribute to the meaning-generating potential of a text.

4.3.i   Metre

When a pattern of stressed and unstressed syllables is regular, we can talk of it in terms of metrical feet. A foot is 'the unit or span of stressed and unstressed syllables which is repeated to form a metrical pattern' (Leech 1969: 112).

In the description of English poetry, four main types of metrical foot are usually singled out: the iamb, the anapest, the trochee and the dactyl. These are illustrated below (x = an unstressed syllable, / = a stressed syllable):

Iamb   x /:   A boat beneath a sunny sky (Lewis Carroll, 1862)
                 x / x /   x / x /

Anapest   x x /: Though I sang in my chains like the sea (Dylan Thomas, 1946)
                    x x / x x   /   x x /

Trochee   / x: Tyger! Tyger! burning bright (William Blake, 1789–94)
                 / x / x /   x   /

Dactyl   / x x: Woman much missed, how you call to me, call to me (Thomas Hardy, 1915)
                  / x   x   /   x x / x x /   x x

4.3.ii The interplay between prose rhythm and metre

A full metrical analysis of the entirety of Hardy's poem from which one line was used above to illustrate dactylic metre will help us see how poets can exploit the interplay between poetic metre and natural speech rhythm. This interplay may be referred to as 'versification' (Leech 1969: 103). Consider the first stanza:

From Thomas Hardy (1840–1928), *Satires of Circumstance, Lyrics and Reveries with Miscellaneous Pieces*, published 1915; brackets indicate pauses required to maintain stress timing:

Woman much missed, how you call to me, call to me,
/ x   x   /   x x / x x /   x x

Saying that now you are not as you were
/ x   x   /   x x x / x x /   (x x)

When you had changed from the one who was all to me,
/   x   x   /   x x / x   x / x x

But as at first, when our day was fair.
/   x x /   x   x / x (x) / (x x)

If we read this poem aloud, it is noticeable that obeying the metrical pattern of stressed and unstressed syllables produces a completely natural reading of the first two lines, whereas the stress on 'when' at the beginning of the third line sounds slightly odd; in ordinary speech, the first stress in 'when you had changed' is likely to fall on 'changed'. In the fourth line, keeping a stress on 'But', produces an even more unnatural reading as compared with ordinary speech rhythm, where the first stress in 'But as at first' would certainly fall on 'first'.

As we read further, it becomes increasingly difficult to maintain the metre, as the rhythm of natural speech asserts itself increasingly forcefully, until, in the final stanza, the metrical pattern breaks down completely:

> Can it be you that I hear? Let me view you, then,
> Standing as when I drew near to the town
> Where you would wait for me: yes, as I knew you then,
> Even to the original air-blue gown!
>
> Or is it only the breeze, in its listlessness
> Travelling across the wet mead to me here,
> You being ever dissolved to wan wistlessness,
> Heard no more again far or near?
>
> Thus I; faltering forward,
> Leaves around me falling,
> Wind oozing thin through the thorn from norward,
> And the woman calling.

An argument can be made here that the degree to which the metre coincides with natural speech rhythm is at least roughly proportionate with the degree to which the speaking voice seems able to believe in the woman's presence and in the image of her as she was in the past. The dactylic metre falters completely at the point when the speaking voice turns away from the image of the woman from the past to become fully conscious and self-reflective of its own thought processes ('Thus I'). In the early stanzas, the woman is a second person addressee, in the final, she leaves the grammatical person system to become 'the woman' heard calling, and it is the image of the wind from the north which is presented with something resembling the force of the metre recalled from stanza 1. Regularity of metre and the interplay between metre and natural speech rhythm is thus employed to reinforce what is expressed through the lexis in this poem.

4.3.iii Practice and discussion

Practice

Consider the following translated poem, from Carl Malmberg's translation, *Havoc* (1968 Madison, Milwaukee and London: The University of Wisconsin Press) of Tom Kristensen's novel *Hærværk* (1930) Copenhagen: Gyldendalske Boghandel (page references to the latter are from the edition of 1968), presented alongside the original:

pp. 53–4	p. 58
Like a ruffian whose hands are bloodied	Som en bisse med blodige hænder
x x / x x / x / x	x x / x x / x x / x
After a brawl and a binge,	efter slagsmaal og spiritusbrand
/ x x / x x /	x x / x x / x x /
I forsake my soft bed of indifference	har jeg rejst mig fra tilfældets leje
x x / x x / x x / x x	x x / x x / x x / x
For a couch at terror's raw edge.	paa en divan ved rædslernes rand.
x x / x / x x /	x x / x x / x x /

Given a sympathetic reading, for example ensuring that 'ruffian' is pronounced as a two-syllable word, the translation can be said to reproduce the metrical pattern of the original, although there is a certain conflict with natural speech rhythm in the third line, where stress would probably fall on both 'soft' and 'bed'. The regularity of metre has been achieved without too great a loss or change of meaning; the original might be glossed as follows:

> like a bandit with bloody hands/ after fighting and alcohol-fire/ have I risen from the coincidence's bed/ on a divan at the horror's edge

The verse above is followed by a piece of narration which reads as follows in the English version:

> Then, farther down the page, almost in a corner of the sheet, and bearing no

relationship other than the rhyme scheme to the stanza above, three more verses had been jotted down hurriedly in small script …:

The verses that follow are reproduced below, alongside their Danish original, with its pattern of stressed and unstressed syllables given and followed by a gloss:

Fear is as strong as a Mongol horde.	Asiatisk i vælde er angsten.
	x x / x x / x x / x
It is ripened with immature years.	Den er modnet med umodne aar.
	x x / x x / x x/
And each day my heart grows heavy,	Og jeg føler det dagligt i hjertet
	x x / x x / x x / x
Foreseeing the continents flooded	Som om fastlande dagligt forgaar.
with tears.	x x / x x / x x /
But my fear must be vented in longing,	Men min angst maa forløses i længsel
	x x / x x / x x / x
In visions of horror and stress,	og i syner af rædsel og nød.
	x x / x x / x x /
I have longed for the final disaster,	Jeg har længtes mod skibskatastrofer
	x x / x x / x x / x
For havoc and violent death.	og mod hærværk og pludselig død.
	x x / x x / x x /
I have longed to see cities burning	Jeg har længtes mod brændende byer
	x x / x x / x x / x
And the races of mankind in flight –	og mod menneskeracer paa flugt,
	x x / x x / x x /
a world rushing headlong in panic	mod opbrud, som ramte alverden,
	x / x x / x x / x
From God's retribution and might.	og et jordskælv, som kaldes Guds tugt.
	x x / x x / x / /

Asiatic in might is the fear/ it is ripened with immature years/ and I feel it daily in the heart/ as if continents daily perish

But my fear must be released in yearning/ and in visions of horror and need/ I have yearned towards shipping disasters/ and towards ravage and sudden death

I have yearned towards burning cities/ and towards human races fleeing/ towards break-ups that struck the whole world/ and an earthquake that was called God's punishment.

The Danish original exhibits slight irregularity of metre in the final verse, where the natural speech form of *Guds tugt*, is so laden with biblical echoes that it is very likely to override the metre of the poem, each syllable receiving a stress. The penultimate line begins with one unstressed syllable only, a breaking of the otherwise very steady metre which interestingly happens on words that mean 'towards break-up'.

Provide a parallel analysis of the translation into English. How regular is the metre in English? Where does it conflict with the rhythm of natural speech? To what extent has the translator managed to make these stanzas do what the prose text claims that they do (namely mirror the previous single stanza's metre)?

Establish the pattern of rhymes in the English version.

Discussion

The English translation reproduces the pattern of rhymes of the original – that is the second and fourth line of each stanza rhyme, but only the original has rhymes in the single stanza poem.

Yet it is not quite the case that the single stanza and the longer poem are related only through metre (even in the English version); both give expression to images of violence: the single verse in association with connotations of sexuality achieved through the image of rising from a bed, the longer poem in association with the yearning for violence born of an existentialist/nihilistic object-less fear.

One other poem, presented as if written by the same character, is included in the novel. It is linked thematically to the single stanza above insofar as it is a love poem, and to both that stanza and the longer poem about fear in virtue of employing the 'opposite' metre to theirs: the first two poems employ anapests (xx/), while the metre in the third poem is dactylic (/xx).

It is not possible to do justice here to the complexities of the personality of the character in the novel who is responsible for these three poems, nor to his relationship to the main character; suffice to say that literary creation and criticism, and the politics associated with both, play major thematic parts in the novel. It is therefore unlikely that the two mirror-image metres have been selected for use coincidentally. Strikingly, the main character has just found the poem below when its author appears on his doorstep. He is invited in, and the main character thinks as follows of his visitor (my translation):

> a form whose face appeared to be divided in two, a dark half turned toward the centre of the room and a light half turned towards the diminishing daylight coming through the windows.

Below are the translation (from pp. 136–7) and the original (p. 140) with a gloss following:

Diminuendo	Diminuendo
Tired of your embrace. Feeling spent and happy,	Træt af dit favntag og udløst og lykkelig
	/ x x / x x / x x / x x
I live but for a kiss against your mouth,	lever jeg kun i et kys mod din mund,
	/ x x / x x / x x /
Feel your lips grow slack and your breath	føler din læbe fortabe sig aandende,
	/ x x / x x / x x / x x
Subside as you drift away into sleep.	Kyssene formløse flyde i blund.
	/ xx / x x / x x /

Tired of your kiss, I caress your soft curves,

Træt af dit kys maa jeg kærtegne formerne,
/   x x /   x x   /   x x / x x

Breasts, hips, firmly with my hand,

brysterne, lænderne, fast med min haand,
/   x x /   x x   /   x   x   /

Shape out of darkness a vase as fragile

skabe af mørket en vase saa dæmrende
/   x x /   x   x / x   x /   x x

As your body, as light as your soul.

lys som dit legem og let som din aand.
/   x   x / x x /   x   x   /

Tired of a caress that reveals how clearly

Træt af et kærtegn, som mærker, hvor
/   x x /   x   x   /   x   x
føleligt
/ x x

Love's calm aftermath has softened your form,

elskovens havblik har mildnet din form
/   x x /   x   x /   x   x   /

I see your face lost among the pillows,

ser jeg, dit ansigt er vældet blandt
/   x   x / x   x /   x   x
puderne,
/   x x

Borne by hair tossed like seaweed after a storm.

baaret af haaret som tang efter storm.
/   x x   /   x   x   /   x x /

Tired of seeing and feeling and loving you

Træt af at se og at sanse og elske dig
/   x x / x x   /   x x / x x

I forsake your bed and your tranquil slumber,

maa jeg forlade din seng og din ro,
/   x   x / x x   /   x x /

Roam through the room and finger its objects,

vandre i kamret og famle blandt tingene
/   x x /   x   x /   x   x   / x x

Feel you here in your peaceful abode.

Føle dig her i dit rolige bo.
/   x x   /   x x / x x/

Anna Marie, you live in these objects,

Anna Marie, du lever i tingene,
/   x   x / x x/ x   x/   x x

Anna Marie so warm and so still,

Anna Marie, saa hvilende varm.
/   x x   / x x   /   x   x /

Anna Marie, now I seek coolness

Anna Marie, nu søger jeg kølighed,
/   x x / x x/   x   x   /   x x

In the crisp fresh air near your windowsill.

Anna Marie, ved vinduets karm.
/   x x / x   x   /   x x /

Gloss

tired of your embrace and released and happy/ live I only in a kiss against your mouth/ feel your lip lose itself breathingly/ the kisses shapeless floating into sleep.

tired of your kiss must I caress the shapes/ the breasts, the loins firmly with my hand/ create of the darkness a vase so spectrally/ bright as your body and light as your mind

tired of an embrace that feels how perceptibly/ love's calm sea has gentled your shape/ see I your face has fallen among the pillows/ carried by the hair like seaweed after storm

tired of seeing and sensing and loving you/ must I leave your bed and your peace/ wander in the room and fumble among the things/ feel you here in your quiet abode

Anna Marie you live in the things/ Anna Marie so restingly warm/ Anna Marie now seek I coolness/ Anna Marie by the window's sill

Practice

Analyse the metre in the English translation above and isolate any rhymes. Compare with the original.

Discussion

In the original, the metre is completely regular. It conflicts with natural speech rhythm in two places. In the opening of line 2, stanza 4, there would probably be a stress on 'maa' in normal speech; and in the final stanza, the stress pattern in the penultimate line would probably be:

Anna Marie, nu søger jeg kølighed
/ x x / x / x x x / x x

These conflicts occur where the poetic voice speaks of leaving Anna Marie's bed.

It seems clear that in the translation of this poem, the translator attended less to the metre and rhyme scheme of the original than he did in the case of the first two poems discussed, where, arguably, the surrounding discourse contains an implicit requirement to do so. As a result, the poems do not contrast as starkly and nor, therefore, are the links between them as clear in the translation as in the original text. Arguably, therefore, the character's poetic production is less closely linked to the contrasts in his personality in the English translation than it is in the original.

NOTES

1. There are rarely completely stable relationships between units of alphabetic scripts and pronunciation. Different accents of a language are represented using the same spelling conventions, and even so-called 'received' or standard pronunciation changes continuously over time, while spelling reforms occur infrequently. Retaining original spellings is a way of storing information about word origins.

2. To make 'Viagra' rhyme with 'Niagara' it is necessary to suppress the second 'a' sound in 'Niagara': 'Niag'ra'.

3. It must be either θ or ð, producing something more Spanish sounding than even the rather alveolar 't' favoured by Tony Blair.

Chapter 5

Words and meanings in translation

5.1 INTRODUCTION

In this chapter, we work with the notions of the word and word meaning. We begin by asking what a word is, before looking at how words have been dealt with in classical translation theory. In section 5.2, we look at word classification. We begin with the kinds of classification typical in linguistics of words according to their part of speech, and we look at a poem by Lewis Carroll in which the characteristics of different parts of speech help to provide meaning. We then analyse translations of the poem. Section 5.3 is devoted to lexical semantics. It sets out the meaning relationships that can be perceived between words and between predicates, describes some characteristics that may be ascribed to words and predicates, and looks at the interesting phenomenon of lexical flexibility. We examine an economics text to see how this flexibility is exploited in order to create particular textual effects and to structure the textual topic in specific ways through the use of metaphors.

5.1.i What is a word?

It is notoriously difficult to provide a definition of the notion, 'word'; we all have a sense that we know what a word is, yet the concept defies anything but the type of working definition standardly used in lexicography: 'any uninterrupted sequence of graphemes that is commonly felt to correspond to a concept' (see Béjoint [1994] 2000: 17–18 and note 22). When it is felt that variations in form dictated by the grammatical systems of a language (such as the variation between, for example, 'man' and 'men' in English or 'alt' and 'alter' in German) do not disturb the relationship between the variant forms and one concept, it is customary to consider the variant forms to belong to one 'base form' or 'lemma' or 'lexeme' (Lyons 1968: 197), which is often written in (small) capitals in order to highlight its status as a term within the theory of words. For example, the verb forms 'shop', 'shops', 'shopped' and 'shopping', denoting the (concept of) the activity of purchasing goods, are all related to the base form or lemma or lexeme, SHOP, whereas the noun 'shopping', in the sense of items bought, relates to a different base form or lemma or lexeme, SHOPPING. Obviously, this definition relies on the notion of the concept, which itself is far from problem free (compare the discussion of the notion of sense in section 5.1.ii below), and as Hunston (2002: 18) points out: 'To a large extent the notion of lemma is a convenience'. Nevertheless, Aichison ([1987] 1994), whose interest is in the mental lexicon, also sets out with a notion of the word derived from dictionary practices. She estimates that an educated adult speaker of English understands and is potentially able to use at the very least 50,000 words, thus defined (Aichison [1987] 1994: 7).

Another potential difficulty associated with the lexicographical definition of the word is that in relying on the notion of the grapheme, it assumes a *written* word. For an illiterate people, we might suppose, the concept of the word might be rather different, or it might not exist at all: fluent speech does not typically pause at each written word boundary, and speech is arguably a more basic and natural form of human language than writing. Robins ([1964] 1989: 185) reports that Malinowski (source not given) 'went so far as to say that words "are in fact only linguistic figments, the product of an advanced linguistic analysis"'. Some weight is lent to this argument when we consider languages such as Finnish and Inuktitut, in which sequences of graphemes regularly get translated into quite a few of the units that count as words in English, as in the following example of Inuktitut to English translation (Ireland 1989: 126): *Iggaaniluguuq qummakkamigiik* ('Without his glasses, his eyes were a pair of lice'). However, Robins ([1964] 1989: 185) maintains that 'diverse experience goes to show that native speakers have an intuitive awareness of word-like entities in their own language, whether written or not'. This is an important issue in linguistic theory, because the word has been seen as 'the unit *par excellence* of traditional grammatical theory' (Lyons 1968: 194).

In contrast, the word is only occasionally and incidentally the effective unit of translation: words in texts tend to operate in unison, and it is generally more helpful to speak of stretches of text (of varying lengths and compositions) when discussing translation units. It is this problem with the notion of the word which underlies the distinction, traditionally drawn in writings on translation, between translation word-for-word and translation sense-for-sense.

5.1.ii Words and meanings in classical translation theory

In his *Libellus de optimo genere oratum* (46 BC) Marcus Tullius Cicero (106 to 43 BC) advocates translation sense-for-sense rather than word-for-word, and Horace (65 to 68 BC) follows suit in his *Ars Poetica* (268; in Dorsch 1965: 83), famously advising against attempting to 'render your original word for word like a slavish translator'. Instead, both Cicero and Horace advise translators to isolate stretches of text that carry 'senses', and then to seek to convey the same senses by means of whatever stretch of the other language might seem most suitable.

As we saw in Chapter 1, word-for-word translation is often associated with literalness and accuracy, and sense-for-sense translation with freedom and creativity; this is why Jerome advocates word-for-word translation of holy scripture even though his preferred method generally is translation sense-for-sense. However, neither method is as easy to follow as it is to recommend. If the intention is to translate word-for-word, difficulties arise because (a) words in different languages do not generally correspond one to one; (b) languages differ in the conceptual distinctions they choose to make explicit by distinct word forms; and (c) it is the morpheme, not the word, that tends to represent a single unit of meaning. Examples a to c below of translations between the Mayan language, Tzeltal, and English (adapted from Levinson 1996: 186), illustrate all these difficulties:

(a)

jipil	*ta laso*	*lo'bal*
hanging	AT rope	banana

'the banana (-fruits) are hanging from the rope'

(b)

k'atal	*ta*	*s-ba*	*s-k'iyojbil*	*kajpei*	*te*	*lo'bale*
lying-across	AT	its-top	it's-drying	coffee	the	banana

'the banana (-trunks) are situated across the top of the coffee-drying patio'

(c)

palal	*lo'bal*	*ta*	*xujk*	*na*
attached-in-bunches	banana	AT	its-side	house

'the banana(-bunches) are against the inside side-wall of the house'

It is, in any case, as Steiner ([1975] 1992: 292) remarks, 'naïve or fictive' to suppose that words in text can be separated from their senses, and the outcome of 'translating' word for word is a line-by-line glossary, as we see above, not a translation proper. Furthermore, since the context in which a word occurs often influences its meaning and can be decisive in determining its gloss in the other language, the line-by-line glossary is, as Steiner ([1975] 1992: 324) maintains, 'contingent': It is contingent on the 'sense' determined by the context.

If the intention is to translate sense-for-sense, the difficulty is to establish exactly what might be meant by the term 'sense' as a unit that a translator can select as his or her focus of attention. Within interpreting studies, scholars belonging to the so-called Paris school associated with the *École Superieure d'Interprètes et de Traducteurs* (ESIT) have developed a so-called '*théorie du sens*' (García-Landa 1981) derived originally from work on consecutive interpreting undertaken by Danica Seleskovitch (1975; extracts reprinted in Pöchhacker and Shlesinger 2002: 121–9, tr. Jacolyn Harmer). Seleskovitch proposed that during (good, successful) interpreting, linguistic units are converted into deverbalised units of sense which are then verbalised in the other language, an idea that was subsequently developed by Seleskovich and Lederer (1989) and adapted for use in written translation studies by Lederer (1994) (see Pöchhacker and Shlesinger 2002: 97). Bell (1991) operates with a similar notion, informed by psycholinguistic accounts of text processing. He assumes (1991: 44) that the translation process operates on the clause, and that a source language clause is first converted into a semantic representation, 'a set of abstract, universal concepts and relationships, which represent the whole of the thought expressed in the clause' and which includes syntactic, semantic and pragmatic information. This is used as the basis for building 'an alternative clause in another language (i.e. a translation) or in the same language (i.e. a paraphrase)' (Bell 1991: 56).

As we saw in Chapter 3, the level of abstraction or specificity at which concepts and relationships may be considered universal is an open question, but it would need to be a fairly high level of specificity before such concepts and relationships could be considered directly helpful during the translation process. However, within the psycholinguistic literature on text processing there is support for the notion that conceptual representations are centrally involved in text and discourse comprehension and production. Research within this paradigm suggests that people's memory for the precise wording of spoken or written text is short-lived (Jarvella 1971), and that when recall is achieved, it normally takes place by means of re-generation of a conceptual representation rather than on the basis of pure memory for what was heard or read (Lombardi and Potter 1992; Potter and Lombardi 1990). Williams (2002: 443–6) provides a good overview of theories about the nature of such representations. However, units of sense, understood as semantic representations, do not seem to be the types of unit that a translator can select as the focus of his or her concentration *in preference* to their linguistic expressions, since semantic representations are generally held to reside at a pre-conscious level. In the relevance theoretic account of text comprehension and production (Sperber and Wilson 1986; Gutt [1991] 2000), for example, it is the fully completed, lexically realised concept that surfaces in the mind. So this account can only work for those parts of the translation process that take place subconsciously and automatically, and with regard to which, therefore, the translator has no choice.

So it seems that any unit of sense that we might identify is either too specific to be universal, in which case concentrating on it in translation would merely push the translation problem one step down, from a verbalisation to a pre-verbalisation stage; or, it is too deeply embedded in pre-conscious language processing to be available for a translator to concentrate on it in the translation process. All in all, then, it seems fruitless to attempt to adhere to a strict separation between sense and expression in translation. Clearly, whatever semantic representations arise in a translating mind do so on the basis of the translator's reading of the text, and must be given expression through the medium of verbal material. In the following, we shall concentrate on the company of words that make up texts and on the basis of which mental representations are formed.

5.1.iii Practice and discussion

This activity can be carried out within a group using either the same or different texts and either the same or different language pairs.

Practice

Select a text or a text extract of around fifty words and attempt to translate it (a) word for word and (b) sense for sense.

Discussion

- What problems, if any, did you encounter when translating word for word?
- And when you translated sense for sense?
- If you encountered any problems, were they caused by the difference between the two linguistic systems or the two cultural systems?
- Were you able to keep the senses separate from the words?
- When you translated sense for sense, did you find yourself tying senses to particular types of linguistic unit (word; phrase or group; clause; sentence)?
- Compare your findings with those of your colleagues who used (a) the same language pair as you and the same text; (b) a different language pair and the same text; (c) the same language pair as you but a different text; (d) a different language pair and a different text.
- Did the results vary with the different combinations of factors mentioned just above?

5.2 WORDS AND MEANINGS IN LINGUISTICS AND TRANSLATION

Although words do not contribute to the meaning of text in simple, cumulative, or invariant ways, they always contribute significantly, and it is important for translators, as language professionals, to be aware of modes of dealing systematically with the organisation of the lexicon and with the relationships words contribute to forming between the propositions that are expressed within texts. These relationships are exploited in the creation of text, whether first-written or translated.

5.2.i Word classification

There are two major ways of classifying words from a grammatical point of view. The first is to draw a distinction between words which belong to closed systems, also sometimes known as function words or grammatical words, and words which belong to so-called open classes, also sometimes known as content words. Closed systems do not admit new members, whereas it is possible to add words to the open classes when the need or wish arises. For example, there are just two members of the article system in standard English, *the* and *a(n)*, and there is a fixed number of demonstratives, *this, those, that* and *these*. If such systems are altered, it is generally considered that a language change has taken place. In contrast, there are thousands of verbs and nouns in English, and new members of these classes, such as 'nylon' for example, are added when new inventions or discoveries are made. Alternatively, items in these open classes can be combined in new ways to cover new inventions and discoveries – for example, 'software', 'term bank' and 'sperm bank' – or their field of coverage can be extended to include them, as when 'hardware' came to be used to refer to computer equipment.

Open class terms may have both technical and general uses; for example, *inspiration* can be used as a medical term for breathing in and also as a term in more general use to denote a process of causing an idea in someone or to denote an object or person which has triggered off such a process. Specialised uses of otherwise general use term are often adopted by special interest groups, for example 'tag' for the 'signature' of a graffiti writer. Similarly, teenagers often adapt open class words for new uses, for example 'fat' as a term of approval. Such new uses may or may not bed down permanently in the language, but the phenomenon of rapid language adjustment to contexts and with speaker groups is one of the reasons why it is considered important for translators to spend time regularly in each of the countries where their languages are spoken. As long as a new usage has currency and may appear in the texts that a translator needs to work with, it is obviously important for the translator to know what the term means and how it is used in its language; that is, the translator must keep abreast of language developments as they occur.

In the case of linguistic innovation in the language of the text to be translated, translators may select one of four major, well known strategies: (a) circumlocution, (b) use of an existing term, (c) invention or (d) importation, with or without accompanying explanation, either intra-textually – for example in brackets after the term in the translation – or in terminological appendices or footnotes. Translators are often at the forefront of linguistic innovation associated with new inventions and new areas of activity, because they are faced with an immediate need to produce documentation and other texts associated with these new fields of activity. In many countries (for example France and Spain) linguistic innovations or importations through translation are eventually placed under the scrutiny and regulation of language academies or committees whose task it is to maintain the integrity and stability of the language in question. But such bodies tend to work at a more sedate pace than the translation industry.

The second major way of classifying words is according to word class, such as the classes of articles and demonstratives mentioned above. These are also known as 'parts of speech'. The parts of speech were originally defined by Priscian in the sixth century on the basis of Greek grammar which he adapted to Latin (see Dinneen 1967: 114–15). For English, *Cambridge International Dictionary of English* (*CIDE*) (1995: xiii–xviii) gives the following ten parts of speech:

1. **nouns**: stand for phenomena of various types
2. **adjectives**: describe and inform about phenomena
3. **pronouns**: can substitute for a noun(-phrase) or proper name
4. **determiners**: used before nouns to indicate definiteness and/or quantity
5. **verbs**: ascribe actions or states to something.
6. **adverbs**: inform about time, place, manner of an action or state
7. **prepositions**: indicate directionality or place and relationships between phenomena.
8. **conjunctions**: link language units (words, phrases, clauses).
9. **exclamations/interjections**: indicate emotions or used conventionally in greetings ('hi') or formulaically ('please').

10. **combining forms**: added to words or parts of words to change or add meaning (prefixes and suffixes (rarely also infixes))

5.2.ii Practice and discussion

Practice

Examine *CIDE*'s information about the above categories, or choose a different dictionary or a grammar and look at the information it provides about word classes.

Discussion

Does your other language have the same categories? Do members of the categories behave in the same way in other languages as they do in English? If not, what are the main differences?

Practice

Dictionaries typically give you this kind of grammatical information about the words you look up. Check in three dictionaries to see how the information is presented.

Discussion

Why do you think dictionaries provide grammatical information? Is the information presented clearly and accessibly in the three dictionaries you looked at?

Example

We recognise the parts of speech as such partly because of their forms and partly because of the ways in which they combine into phrases and clauses. This recognition and understanding enable us to make sense of nonsense poetry like Lewis Carroll's famous poem, *Jabberwocky*, from *Through the Looking-Glass* (1896), Ch. 1, 'Looking-Glass House':[1]

> JABBERWOCKY
> 'Twas brillig, and the slithy toves
>   Did gyre and gimble in the wabe:
> All mimsy were the borogoves,
>   And the mome raths outgrabe.
>
> 'Beware the Jabberwock, my son!
>   The jaws that bite, the claws that catch!
> Beware the Jubjub bird, and shun
>   The frumious Bandersnatch!'

He took his vorpal sword in hand:
　　Long time the manxome foe he sought –
So rested he by the Tumtum tree,
　　And stood a while in thought.

And, as in uffish thought he stood,
　　The Jabberwock, with eyes of flame,
Came whiffling through the tulgey wood,
　　And burbled as it came!

One, two! One, two! And through and through
　　The vorpal blade went snicker-snack!
He left it dead, and with its head
　　He went galumphing back.

'And hast thou slain the Jabberwock?
　　Come to my arms my beamish boy!
O frabjous day! Callooh! Callay!'
　　He chortled in his joy.

'Twas brillig, and the slithy toves
　　Did gyre and gimble in the wabe:
All mimsy were the borogoves,
　　And the mome raths outgrabe.

Discussion

In this poem, we can work out what classes most of the words belong to, either because of their form or because of their place in a larger structure, whereas it is not always possible to be precise about the kind of phenomenon individual words refer to. In the first verse, we recognise ''Twas' as a conventional poetic device for shortening 'It was' when required. 'Brillig' following 'Twas' may be either an adjective (like 'dark', 'light', 'early', 'late') or a noun (like 'morning', 'evening', 'noon', 'dawn') or a weather verb (like 'snowing' or 'raining'). According to Carroll (see Gardner [1960] 1970: 191), it is a noun referring to the time of broiling dinner, i.e. late afternoon.

We know that the following 'the' must introduce a noun phrase (NP). It is not immediately obvious whether the NP ends with 'slithy', which would then be a noun in the singular, having 'toves' as its present tense verb; given the past tense on the preceding ''Twas', however, this reading is unlikely to be the preferred one. A better parsing of this text part would take the NP to be all of 'the slithy toves', understanding 'toves' to be a noun having the plural ending, '-s' and 'slithy' to be an adjective having the '-y' ending. This reading is confirmed by the obviously verbal 'Did gyre': Given 'Did', 'gyre' and 'gimble' must both be verbs in a formally archaic but easily recognisable verb phrase (VP). After that, 'in' before 'the wabe' (clearly recognisable as an NP because of the definite article, 'the') suggests place or time, with place likely to be given preference because 'brillig' has already given us time.

Practice

Analyse the remainder of the poem, following the patterns provided above for the first two lines.

Do the nonsense words suggest any kinds of meaning to you?

Discussion

It should be possible to provide a complete parts of speech analysis for the words in the poem. Carrying out an analysis of this type is part of any comprehension process, though we tend not to be aware of it in the case of texts that do not contain a significant proportion of unknown words, or which are not especially complex syntactically.

In the Carroll poem, the nonsense words tend to echo the sounds of known words and this may lead readers to assign hints of meanings to them (see the discussion of phonaesthesia in Chapter 4). It may be more important to translate these terms into terms of the other language with similar phonaesthetic resonances, rather than into terms that simply sound similarly in the other language. Carroll himself provides explanations of the pretended derivations, resonances and meanings of the words (see Gardner [1960] 1970: 191–7).

Activity

Translate the first verse of the poem.

Discussion

Gardner's edition of Carroll's *Alice* books provides a French and a German version of 'Jabberwocky' ([1960] 1970: 193–4), and Keith Lim's website (http://www76.pair.com/keithlim/jabberwocky/index.html) provides a total of fifty-eight translations in twenty-nine languages, including, for French and German, the translations reproduced by Gardner. Below you will find the three French versions, the three German versions and two of the Spanish versions. Two of the French versions are by the same translator, with publication details available for one. Publication details are available for each of the Spanish translations:

French versions

Frank L. Warrin, *The New Yorker*, 10 January 1931 (see Gardner 1960/1970: 193), plus the further two available on the website mentioned above):

> LE JASEROQUE
> Il brilgue: les tôves lubricilleux
> Se gyrent en vrillant dans le guave,
> Enmîmés sont les gougebosqueux,
> Et le mômerade horsgrave.

Garde-toi du Jaseroque, mon fils!
Le gueule qui mord; la griffe qui prend!
Garde-toi de l'oiseau Jube, évite
Le frumieux Band-à-prend.

Son glaive vorpal en main il va-
T-à la recherche du fauve manscant;
Puis arrivé à l'arbre Tè-Tè,
Il y reste, réfléchissant.

Pendant qu'il pense, tout uffusé
Le Jaseroque, à l'œil flambant,
Vient siblant par le bois tullegeais,
Et burbule en venant.

Un deux, un deux, par le milieu,
Le glaive vorpal fait pat-à-pan!
La bête défaite, avec sa tête,
Il rentre gallomphant.

As-tu tué le Jaseroque?
Viens à mon cœur, fils rayonnais!
O jour frabbejeais! Calleau! Callai!
Il cortule dans sa joie.

Il brilgue …

Henri Parisot:

JABBERWOCKY
Il était grilheure; les slictueux toves
Gyraient sur l'alloinde et vriblaient:
Tout flivoreux allaient les borogoves;
Les verchons fourgus bournifaient.

«Prends garde au Jabberwock, mon fils!
A sa gueule qui mord, à ses griffes qui happent!
Gare à l'oiseau Jubjube, et laisse
En paix le frumieux Bandersnatch!»

Le jeune homme, ayant pris sa vorpaline épée,
Cherchait longtemps l'ennemi manziquais …
Puis, arrivé près de l'Arbre Tépé,
Pour réfléchir un instant s'arrêtait.

Or, comme il ruminait de suffèches pensées,
Le Jabberwock, l'oeil flamboyant,
Ruginiflant par le bois touffeté,
Arrivait en barigoulant.

Une, deux! Une, deux! D'outre en outre!
Le glaive vorpalin virevolte, flac-vlan!
Il terrasse le monstre, et, brandissant sa tête,
Il s'en retourne galomphant.

«Tu as donc tué le Jabberwock!
Dans mes bras, mon fils rayonnois!
Ô jour frabieux! Callouh! Callock!»
Le vieux glouffait de joie.

Il était grilheure; ...

Henri Parisot, *De l'autre côté du miroir*, Traduction par Henri Parisot. Aubier Flammarion, 1971.

JABBERWOCHEUX
Il était reveneure; les slictueux toves
Sur l'allouinde gyraient et vriblaient;
Tout flivoreux vaguaient les borogoves;
Les verchons fourgus bourniflaient.

«Au Jabberwoc prends bien garde, mon fils!
A sa griffe qui mord, à sa gueule qui happe!
Gare l'oiseau JeubJeub, et laisse
En paix le frumieux, le fatal Bandersnatch!»

Le jeune homme, ayant ceint sa vorpaline épée,
Longtemps cherchait le monstre manxiquais,
Puis, arrivé près de l'arbre Tépé,
Pour réfléchir un instant s'arrêtait.

Or, tandis qu'il lourmait de suffèches pensées,
Le Jabberwoc, l'oeil flamboyant,
Ruginiflant par le bois touffeté,
Arrivait en barigoulant!

Une, deux! une, deux! Fulgurant, d'outre en outre,
Le glaive vorpalin perce et tranche : flac-vlan!
Il terrasse la bête et, brandissant sa tête,
Il s'en retourne, galomphant.

«Tu as tué le Jabberwoc!
Dans mes bras, mon fils rayonnois!
O jour frableux! callouh! calloc!»
Le vieux glouffait de joie.

Il était reveneure; ...

German version by Robert Scott, *Macmillan's Magazine* February 1872 (see Gardner 1960/1970: 193–4) and the two further translations found on the website mentioned above:

DER JAMMERWOCH
Es brillig war. Die schlickte Toven
    Wirrten und wimmelten in Waben;
Und aller-mümsige Burggoven
    Die mohmen Räth' ausgraben.

Bewahre doch vor Jammerwoch!
    Die Zähne knirschen, Krallen kratzen!
Bewahr' von Jubjub-Vogel, vor
    Frumiösen Banderschnätzchen!

Er griff sein vorpals Schwertchen zu,
    Er suchte lang das manchsam' Ding;
Dann, stehend unten Tumtum Baum,
    Er an-zu-denken-fing.

Als stand er tief in Andacht auf,
    Des Jammerwochen's Augen-feuer
Durch tulgen Wald mit wiffek kam
    Ein burbelnd ungeheuer!

Eins, Zwei! Eins, Zwei! Und durch und durch
    Sein vorpals Schwert zerschnifer-schnück,
Da blieb es todt! Er, Kopf in Hand,
    Geläumfig zog zurück.

Und schlugst Du ja den Jammerwoch?
    Umarme mich, mein Böhm'sches Kind!
O Freuden-Tag! O Halloo-Schlag!
    Er chortelt froh-gesinnt.

Es brillig war, etc.

Lieselotte and Martin Remane in an edition of 'Through the Looking Glass', published by Reclam – Kinderbuchverlag Berlin 1976 .

BRABBELBACK
Es sunnte Gold, und Molch und Lurch
krawallten 'rum im grünen Kreis,
den Flattrings ging es durch und durch,
sie quiepsten wie die Quiekedeis.

»Nimm dich in acht vorm Brabbelback,
mein Sohn! Er beißt, wenn er dich packt.

Reiß aus, reiß aus vorm Sabbelschnack,
vorm Jubjub, der dich zwickt und zwackt!«

Er aber schwuchtelt mit dem Schwert,
trabaust dem Unhold hinterdrein.
Doch beim Tumtumbaum macht er kehrt
und grübelt: Wo, wo mag er sein?

Und während er so duselnd stand,
kam feuerfauchend Brabbelback
quer durch den Dusterwald gerannt,
der Brabbelback, der Sabbelschnack!

Komm 'ran, komm 'ran! Und schwipp und schwapp
haut er das Schwert ihm ins Genick,
der Unhold fiel, sein Kopf war ab,
der Held kam mit dem Kopf zurück.

»Ermurkst hast du den Brabbelback!
Umarmen wird man dich zu Haus!
Callu, callei! Mit Sabbelschnack
und seinem Tratschen ist es aus!«

Es sunnte Gold, …

Christian Enzensberger; source unknown

DER ZIPFERLAKE
Verdaustig war's, und glaße Wieben
rotterten gorkicht im Gemank.
Gar elump war der Pluckerwank,
und die gabben Schweisel frieben.

»Hab acht vorm Zipferlak, mein Kind!
Sein Maul ist beiß, sein Griff ist bohr.
Vorm Fliegelflagel sieh dich vor,
dem mampfen Schnatterrind.«

Er zückt' sein scharfgebifftes Schwert,
den Feind zu futzen ohne Saum,
und lehnt' sich an den Dudelbaum
und stand da lang in sich gekehrt.

In sich gekeimt, so stand er hier,
da kam verschnoff der Zipferlak
mit Flammenlefze angewackt
und gurgt' in seiner Gier.

Mit Eins! und Zwei! und bis auf's Bein!
Die biffe Klinge ritscheropf!
Trennt' er vom Hals den toten Kopf,
und wichernd sprengt' er heim.

»Vom Zipferlak hast uns befreit?
Komm an mein Herz, aromer Sohn!
Oh, blumer Tag! Oh, schlusse Fron!«
So kröpfte er vor Freud'.

Verdaustig war's, …

Spanish version by Francisco Torres Oliver, from *Alicia anotada, edición de Martin Gardner de Alicia en el País de las Maravillas & A través del espejo*. Akal Editor, Madrid, 1984.

JERIGÓNDOR
Cocillaba el día y las tovas agilimosas
giroscopaban y barrenaban en el larde.
Todos debirables estaban los burgovos,
y silbramaban las alecas rastas.

"Cuídate, hijo mío, del Jerigóndor,
que sus dientes muerden y sus garras agarran!
!Cuídate del pájaro Jubjub, y huye
del frumioso zumbabadanas!"

Echó mano a su espada vorpal;
buscó largo tiempo al manxomo enemigo,
descansó junto al árbol Tumtum,
y permaneció tiempo y tiempo meditando.

Y, estando sumido en irribumdos pensamientos,
surgió, con ojos de fuego,
bafeando, el Jerigóndor del túlgido bosque,
y burbulló al llegar!

!Zis, zas! !Zis, zas! !Una y otra vez
tajó y hendió la hoja vorpal!
Cayó sin vida, y con su cabeza,
emprendió galofante su regreso.

"!Has matado al Jerigóndor?
Ven a mis brazos, sonrillante chiquillo,
!Ah, frazoso día! !Calós! !Calay!"
mientras él resorreía de gozo.

Cocillaba el día y las tovas agilimosas
giroscopaban y barrenaban en el larde.
Todos debirables estaban los burgovos,
y silbramaban las alecas rastas.

Spanish version by Mirta Rosenberg and Daniel Samoilovich, from *Diario de Poesia*
43, September 1997. *Diario de Poesia* is an illustrated poetry quarterly published in
Buenos Aires, Argentina.

JABBERWOCKY

Asardecía y las pegájiles tovas
Giraban y scopaban en las humeturas;
Misébiles estaban las lorogólobas,
Superrugían las memes cerduras.

!Con el Jabberwock, hijo mío, ten cuidado!
!Sus fauces que destrozan, sus garras que apresan!
!Cuidado con el ave Jubjub, házte a un lado
Si vienen las frumiantes Roburlezas!

Empuñó decidido su espada vorpal,
Buscó largo tiempo al monxio enemigo –
Bajo el árbol Tamtam paró a descansar
Y allí permanecía pensativo

Y estaba hundido en sus ufosos pensamientos
Cuando el Jabberwock con los ojos en llamas
Resofló a través del bosque tulguiento:
!Burbrujereando mientras se acercaba!

!Uno, dos! !Uno, dos! !A diestra y siniestra
La hoja vorpalina silbicortipartió!
El monxio fue muerto, con su cabeza en ristre
El joven galofante regresó.

"!Muchacho bradiante, mataste al Jabberwock!
!Ven que te abrace! !Que día más fragoso
!Me regalas, hijo! !Kalay, kalay, kaló!"
Reiqueaba el viejo en su alborozo.

Asardecía y las pegájiles tovas
Giraban y scopaban en las humeturas;
Misébiles estaban las lorogólobas,
Superrugían las memes cerduras.

Practice

Find as many translations as you can of this poem into a language of your choice. Fill in the words corresponding to the original words in a list like the one below:

English	French	Spanish
brillig		
slithy		
toves		
gyre		
gimble		
wabe		
all mimsy		
borogoves		
mome		
raths		
outgrabe		

Do these selections mirror your own?

Do the translators seem to have prioritised meaning-echoes over sound-echoes of the original?

Compare the translations from the points of view of (i) their use of parts of speech; (ii) phonaesthesia; (iii) relationships with the original.

Discussion

It is striking that both the French and German versions reprinted in Gardner (1960/1970: 193–4) replicate very closely the original's nonsense-words, generally altered only just enough to take account of French and German spelling and grammatical conventions, respectively:

English	French	German
brillig	brilgue	brillig
slithy	lubricilleux	schlichte
toves	tôves	Toven
gyre	gyrent	wirrten
gimble	vrillant	wimmelten
wabe	guave	Waben
all mimsy	enmîmés	aller-mümsige
borogoves	gougebosqueux	Burggoven
mome	*môme*rade	mohmen
raths	môme*rade*	Räth'
outgrabe	horsgrave	ausgraben

Notice that priority seems to be given to meaning-echoes, whether phonaesthetically or morphologically provided, over formal/phonological similarity, when a choice has been felt necessary. Thus 'slithy', which may echo 'slimy' and 'lithe' is given in French as 'lubricilleux' and 'gyre', which is reminiscent of 'gyrate', is given as 'wirrten' (though Carroll's explanation of 'gyre' relates it to scratching like a dog; see Gardner [1960] 1970: 191).

5.3 WORDS IN LEXICAL SEMANTICS

In the sections above, we have looked at the grammar of words. In this section, we begin to study the notion of word meaning.

5.3.i Words and classification

Words play an important part in human efforts to order and control the environment through classification. Consider the following text extract From the *Times Higher Education Supplement* of 14 June 1985:

> The voluntary licensing authority set up to oversee *in vitro* fertilization research has proposed a new term – the 'pre-embryo' – to clarify the debate about work on early stages of human development ...
>
> The guidelines suggest that the group of cells growing from a fertilized human egg be called the pre-embryo until the first signs of individual development appear. The term has no currency among biologists ...
>
> However, the definition is consistent with the Warnock report's argument for a 14-day limit on research on human embryos ...

This text provides an example of the use of a new term, 'pre-embryo', to help turn the notion of a group of cells growing from a fertilised human egg before the first signs of individual development have appeared, into a more sharply defined concept having one term associated with it and with it alone. It shows that we do not simply assign labels to pre-existing categories, but that many categories are recognised as such because they seem appropriate to human purposes.

Types of category

Some of the categories we operate with are so-called natural kinds, e.g. mammals, lemons, gold and so on – categories which we tend to consider identifiable in virtue of particular genetic, chemical or other structures or physical characteristics given naturally and objectively. Other categories are more culturally than naturally determined, e.g. clergy, philosophical theories, literary 'schools' and political movements. Some categories arise as a result of attempts to make sense, in psychological terms, of human behaviour and of physio-chemical changes, e.g. emotions and mental states; and there are of course also innumerable classes of humanly manufactured objects, e.g. computers, cutlery, crockery, vehicles, buildings and so on (see Figure 5.1 below).

Natural kinds: mammals, lemons, gold ...
Cultural kinds: clergy, philosophical theories, literary schools; political movements ...
Psychological kinds: emotions, mental states ...
Manufactured kinds: computers, cutlery, crockery, vehicles buildings ...

Figure 5.1   Kinds of kind.

It is likely that there will be most overlap between languages and cultures in the case of natural kinds, followed by manufactured kinds, and least in the case of cultural kinds and psychological kinds (see, however, Putnam [1970] 1975 on natural kinds, and see Gallie 1955–6 on cultural kinds).

Semantic fields and lexical sets

We may consider all of these categories of phenomenon to constitute different semantic fields or spheres of activity or interest, and we shall consider the sets of words that stand for phenomena within a field to constitute lexical sets (see Figure 5.2 below):

Semantic fields: groups of phenomena of a certain kind, e.g. mammals, fish, colours, days of the week, months of the year, emotions, political movements ...
Lexical sets: The sets of words that stand for phenomena within a field

Figure 5.2   Semantic fields and lexical sets.

Mutual incompatibility

The various terms within lexical sets cannot simultaneously be ascribed to one and the same object, e.g.: If the animal in the cage is a lion, it cannot also be a horse; if the fish in the aquarium is a cod it cannot also be a plaice; if a piece of material is red it cannot also be blue; if today is Tuesday, it cannot also be Wednesday; if we are in April, we cannot also be in May. Because of this feature of terms within lexical sets, they are known as mutually incompatible terms. If two utterances that refer to the same are identical except that one contains one of two incompatible terms and the other utterance contains the other term in the pair, then the sentences will be mutually contradictory: 'The animal in that cage is a lion' contradicts 'the animal in that cage is a tiger'.

Gradability

The terms we have looked at so far are non-gradable in principle. You cannot be more or less a lion, horse, etc., a day cannot be more or less Tuesday; a month cannot be more or less April, and so on.

In contrast. some lexical sets, such as the set of terms for temperatures, consist of gradable terms, e.g. 'cold', 'cool', 'warm', 'hot'. These can cause difficulties for translators because the gradations that can be lexicalised are not the same in all languages. They do, however, allow for variations in opinion, and the two utterances 'this liquid is cool' and 'this liquid is warm', although contradictory, at least allow for negotiation between utterers about the most suitable description given various sets of surrounding circumstances.

Practice

Consider the other languages you know, and whether they have the same sets of gradable terms as English. Do the nuances picked out by the terms correspond between the languages?

5.3.ii Words and typicality

There is evidence to suggest that people are able to grade the members of semantic fields according to their typicality as members of that field (see e.g. Rosch 1973, 1977, 1978 and Aichison [1987] 1994, Chapters 5 and 6 for a review of work on this topic, known as prototype theory). Fruits considered typical by speakers of American English include e.g. apples and pears; typical birds include e.g. robins, sparrows, canaries, blackbirds, doves and larks; typical vegetables include peas, carrots and cauliflower; typical pieces of furniture includes chairs; typical clothing includes shirts, dresses and skirts; typical weapons include guns and daggers; typical carpenters' tools include hammers and screwdrivers. In other cultures, proto-typicality judgements differ, and it is useful for translators to bear this in mind. For example, a mention of birds is likely to call very colourful creatures to the minds of people among whom parrots are prototypical birds, whereas for members of northern hemisphere cultures, the image is likely to be more modest.

5.3.iii Words and relationships

Apart from the organisation of words into lexical sets in virtue of the classification of the phenomena in the world that words relate to, lexical semantics also provides an account of relationships between words, known as sense relations.

Hyponymy

Terms that are used to denote a class, e.g. 'mammal', 'fish', 'vehicle', typically stand in a relationship of hyponymy with the terms that can be used to denote subtypes of the members of the class. For example, 'mammal' is the 'superordinate term' for its 'hyponyms', 'tiger', 'wolf', 'whale' and so on, and these latter, in turn, are 'cohyponyms' of each other. There are layers of hyponymy, and the relationship between a higher and a lower layer is always such that any member of a layer lower down is an example of the kind named by the superordinate term, whereas the

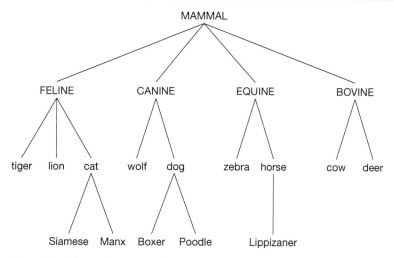

Figure 5.3   A (partial) representation of the hyponymy relationship between terms for mammals.

reverse is not the case: All Siamese cats are kinds of cat, but all cats are not Siamese cats; all cats are felines, but all felines are not cats; all felines are mammals, but all mammals are not felines. Figure 5.3 depicts a hyponymy relationship in the form of a tree structure.

Many hyponymy relationships are organised differently in different languages. For example, most English people consider a potato to be a (root) vegetable, whereas most French people do not consider a *pomme de terre* to fall into the *legume* category.[2]

Synonymy or sameness of meaning

It is extremely difficult to find total synonymy between terms within one language, because languages appear to resist redundancy of this type. Thus, when terms are imported into a language from another so that, for a while, there may be two terms for the same phenomenon, their uses soon begin to diverge. For example, 'infant', which derives from the French word for 'child', *enfant*, is now used in English to denote very young children only. Synonymy does, nevertheless, seem to exist between some pairs of predicates (i.e. a verb with complementation) which ascribe the same property to a phenomenon; for example, because being dead is the same as not being alive, 'is dead' means the same as 'is not alive'. Because we decide to call men who have never married, 'bachelors', 'is a bachelor' means the same as 'is a man who has never married'. Because we call a vixen 'a female fox', 'is a vixen' means the same as 'is a female fox'. We may then say that 'bachelor' and 'man who has never married' and 'vixen' and 'female fox' are pairs of synonyms.

Antonymy

Along with synonymy goes antonymy, which is often, metaphorically, referred to as 'oppositeness of meaning' ('metaphorically', because meanings are not physical entities and cannot, therefore, strictly speaking be arranged in physical space, as implied by the term 'opposite'). Antonymy holds between pairs of terms that are used to predicate characteristics in the case of which a phenomenon either displays them or does not display them, provided that the characteristics are applicable to it. For example, any animate creature must be either alive or dead, so 'is dead' and 'is alive' are antonymous predicates – though it makes no sense to try to predicate either of e.g. a stone. 'Is true' is antonymous with both 'is false' and 'is untrue', but since the two latter predicates are synonymous, this does not destroy the binary nature of the antonymy relationship. The problem with the relationship, is, rather, that in reality there are very few clear dividing lines to be drawn in human affairs: We often feel that there really are half-truths and cases in which it is simply not possible to assign truth and falsity absolutely. And what are we to do with concepts like brain-death?

It is also important to be aware that although some predicates realise relationships like hyponymy, synonymy and antonomy very regularly – and I have used such predicates for exemplification in this section – it is very common to see a far wider variety of terms realising the relationships in texts. Sense relationships, in common with grammatical relationships, provide a fixed framework consisting of a limited number of relationships which can however be used to create an infinite number of different texts in which an infinite number of terms can be placed in the relationship in question. In the first paragraph of the banking text at the end of this chapter, for example, what we may term a text-local hyponymy relationship is set up between the superordinate term 'source of wealth' (sentence 3), text-locally synonymous with 'factor' (sentence 2), and the hyponyms 'trickle down effect of large government budgets' and 'boom in value', the latter in turn having three hyponyms of its own, 'share market value', 'local property value' and 'local land value' (sentence 2) (see Figure 5.4).

Symmetry, transitivity and converseness

Further types of predicate characteristic or relationship between predicates include symmetry, transitivity and converseness. Symmetric predicates like 'is married to', 'is near (to)', and 'is next to' work in such a way that (where P stands for the predicate and x and y for individuals) if xPy, then yPx; e.g. if a is married to b, then b is married to a. Transitive predicates, like 'is in front of' and 'is taller than' work in such a way that if xPy and yPz then xPz; e.g. if a is in front of b and b is front of c, then a is in front of c. Converse or relationally opposite predicates, like 'is a parent of' and 'is a child of' work in such a way that (where P and R stand for converse predicates), if xPy then yRx; e.g. if a is a child of b, then b is a parent of a.

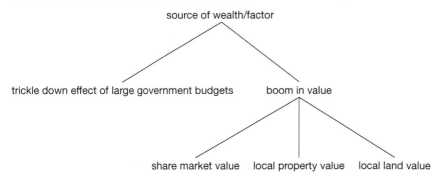

Figure 5.4.   A text-local hyponymy relationship.

5.3.iv Words and flexibility

Just as the sense relationships we looked at above are not restricted in their realisations to a fixed set of terms, no term in any language is restricted to one meaning or use. Flexibility is the norm in language, rather than the exception, and there are a variety of ways of describing and referring to different types of lexical flexibility.

Ambiguity (lexical; syntactic; process/product)

Ambiguity is a property of predicates which will affect sentences in such a way that those sentences in which the predicates are used will be capable of two quite different interpretations. For example, 'James was looking carefully at the coach' has an interpretation under which James is observing a large vehicle and another under which he is observing a person who trains others, usually in sporting activities. Put simplistically, 'coach' is ambiguous between the meanings 'person who trains others, usually in a sport' and 'large passenger carrying vehicle; bus'.

Ambiguous words or phrases have more than one extension (set of things they denote) and these extensions comprise quite different things or phenomena. This means that an ambiguous sentence has more than one potential sets of quite different, unrelated truth conditions at any one time that it is being used (Quine 1960: 131). Usually, properly ambiguous words or phrases will be given one entry for each of their extensions in a dictionary. For instance, there will typically be individual entries for each of the meanings of 'coach', 'trunk' and 'lift'.

If ambiguity pertains to both the spoken and written form of a term, as in the case of 'bank', the term is said to be homonymous. If ambiguity pertains to the spoken form only, the two differently written forms are said to be homophones, for example, 'site'–'sight'; 'rite'–'right'; 'there'–'their'. If, on the other hand, terms are only ambiguous when written down, they are said to be homographs. An example would be 'lead', which may denote either a dog's lead or the metal, lead.

An ambiguous predicate such as 'is light' may produce a sentence which is at once clearly true and clearly false, when predicated of an object. For example, if we predicate 'is light' of a dark feather, then the sentence 'this feather is light' is clearly true in the weight-sense of 'light', and clearly false in the colour-sense. Sometimes the ambiguity of a word is resolved by the rest of a sentence that contains it; thus 'light' is generally taken to mean 'not heavy' when followed by 'as a feather'. When the ambiguity of a term infects the containing sentence, as in 'our mothers bore us', it can sometimes be resolved by the surrounding discourse (Quine 1960: 129).

There are some types of word that are systematically ambiguous. For example, some verbal nouns display systematic ambiguity between process and product. The form, 'utterance' has caused much disquiet in linguistics because it is ambiguous between the act of uttering and the utterance thereby produced (see Lyons 1996: 12). The form 'assignment' can be used to denote the act of assigning or the thing assigned, 'arrangement' to the act of arranging or to the things arranged; 'shopping' can denote the act of shopping or things bought. Other verbal nouns display ambiguity between action and custom. For example, 'skater' can denote a person who is skating now (and therefore has to be awake, for instance), or a person who often skates (but may at this very moment be asleep) (Quine 1960: 130).

The examples discussed so far have been examples of lexical ambiguity, so called because the ambiguity of the sentences in which they occur arises because individual words have two or more extensions. However, we also often encounter what is known as 'structural ambiguity', as in 'the chicken is ready to eat'; 'visiting relatives can be a nuisance' and 'flying planes can be dangerous' (attributable to Chomsky) and 'the police were ordered to stop drinking after midnight' (probably first used by Halliday). The ambiguity of such sentences arises because one graphological form is used to realise different syntactic structures. For example, the phrase 'visiting relatives' may be understood either as a Noun Phrase in which 'visiting' is an adjective modifying the noun, 'relatives', and which functions as a straightforward clause subject. Or, it may be understood as a participial or nominal '-ing clause' occurring in subject position and having 'visiting' as its verb and 'relatives' as its object.

Polysemy

Whereas ambiguity affects sentences or words that have two completely different meanings, a polysemous term has several shades of meaning, more or less clearly separable, but with a basis in similarity. For example 'foot' (of the bed or a mountain), 'hand' and 'face' (of a clock), 'leg' (of a table) each resembles in some respect a human body part.

One way of trying to differentiate between ambiguity and polysemy is the so called 'co-ordination test' (Palmer 1981: 106) also known as the 'to do so too test' (Kempson 1977). Whereas it is just about acceptable to say 'John has a bright face and so has the clock on the wall', it is not acceptable to say 'Jane went to the bank and so did Samantha' if one went to get some money and the other went fishing.

Vagueness

Although it is not difficult to produce sentences which look ambiguous in isolation, in use, utterances are in fact rarely ambiguous. Although we sometimes need to check each others' meanings, most of the time, we understand which of several potential meanings is the intended one in any one instance of use. It is fortunate indeed that we have this ability to relate utterances and written sentences to their co-text and context in such a way that we understand the utterer's intentions most of the time, because it is also true that almost any linguistic item can be used in many ways and with many functions. For this reason, it is useful to try to keep the notion of ambiguity apart from another property of terms, which we might prefer to call vagueness. Ambiguity can then be reserved for terms that have the potential, on each occasion of their use, to be both quite clearly true of what they are predicated of, and clearly false of what they are predicated of. Vague terms, on the other hand, might be said to be 'dubiously applicable to marginal objects' (Quine 1960: 129).

It is not clear, for instance, exactly how far down the spectrum toward yellow or up toward blue a thing can be and still count as green. It is not always clear whether something is a wood or a forest. It is not clear how wide or long or deep a watercourse has to be in order to be a river rather than a stream, or a stream rather than a ditch. Nor may it be clear when muddy water becomes wet mud. So 'green', 'wood', 'forest', 'water', 'mud', 'river', 'stream' and 'ditch' and numerous other terms may be said to be vague. Furthermore, personal perception can play a part here: To someone from e.g. China or from another country where rivers are of such magnitudes that it can be impossible to see one bank from the other, famous English rivers, such as the Cam, might seem more like large ditches (I am indebted to Huang Ai-Feng for this insight). It is interesting to note that diversities in the ways in which different languages divide up semantic fields are especially obvious in the case of lexical sets of vague terms like the ones listed here; see the examples from the sets of terms for colours in Chapter 3.

Vagueness can also be said to obtain when it is unclear which of a number of possible relationships or characteristics a speaker might be intending to refer to by a term on a particular mention. Take, for example, 'John's book'. The possessive here might be intended to indicate that the book in question belongs to John, was written by John, is being read by John, or has just been mentioned by John. In the case of 'she has good legs', 'good' may be meant to indicate that the legs are beautiful or that they are strong or even, given a particular outlook on the world, that they are quite unremarkable. In the case of 'John hit Bill', 'hit' may be being used to indicate different ways of hitting, e.g., with a flat hand, with a fist, with a club, and so on (see Kempson 1977: Ch. 8).

Metaphor

Linguistic flexibility culminates in the phenomenon of metaphor. Metaphor has traditionally been considered a trope, or figure of speech, along with irony and synecdoche. A trope may be roughly defined as a linguistic device that involves 'alteration of the normal meaning of an expression' (Leech 1969: 74). Using this as a working definition here, let us examine the banking text printed below.

5.3.v Practice and discussion

Practice

Make a list of all of the expressions in the banking text on pp. 112–14 which you think are being used in ways or with meanings that differ from the normal meanings/uses of the expressions.

Discussion

Perhaps the beginning of your list looks more or less like this:

(1) the Suq al Manakh crash ['crash' often means a crashing together of items like cars or train carriages in an accident; here it is used about the economy, which is neither a vehicle nor a physical entity].

(1) Kuwait's economy is now at a crossroads [a crossroads is a place where two roads meet and cross over one another. Normally vehicles find themselves at crossroads. Here, however, since it is the economy that is at a crossroads, the meaning must be the derived meaning of being in a situation where a choice has to be made about which direction to take – again using direction metaphorically. The meaning is perhaps that there are a number of actions that can be taken by people running the economy, and the choices have to be made now if any progress is to be made.]

(2) the state's economy has been largely based on three factors ['be based on' suggests a physical structure with a base. But physical structures are based on, for example, concrete foundations; here, it is non-physical factors which form the base, and it is the non-physical economy that is conceptualised as being based on them].

(2) the trickle down effect of large government budgets [literally, it is physical substances that trickle down; but whatever the effects of large budgets, making substances trickle down (down where and along what?) is not among them].

(2) the boom in values in the share market and in local property and land [what does 'boom' mean here?].

(4) the decline in world oil demand ['decline' provides a physical understanding of the fact that there is less demand for oil].

(5) maintain production at the levels set by OPEC [again, 'levels' suggest a physical mass of oil which reaches up to for example a certain mark on a measuring stick].

(6) Oil revenues were expected to be in the region of Kd2.9 billion ['region' also suggests a physical space, when in reality what is at issue is a monetary value].

What this brief, partial analysis already suggests is that there is a strong tendency in this text to use terms metaphorically in order to be able to impose an understanding derived from our experience of concrete, physical phenomena on the more ephemeral subject of the economy.

Does your own interpretation support this suggestion?

Practice

Translate the text (or a part of it) into another language for publication in a journal similar to *The Banker*. Do you use the same metaphors as you found in the source text, or do you use different metaphors? Or no metaphors? What determines your choices of expression?

Discussion

Sentence-level metaphors such as the ones identified in the discussion section above are often explained in terms of their difference from simile: A simile is a statement of similarity which includes a term such as *like, similar, resembles*, and so on, whereas a metaphor implies similarity but includes no such term. For example, 'You are like sunshine to me' is a simile whereas 'You are my sunshine' is a metaphor. Both are supposed to be grounded in similarity, and neither makes it explicit in which respects the two subjects are similar. This indeterminacy, however, is usually seen as an advantage of metaphor: A metaphor can express something which simply cannot be said as precisely in literal terms, and paraphrase (as seen in the explanations in the activities section above) is never total, any more than it can be total and completely satisfactory in the case of paraphrase of poetry.

There are many views on the nature of metaphor, but they tend to fall into one of two major kinds: Constructivist and non-constructivist views. Briefly described, non-constructivists tend to see metaphors as ornamental at best and as misleading near-falsities at worst, and to prefer the precision of what they tend to see as the opposite of metaphor, namely literal language. Constructivists consider metaphor to be an important linguistic means of constructing a particular understanding of phenomena, and they tend not to distinguish between metaphors and other tropes such as similes. They do, however, distinguish between what we might speak of as visible metaphors, which appear in sentences or utterances, and the underlying metaphor, which gives rise to a variety of sentence level metaphors. Such a view is to be found in George Lakoff and Mark Johnson's *Metaphors We Live By* (1980), the title of which nicely hints at the view it expresses. According to Lakoff and Johnson, the way of life of a people – its values and modes of interpreting the world – is reflected in its metaphors. The banking text illustrates the distinction between sentence level and underlying metaphors rather well: The underlying metaphor that gives rise to the sentence level metaphors, 'crash' and 'at a crossroads' (sentence 1) and 'heading for a tailspin' (sentences 17 and 20) is of the economy as some kind of vehicle which can be steered and maintained with due care and skill but which, if it is not, can come to grief.

According to terminology developed by Richards (1936), the phenomenon that is the main referent of the metaphor, in this case Kuwait's economy, is called the Topic or Tenor of the metaphor, the phenomenon that it is being seen as, in this case, as it happens, the vehicle, is called the Vehicle. A third term in Richard's account is the 'Ground', by which is meant the basis on which it is possible to see the Topic in terms of the Vehicle.

A major issue in the theory of metaphor relates to the notion of the Ground. Does the basis on which the Topic is understood in terms of the Vehicle pre-exist the making of the metaphor, or is it created in the making of the metaphor? If I say 'you are my sunshine', do I do so because there is some similarity between you and sunshine, or do I 'construct' such a similarity in saying it? And, if the latter, do your characteristics get projected onto the sunshine, or is the projection all the other way? According to Lakoff and Johnson, most underlying metaphors are based on the human condition. For instance, because we walk upright when we are in good condition but are prostrate when unwell or weak, UP is good whereas DOWN is bad.

According to the interaction view of metaphors expressed by Black (1979), characteristics of the Topic affect the selection of Vehicle characteristics that someone who hears or reads a metaphor will pay attention to; but these Topic characteristics are in turn reinterpreted in light of the characteristics of the Vehicle. It is less clear exactly how the maker of a metaphor makes the connection between Topic and Vehicle in the first place, but then it is never easy to say what triggers off linguistic creativity.

For an excellent collection of writings on metaphor, see Ortony, 1979.

Text by Kathy Evans from *The Banker*, March 1985 (sentence numbers added):

KUWAIT ECONOMY

At the crossroads

(1) Three years after the shock of the Suq al Manakh crash, Kuwait's economy is now at a crossroads. (2) For years the state's economy has been largely based on three factors – the trickle down effect of large government budgets, and the boom in values in the share market and in local property and land. (3) Now, all three of these principal sources of wealth in Kuwait are in jeopardy.

(4) The government has itself been hit by the decline in world oil demand, and production in the last four years has been halved. (5) Yet, as a producer of medium heavy crude oil, Kuwait's oil output has suffered less than those states producing light crudes and, unlike other states in the Gulf, Kuwait has at least managed to maintain production at the levels set by OPEC. (6) Oil revenues were expected to be in the region of Kd2.9 billion (US$9.4 billion) in the current fiscal year, though with the quota cut, these expectations are likely to slip.

(7) In view of the declining revenues from oil, Kuwait's finance ministry likes to maintain the pretence that there is a deficit in the budget. (8) However, only oil revenues can be counted as income into the budget – investment returns are excluded. (9) (They are currently about Kd1.2 billion a year). (10) Even excluding this factor, the budget deficits are still theoretical, for in the last fiscal year of 1983–84, the projected deficit of Kd704 million turned out to be a surplus of

Kd100 million, due to under-spending and postponements.

(11) The government did not emerge unscathed from the Manakh disaster. (12) Some $7.3 billion of investment assets have had to be liquidated and brought home to pay for the various schemes arranged by the government to help the private sector get out of the Manakh morass. (13) Not surprisingly, investment revenues fell by 20% in the year ending June 1984. (14) Nevertheless, foreign assets still stand at $71 billion.

(15) This cushion will make it harder for the government to tackle the fundamental questions now being raised about the future direction of Kuwait's private sector economy. (16) Local merchant circles are now urging the government to reactivate the economy so that share values and land prices can return to their former levels of fantasy.

Domino effect

(17) Some experts believe that if the government does nothing to provide the necessary spark to share prices, then the economy could be heading for a tailspin. (18) Share and land provide the two principal forms of bank collateral in Kuwait, and if the values of those continue to fall, then further foreclosures by the banks are threatened. (19) With the onset of further bankruptcies, the domino effect comes into play.

(20) The signs of this tailspin can already be seen. (21) Share prices have dropped 50% in the last 12 months, and some have fallen a further 30% since the beginning of this year. (22) Rents and land prices have declined by 30% and 50% respectively. (23) Money supply has fallen, bank credit is barely rising, and the outflow of capital continues.

(24) Most local financial executives believe that the return of confidence in Kuwait is going to be a long slow process, and probably will only start with the ending of the Gulf war, or something equally dramatic and energising. (25) Various palliatives have been suggested by local commercial circles – such as further purchases of equity by the government, or greater tariffs to protect local industry, or the establishment of free zones. (26) But most concede that these schemes are not going to transform conditions.

(27) Stockbrokers point out that while share prices are falling, they still have a long way to go before they hit any semblance of their real value. (28) Any further purchases of stock by the government to boost prices would be difficult in view of the fact that the state already owns more than 50% of the market anyway.

(29) Real estate agents say that the land values will continue to experience erosion in the next year, for there is already enough empty accommodation to soak up two years of demand. (30) Land values, too, have a long way to go down before they reach the pre-Manakh levels, for during the boom days, buildings and land were being bought and sold with post-dated cheques.

(31) In the months ahead, the government will be coping with the potential fall-out of the recession and the post-Manakh problems, and it will be doing this with a new Parliament and new cabinet of ministers. (32) Innocent people have

been affected by the Stock Exchange collapse, and the government may feel some moral obligation to those families who bought stock as a long-term family investment. (33) After all, it was the lack of state control that allowed the bonanza in forward deals to occur in the first place.

(34) The government is likely to concentrate on healing the social and commercial wounds that the disaster has caused, and it therefore may be tempted to look at ways to boost share and property prices, (35) The experts may say that by doing this, they will miss the chance of achieving an economy with a really solid basis. (36) But certainly that way will be less painful. (37) After 30 years of growing prosperity, anything else would be very difficult for the Kuwaitis to accept.

NOTES

1. This poem is often used in linguistic discussions. See, for example, Traugott and Pratt (1980: 88–9).

2. I am grateful to Keith Mitchell for this example.

Chapter 6

Words in company

6.1 INTRODUCTION

In Chapter 5, we looked at properties of lexical items and expressions, and at relationships between them. Essentially, these properties and relationships were defined in terms of the connection between linguistic items and those aspects of the world that they are used to speak about, and this relationship has traditionally been thought of as basic to semantics, the study of meaning. Dictionaries provide meanings of terms and expressions by means of definitions that explain what kind of phenomenon a given term can be used to refer to and there may be pictures of the phenomenon in question as well as perhaps examples of the use of the term. In recent years, however, the attention of many linguists has turned to the co-occurrence relationships between words and to the question of the relationship between this phenomenon and the phenomenon of meaning.

In this chapter, we begin by looking at dictionaries in section 6.2.i before turning our attention, in section 6.2.ii to the notion of a corpus. In section 6.3, we shall examine the notion of collocation, and in section 6.4, at the interesting associated phenomenon of semantic prosodies, or 'connotation by association'. Finally, in section 6.5, we shall introduce some notes of caution, though tempered with optimism, which it is useful to bear in mind when working with corpora.

6.2 WORDS IN DICTIONARIES AND IN CORPORA

6.2.i Dictionaries

Although dictionaries provide the kinds of information about word grammar that we looked at in Chapter 5.2, their main function is to provide word meaning: to say what concept or sense a word is related to and to provide examples of how the word can be used.

Dictionaries come in many types and sizes (for an exhaustive overview, see Béjoint [1994] 2000, Ch. 1), but the following broad distinctions between kinds of dictionary (Béjoint [1994] 2000: 37–8) are especially relevant for translators:

- General versus specialised: A *general dictionary* includes a representative section of the lexicon of a language, including its current standard and non-standard vocabulary and the vocabulary of all of its varieties, including archaic and obsolete varieties. It lists words of all classes. For English, Béjoint mentions the *Oxford English Dictionary* as an example of a general dictionary. A *specialised dictionary* is restricted to one variety, dialect or word class. Translators of specialised texts have available to them a vast array of specialised dictionaries which cover the terminology of, e.g., business, chemistry, commerce and finance, construction and civil engineering, electrical engineering and electronics, environmental technology, information technology, telecommunications, law, medicine, and so on.
- Monolingual versus bilingual. Monolingual dictionaries describe the language that is also being used in the description; bilingual dictionaries use one language in the description of another language. Monolingual and bilingual dictionaries may be either general or specialised.

Lexicographers rely on introspection, experiment and observation in deciding which words to include in a dictionary and in order to create the entries in which words are defined (see Ilson 1991). Since the 1980s, lexicographical observation has increasingly come to include observation of computerised corpora of language in use in texts – initially written text but more recently also including speech. The first dictionary to be compiled on the basis of a computerised text corpus was the COBUILD dictionary, published by Collins in 1987, and development in this field has been rapid. Few if any serious dictionaries published since 1990, at least for English, have been compiled without reference to an electronic corpus, and several corpora are available on the worldwide web so that translators and other interested persons can explore them for themselves. There are also a number of on-line dictionaries available there.

6.2.ii Corpora

A corpus is a collection of texts used for language-related research or lexicographical purposes. Since the 1960s, it has become increasingly common to both store and explore corpora electronically using computerised storage and search facilities, parsers and concordancing programmes.

Hunston (2002: 14–16) lists the following types of corpus:

- Specialised corpora of texts of a particular type, such as for example newspaper editorials, textbooks or research articles on particular topics, student essays, or casual conversations.
- General corpora that include texts of many types. To be representative, such a corpus has to be very large. For example, Hunston reports that in January 2001, the British National Corpus (http://info.ox.ac.uk/bnc.htm) stood at 100 million words and the Bank of English (http://titania.cobuild.collins.co.uk.htm) stood at 400 million words.
- Comparable corpora: Two or more corpora of different languages or language

varieties which include similar proportions of similar text types. These are often used in translator training (see e.g. Zanettin, Bernardini and Stewart 2003) and can be important resources for working translators.

- Parallel corpora of source texts and translation. These, again, are useful in translator training and in translating practice, offering evidence of past translator behaviour. Examples include for instance the Chemnitz corpus (http://www.tu-chemnitz.de/phil/english/real/transcorpus/index.htm) of English and German texts and translation, and the English-Norwegian Parallel Corpus of English and Norwegian texts and translations (http://www.hf.uio.no/iba/prosjekt/). Given that most translators (and also students of translation) produce their translations and often receive their source texts in electronic form, it is relatively easy for them to create their own corpora, which can prove invaluable sources for future reference.
- Learner corpora which contain, for example, student essays.
- Historical corpora of texts from different periods.
- Monitor corpora designed to track language changes as they occur.

In addition, a corpus of original texts in English and of texts translated into English is held at the University of Manchester. This has been used to explore the possibility that the process of translation causes translated texts to differ systematically from non-translated text (see Baker 1993, 1995, 1999 and Laviosa 1997). For example, Laviosa (1998: 557) finds that translated newspaper articles display the differences from non-translated newspaper articles shown in Figure 6.1 below:

	Translated text	Non-translated
TYPE-TOKEN RATIO	Higher	Lower
LEXICAL DENSITY	Lower	Higher
USE OF FREQUENT WORDS	Higher	Lower
CONVERGENCE	Higher	Lower

Figure 6.1   Aspects of translated versus non-translated newspaper articles.

This suggests that translated text of this genre may generally be more accessible than non-translated text: A high type-token ratio suggests frequent use of the same terms; low lexical density – that is a lower ratio of content to non-content words – suggests that relationships between ideas are made explicit; use of frequent words suggests that readers are likely to be familiar with most of the terms in the text; and finally convergence, which is towards text that is 'normal' for its genre, suggests that readers will not meet with surprising lexis and syntax in translated text.

An extensive list of corpus resources is available in Meyer (2002: Appendix 1) and both Meyer (2002) and Hunston (2002) provide good guides to corpus construction and exploration.

6.2.iii Practice and discussion

In the Practice below, we explore dictionaries and corpora in order to see how they can help solve some potential difficulties a translator might experience during the translation of the text on economics printed at the end of Chapter 5.

Practice

Read the economics text by Kathy Evans which is printed at the end of Chapter 5. As you read, list any words and expressions that you would like to look up in a monolingual or bilingual lexicographical resource to help you to translate the text for publication in a specialist journal similar to *The Banker*. Next, look up these words in a selection of dictionaries and electronic resources.

How does each resource deal with the words and expressions you have looked up? In which way does each help you to translate?

Discussion

Say that your list of terms includes the following:

crude
tailspin
foreclosures

Of these, one term is subject specific ('crude'), one is transferred from another topic field ('tailspin') and used metaphorically in this text, and the last is a technical term from the discourse of economics and finance ('foreclosures'). These terms are treated as follows in the *Longman Dictionary of the English Language* (1984) (*Longman*), the *Collins Cobuild English Language Dictionary* (1987) (*Cobuild*) and the *Cambridge International Dictionary of English* (1995) (*CIDE*) (pronunciation and etymological information not reproduced):

Longman	*Cobuild*	*CIDE*
crude *n* a substance in its natural unprocessed state; *esp* unrefined petroleum.	**crude oil** is oil that is in a natural state and has not yet been processed or refined. EG *The Soviet union was the world's leading crude oil producer.*	**Crude** or **crude oil** is oil in a natural state that has not yet been treated: *70 000 tonnes of crude oil has poured out of the damaged tanker into the sea.*

Each entry provides information that will enable readers to understand the term as it is used in the banking text. It is noticeable that *Longman* provides no examples, though it singles out unrefined petroleum as the substance most likely to be referred to as crude.

Longman	Cobuild	CIDE
tailspin *n* 1 SPIN 2a (aerial manoeuvre) 2 a mental or emotional collapse; loss of capacity to cope or react 3 a sharp financial depression <*may tip the economy into a –* *– Newsweek*>	If a plane goes into a **spin**, it falls very rapidly towards the ground in a spiral movement.	(*fig.*) *The country's economy seems to be spinning **out of control*** (= experiencing fast change in an uncontrolled way).

In this case, the only dictionary to include the search term is *Longman*, and in this case, an example which happens to be peculiarly appropriate for the banking text is provided. In the case of *Cobuild* and *CIDE*, a search for the term *spin* uncovered some information that might be helpful for understanding the term as it is being used in the banking text, but the information provided in *Longman* is more to the point, and was found under the actual term that occurs in the text.

Longman	Cobuild	CIDE
foreclosure *n* an act or instance of foreclosing; *specif* a legal proceeding that bars or extinguishes a mortgagor's right of redeeming a mortgaged estate.		**foreclosure**
foreclose *vt* 1 to deprive (a mortgagor) of the right to redeem property, usu because of nonpayment 2 to take away the right to redeem (a mortgage or other debt) *– vi* to foreclose a mortgage or other debt.	**foreclose, forecloses, foreclosing, foreclosed.** If the person or organization that lent someone money **forecloses**, they take possession of the property that was bought with the borrowed money, for example because regular repayments have not been made; a technical term. EG *My bank foreclosed on me.*	**foreclose** *v specialised* (esp. of banks) to take back property that was bought with borrowed money because the money was not being paid back as formally agreed. *In a recession banks tend to foreclose* **on** *businesses that are in financial difficulty.* [I] *Their building society has foreclosed their mortgage.* [T]

In this case, both *Longman* and *CIDE* list the actual search term, but only *Longman* provides any information in its entry. This information may be sufficient for our purposes, but, if not, we can go to the entry for 'foreclose'. In the case of *CIDE*, it is necessary to do this to obtain any information at all, and in the case of *Cobuild*, the reader needs to make the link between the search term and the entry for 'foreclose'. Arguably, *CIDE*'s examples are the most helpful.

The idea of this comparison is not to judge one dictionary as superior or inferior to the others – which would certainly be absurd on the basis of three search terms

only – but to note that different dictionaries prioritise different kinds of information and different kinds of user, and that this obviously affects their content. The
Longman dictionary is designed primarily with native speakers of English in mind,
who may be expected to read a variety of semi-technical and semi-professional texts,
and to seek information about a large variety of types of word. They might, however,
be expected to have a fairly good sense of how to use expressions in text, so examples,
when used, are more likely to help with definition than with use.

Cobuild and *CIDE*, in contrast, are marketed as learners' dictionaries, so they
contain fewer technical, semi-technical and archaic terms than *Longman*, and they
rely more heavily on examples to illustrate use. Both *Cobuild* and *CIDE* are based on
electronic corpora, whereas *Longman* was compiled using more traditional methods
of data exploitation.

It is possible to access dictionaries of similar types to these on internet sites
such as http://www.yourdictionary.com/. It is also possible to access a number of
corpora directly. Most of these require a subscription fee though the British National
Corpus (BNC) can be sampled for free. The BNC sampler will provide up to forty
listings at a time for a given term from the corpus accessible via the BNC homepage.
A similar service used to be accessible through the Collins COBUILD home page.
Examples from the Collins COBUILD corpus are presented as so-called Key Word
in Context or KWIC concordances. On 19 April 2003 searches for our three focal
terms in the Cobuild concordance sampler provided the following concordance
lines:

Crude

The market price of North Sea Brent	crude	has moved above thirty-four-dollars
in New York and for North Sea Brent	crude	in London, and West Texas
spilling at least 4,000 barrels of	crude	in Colombia's central middle
of energy futures, including Brent	crude	oil, Dubai sour crude oil, gas oil,
President Bush ordered the sale of	crude	oil from the United States
release of five million barrels of	crude	oil from United States reserves in
average. The price that you pay for	crude	oil is greater at the moment than
announced that it has increased its	crude	oil production to six-hundred-and-
if all of her 147,000 tonnes of light	crude	oil are washed ashore. [p] If the
impact on oil prices. The price of	crude	oil closed near record levels today
report showing a large drop in US	crude	oil supplies and comments by a
[p] Now that the crisis has made	crude	oil a hot commodity, the New York
In London, Britain's North Sea Brent	Crude	oil fell to $ 23.50 a
decline. Carl Kasell, newscaster: [p]	Crude	oil prices fell to a seven-month
s main indicators – North Sea Brent	crude	– rose by one and a half dollars

The corpus (like the dictionaries) provides listings for a number of senses of *crude*
other than the one relevant to oil production (and we know this is the sense we want,
because the text provides the expressions, in sentence 5, 'as a producer of medium
heavy crude oil'). These other senses have been deleted here. The concordance lines
confirm that 'crude' can be used either as a noun in its own right, as in sentence 5 of

the text, 'producing light crudes', or as an adjective modifying the noun 'oil'. In these concordance lines, the most common left collocate (word occurring immediately preceding the search word) is 'Brent' with or without 'North Sea' preceding it, but this is likely to be because the lines are drawn from British texts whose concerns are mainly domestic. The presence of the instance of left collocation with 'US' at least confirms that there are other kinds of crude than North Sea Brent, and there is also mention in the lines of 'crude oil from the United States', and the interestingly described 'Dubai sour crude oil'. The most common right collocate (word occurring immediately after the search term) for crude is clearly 'oil'.

Tailspin

efforts. Throw your skin into a	tailspin	all over again. [h] That's where
yesterday. [p] Shares went into a	tailspin	and sentiment was battered even
Soviet Union out of its economic	tailspin.	Justin Burke has details from
like his car, is not in a permanent	tailspin,	particularly as Coulthard's
the European bond market into a	tailspin.	Quantum is to be commended for
effect, the economy could go into a	tailspin.	The president has wooed Federal
knocked world stock markets into a	tailspin.	This Good Friday the US
suicide sent the shares into a	tailspin,	undermining bank loans. The

The clauses in which 'tailspin' occurs in the banking text are 'the economy could be heading for a tailspin' (from sentence 17) and 'The signs of this tailspin can already be seen' (sentence 20). Since sentence 21 elaborates on sentence 20 by listing a number of economic factors, it is clear (as it is from the anaphoric 'this' in 'this tailspin') that the tailspin in question in sentence 20 is the same as that mentioned in sentence 17, which of course links 'tailspin' directly to economic affairs. The concordance listings provide a number of economy-related terms to the left of the search term ('shares,' economic', 'bond market', 'economy', 'stock markets'), confirming that the word is common in this context – in fact it seems to be the most common context for it. In addition, the listings include one that mentions skin in a tailspin, as well as a car.

Foreclosure

no calling in of loans, no	foreclosure.	[p] The notion of the air as a
that if left unpaid can result in	foreclosure.	[p] [f] Back ratios [f] include
a situation that can result in	foreclosure.	[p] Not all second trusts are
can regain possession without a	foreclosure.	[p] Why no foreclosure? Because
no commitment has yet been made.	Foreclosure:	A commitment has been made
property would have fallen into	foreclosure.	As a practical matter, Sinclair
report indicates a bankruptcy,	foreclosure,	attachment, garnishment,
report indicates a bankruptcy,	foreclosure,	attachment, garnishment,
without a foreclosure. [p] Why no	foreclosure?	Because a land contract
no home and therefore faced no	foreclosure.	Being on the road was in many
it will lose money on the deal.	Foreclosure	expenses, coupled with lost
s traditional enforcement tool,	foreclosure,	may be unworkable. [p] Imagine

offer to a homeseller who faces	foreclosure	may be regarded as '
Harshburger wants a four-month	foreclosure	moratorium and is investigating
troubles. [p] I was looking at	foreclosure	on my house in January and now I'
and I'm concerned about	foreclosure	proceedings on The Antibes that
Mrs. Sklar had recently promoted,	foreclosure	proceedings had been avoided in
and unpaid liens can lead to	foreclosure.	Since condo associations
people at every age were in the	foreclosure	status, which may indicate that
Marcia's formulation is that the	foreclosure	status is less developmentally
than are those in the diffusion or	foreclosure	statuses (Leadbeater & Dionne,
missed mortgage payments and face	foreclosure	will often sell at discount, but
culture. Key Terms androgyny (xx)	foreclosure	(xx) gender concept (xx) gender

It is interesting that while the concordance listings for 'crude' and for 'tailspin' provide excellent evidence of use, they do not really help with meaning. None of the concordance listings for 'crude' reveals that crude oil is oil that is untreated; none of the listings for 'tailspin' indicates what it means. In contrast, the listings for 'foreclosure' link the term with the calling in of loans, leaving something unpaid, property, bankruptcy, land contracts, homesellers, houses and mortgage payments. Cumulatively, they provide a pretty good indication of what foreclosure might involve, though, again, it is necessary to go to a dictionary for a clear definition.

What this suggests is that for a unknown word, a good sized dictionary is likely to provide the best quick guide to meaning, whereas a corpus can provide essential information about use – the kind of information that will help us decide which of the senses for a term listed in a dictionary is likely to be the one at issue in a particular text example. In addition, it suggests that once a translator has determined which term to use in the language being translated into, a corpus can provide good guidance on the kinds of structure in which the term fits appropriately. This information can be especially important in translating into an L2 (language that is not one's native language or language of habitual use), but it can also help translators into L1 to avoid inappropriate transfer from the language of the source text.

6.3   COLLOCATION

Searches such as those we looked at in the previous section, where the focus is on the tendencies of word to occur together, are in effect searches for word 'collocation', the term coined by J. R. Firth (1957) to stand for the study, which he pioneered, of the tendencies of certain sets of words to occur regularly in fairly close proximity.

Corpora can be explored to establish frequencies of occurrence, in texts of the types stored in the corpus, of words, phrases and structures, and also details of phraseology. As Hunston (2002: 21) points out, even native speakers are often not able to introspect reliably about these phenomena; for translators it can be even harder, if they are translating into a non-native language or if they find that the presence of the non-native source text clouds their judgement, or if they are translating into text types with which they are relatively unfamiliar. In such cases, a look in a corpus can be very helpful. Consider, for example, the following extract from an information folder about the University Residential Centre at Bertinoro, Italy:

> Il simbolo dell'ospitalità di Bertinoro è la colonna degli anelli, posta di fronte al Palazzo Comunale ed eretta dai signori del luogo, nel 1300 circa, per porre fine alle continue dispute che sorgevano fra le famiglie nobili del tempo per dare ospitalità ai forestieri che raggiungevano il paese. Alla colonna furono affissi tanti anelli quante erano le famiglie del posto: il forestiero che arrivava in paese legave il suo cavallo ad un anello e diventava automaticamente ospite della famiglia cui l'anello apparteneva.

The passage is translated as follows:

> The symbol of Bertinoro hospitality is the Column of the rings, sited in front of the Town Hall and raised, in about 1300, by the Princes of the town to put an end to the continuous controversies which arose among the noble families of that time because of their wish of giving hospitality to the foreigners which reached their little town. Some rings, the same number of the families living in Bertinoro, were hung to the column: when the foreigner arrived he fastened his horse to a ring and he automatically became the guest of the family which that ring belonged to.

Among the problematic expressions in the translation are the following:

> their wish of giving
> rings … were hung to the column

It is notoriously difficult for non-native speakers of a language to attach the appropriate preposition to verbs, and dictionaries do not always provide clearly contextualised examples that will cover every eventuality. In such cases, a corpus can be extremely helpful. A look at the British National Corpus's free sampler (28 May 2004) provided the following fifty-three examples of the use of 'wish'. The examples are selected randomly from 11,448 examples found by the search engine (some of the co-text has been removed and the search term has been separated from the remaining co-text by spacing). The search engine provides fifty text examples for each search term, but 'wish' occurred twice in three of them:

Few readers will	wish	to make wood blades
what their ablest teachers	wish	to give them.
I	wish	I could say the same for ours
if you	wish	your child or partner to desist
(or a simple mains unit if	wish)	are fixed to the base
We would not	wish	to underestimate the difficulties
I … am beginning to	wish	that I did
I have no	wish	to be seen like this
I	wish	it would happen more often.';
motorists who	wish	to halt and admire the superb view across to Skye
Do you ever	wish	you were someone else?
unless you	wish	to make a serious request.

the charity you	wish	to help direct.
in view of my	wish	to make some sort of contribution
one party may	wish	to inspect documents
initiating from the	wish	of people to have greater
free to indulge, if they so	wish,	in areas outside of productive work, such as
education, but also those who	wish	to use the money from their labour
The photographs … seem to	wish	to express some more personal aesthetic statement.
The applicants	wish	to know the nature and extent of their receivership
I really	wish	I'd been told that I looked disgusting!
Oh god, I	wish	the shops were open,
you can go on home if you	wish.	
We	wish	to focus on two issues
artists who	wish	to combine images
fees for … only apply if they	wish	to take part in the main competitions.
She didn't	wish	Roman's company any harm at all
representatives might	wish	to see a general extension of legal services they
would not	wish	the value of their own legal services to members to
I	wish	you a profitable day.
With every good	wish	from us all here
we	wish,	following Cauchy, to set up a molecular theory
things he would surely	wish	to know.
If you	wish,	we can let the matter drop
You	wish	to see me
those who	wish	to direct their care and attention to the living.
you surely	wish	to please the Master
I	wish	to refute Alan Davidson's comment
I	wish	to rest now.'
people who	wish	to claim backdated benefits.
they	wish	to take early retirement,
The .. countries stressed their	wish	to join the EC
If you	wish	me to give evidence
If you	wish	to base the current SPR on an existing SPR
government appears to	wish	to introduce a benefit-related tax
whether they	wish	to include the words in square brackets.
The teacher may	wish	to introduce pupils to evidence from archaeology
I	wish	to differentiate between
the tenant will	wish	to deal with the premises
the landlord will	wish	to exercise fairly strict control over alienation
groups which … did not	wish	to be involved in these narrow manoeuvres.
I don't	wish	to hear this
	Wish	I could afford a new car

The problematic expression we are interested in is 'their wish of giving'. The first thing to notice about the corpus examples is that there is only one instance in which 'wish' is followed by 'of': 'wish of people to have greater'; in all but one case in which 'wish' is followed by what looks like a preposition, the preposition is 'to' and it functions as an infinitival participle. The odd instance is: 'free to indulge, if they so wish, in areas ...', and here, 'in' belongs to 'indulge', not to 'wish'. There are two instances in which 'wish' is preceded, as in the problematic expression, by a possessive determiner: 'in view of my wish to make some sort of contribution', 'the ... countries stressed their wish to join'. In both cases, 'wish' is followed by 'to', followed by a verb in the base form, 'make' and 'join', respectively. The instance of 'wish' + 'of' is followed by 'people' – a noun, not a verb, and 'wish of people' is in fact an instance of the possessive with 'of'. There are no instance is which 'wish' is followed by 'of' + 'VERBing'. In light of such evidence, an uncertain translator might feel justified in producing 'their wish to give'.

6.3.i Practice and discussion

Practice

In the Bertinoro translation, 'their wish of giving' is followed by 'hospitality'. An examination of the concordance lines for 'wish' persuaded us that a more natural expression in English might be 'their wish to give'. But the expression is followed by 'hospitality' as the object of 'give'. Do you think that 'give' is a suitable verb to precede 'hospitality'?

Search the BNC or a similar resource for 'hospitality' to check your intuition. If your search is unsuccessful or provides unconvincing results, think of other ways of trying to ensure that you produce the most appropriate construction for the co-text in question.

Discussion

A search of the BNC's free sampler on 30 May 2004 revealed three verbs for the VERB + 'hospitality' construction, namely 'show hospitality', 'provide hospitality' and 'return hospitality'. The third is inappropriate in the context of the Bertinoro text, which does not indicate that the town's noble families have already visited the people to whom they wish to be hospitable. There was only one example of SHOW + HOSPITALITY (recall that small caps indicate a lemma – see Chapter 5 above; the corpus was searched for 'show/shows/showed/showing/ hospitality') which is not sufficient to be convincing. For PROVIDE + HOSPITALITY, with 'hospitality' as direct object of the verb, the following are all of the examples in the whole corpus:

> Some details of this tenure are reminiscent of a former age, not least the obligation to provide hospitality (gîte) and domestic service to the king-duke when he visited Aquitaine.

> Rotary committee chairman Tony Dennett said: ';The lunch is an ideal opportunity for us to provide hospitality to these students

> They provided hospitality to travellers

> Under the same management as the Villa San Paolo down the road, it shows the

same ability albeit in a different category, to combine taste and comfort in providing hospitality.

The town has also ar [sic] institution called the Spittel, built from an endowment of 1225 which laid an obligation upon the Teutonic Order to maintain a hospice for tending the poor and providing hospitality to pilgrims.

Introspection or a dictionary search might suggest to you that EXTEND + HOSPITALITY and OFFER + HOSPITALITY are other possible combinations. The following examples are to be found in the BNC:

EXTEND + HOSPITALITY

The prioress … and asked one of the sisters to extend hospitality to the pedlar.

There must therefore have been a certain piquancy for him in now extending hospitality to the fallen monarch.

Richmond Town Council is to send a town crest shield to the council in the city of Marong, Australia, after its mayor extended hospitality to Coun John Blenkiron, mayor elect of Richmond, during his visit to the area.

OFFER + HOSPITALITY

We … would also like to be able to offer hospitality in local members' homes.

It was one thing to offer hospitality, quite another to extend the boundaries of tolerant understanding to dark moods and sudden rages

Instead she told herself that it was only fair to offer hospitality.

You may be kind of blackmailing people to perhaps indiscriminately offer hospitality.

Explain situation to Elaine, who though clearly suffering from flu, offers hospitality, tea, TV for kids, etc.

A woman who offers hospitality to guests is more honourable than one who has to take in lodgers for a fee.

Others in the local community joined in with this socialising process, offering hospitality and a chance to mix with adults and children on a day-to-day basis.

The rites of entertaining and offering hospitality.

In previous years the banks have been lined with marquees offering hospitality as riverside farmers cash in on the regatta … even though they have virtually nothing to do with it.

Nevertheless, the O'Rourke of the day offered hospitality and refuge to Captain Francisco de Cuellar and his crew.

Borrow was not apparently disconcerted to find the coach meeting the train at

Plymouth was full but set out accordingly on foot to St. Cleer, where he was offered hospitality by the Taylor family at Penquite Farm.

The patrons of the first and second kinds offered hospitality, reward and (in some cases of the second kind) direct monetary exchange,

Tweeddale District Council has kindly offered hospitality in the form of a Cocktail Party prior to dinner.

For GIVE + HOSPITALITY, in contrast, the entire BNC provides only three examples, which are all in the past tense and which seem to derive from historical accounts:

In the time of Henry VII he had stripped the whole of Fife of oak and fir trees in order to build a huge man-of-war, the Great St Michael, and had given hospitality to the impostor Perkin Warbeck as son of Edward IV and therefore rightful king of England.

Tudor England was no cultured and sophisticated Italian state, but the country did feel the influence of the humanists and gave hospitality to Erasmus.

In 1853 Mrs Reid gave hospitality to Harriet Beecher Stowe, who had come to England to speak about slavery at private gatherings of women, and in 1860 she shared her home with Sarah Redmond, the first black woman to undertake a public lecture tour in Britain on the slavery question, who later studied at Bedford College.

Next, let us see whether the BNC can help with the proposition for 'rings ... were hung to the column'. In this case, the search term was 'were hung', and the search produced a random selection of fifty of sixty-six examples found in the corpus:

The walls	were hung	with competent oils.
a space in which the pockets	were hung	and for stoking the fires in the kilns.
on which ... paintings ...	were hung,	
rails where wet clothes	were hung	to dry
the walls	were hung	with dead rabbits
The walls	were hung	with posters
the walls ...	were hung	with a miners' banner and posters
the ... ringleaders	were hung,	and the Indians' lands opened
The bodies ...	were hung	upside down from a girder
their bodies	were hung	in chains at various crossroads on the moor.
the tall windows	were hung	with red velvet draperies
Finished cloth and yarn	were hung	out for the approval of the merchants
Three of them	were hung.	
garden implements	were hung	on hooks outside, below the fascia.
doors ...	were hung,	the locks and handles fitted and ...
the walls	were hung	with some of Hugo's collection
The walls	were hung	with furs
her underclothes	were hung	over a chair.
The walls	were hung	with abstracts.

Around the frames	were hung	walls of lath and plaster,
the small boxes	were hung	from the top edge of the dash either side.
portraits, which	were hung	on the gallery walls.
the lime trees	were hung	with pale, yellow-green, dangling flowers.
all four walls	were hung	with gun racks.
At Chalton the doors	were hung	inside the building
the two … horizontal pieces	were hung	while everything was still wet and workable.
On the walls	were hung	religious pictures of Christ
Perhaps nets	were hung	over windows and doorways in the temples
before they	were hung.	
His jackets	were hung	on the backs of chairs
The walls	were hung	with elaborate textiles,
several grotesque fish …	were hung	on hooks beside dried roots.
they	were hung	up to be smoked.
The trophies	were hung	according to their comment
birds in cages	were hung	from lamp posts,
All the walls	were hung	with hunting prints
to ensure that they	were hung	together,
Braque's entries …	were hung	in the Fauve room.
the walls of her hall	were hung	with examples of her work.
walls which	were hung	with oleographs of old sailing vessels.
round the horses' necks	were hung	the bloodstained cloaks and trophies
Fairy lights	were hung	over many of the mosques and houses.
torsion balance from which	were hung	masses made of the two materials
the high walls of the hallway	were hung	with modern tapestries
new shoots	were hung	along the branches of each tree
huge beautiful things that	were hung	from the ceilings on bits of thread.
the other walls	were hung	with home-produced charts
All his suits	were hung	in the wardrobes in covers.
they	were hung	at different heights
Well they	were hung	up on the board in OSD on Friday

Our problematic expression is 'rings … were hung to the column'. Sixteen of the examples provided by the BNC are of the 'walls were hung with' kind. In this construction, 'hung with' suggests near-total cover of the item denoted by the grammatical subject ('walls'), and the sense is somewhere between that of 'decorated with' and that of 'covered with '. This is not the sense of 'hung' (as translation of 'affissi') that is at issue here, and it cuts out 'with' as an appropriate preposition to follow 'hung'. The examples also include a number of preposition-less cases of 'hung', where the context indicates that the sense is that of a person being hung by the neck until dead, or of doors or other large planes being suspended in position. The remaining examples with prepositions are (disregarding 'rails where wet clothes were hung to dry', which pays no attention to the manner of fixing the clothes; in fact, it is not clear that the clothes are in contact with the rails at all – the full context provided being: 'There were several hot-water pipes leading off from the stove, heated rails where wet clothes were hung to dry and plates of food were left to keep warm after serving'; disregarding also two instances of 'hung up'):

a space in which the pockets	were hung		(in)
on which … paintings …	were hung,		(on)
The bodies …	were hung	upside down from a girder	(from)
their bodies	were hung	in chains	(in)
garden implements	were hung	on hooks outside	(on)
her underclothes	were hung	over a chair.	(over)
the small boxes	were hung	from the top edge	(from)
portraits, which	were hung	on the gallery walls.	(on)
On the walls	were hung	religious pictures of Christ	(on)
Perhaps nets	were hung	over windows and doorways	(over)
His jackets	were hung	on the backs of chairs	(on)
several grotesque fish …	were hung	on hooks beside dried roots.	(on)
birds in cages	were hung	from lamp posts,	(from)
Braque's entries …	were hung	in the Fauve room.	(in)
round the horses' necks	were hung	the bloodstained cloaks	(round)
Fairy lights	were hung	over many of the mosques	(over)
torsion balance from which	were hung	masses	(from)
new shoots	were hung	along the branches	(along)
huge beautiful things that	were hung	from the ceilings on bits	(on)
All his suits	were hung	in the wardrobes in covers.	(in)

There are three cases where 'in' is the chosen preposition, and in two of these, it indicates a contained space (a room; a wardrobe). In the third, 'hung in chains', what is at issue is the fact that the material used to suspend the bodies is chains. None of these situations is relevant to our rings and column. Each of the instances with 'over' are of material that is soft enough to drape (fairy lights are attached to flex), which is not so in the case of our rings. It is possible, but unlikely, that the rings will go right around the column, in the way that cloaks can be hung around the necks of horses. Removing the unlikely examples, we are left with seven instance of 'hung on', four instances of 'hung from' and one instance of 'hung along'. But 'along' suggests a horizontal surface, as branches indeed often are, whereas a column is vertical. The examples with 'from' suggests free, perpendicular suspension – from a girder; from the top edge; from lamp posts; (less obviously) from a torsion balance – which, again, will not be the case of our rings in relation to the column. It is true that some of the examples with 'on' also suggest free suspension, but they do not all suggest this (on walls; on backs of chairs), so our translator might, after a search and examination like this, decide to write, 'rings … were hung on the column'; but even 'rings … were hung from the column' would be preferable to 'rings … were hung to the column'.

Practice

In fact, it may be that 'hung' is not the best verb to select to represent 'affissi' in this context. Can you suggest alternatives? If Italian is not your native language, try out an internet translation provider such as 'Babelfish' to obtain a quick translation. Devise a way to use the BNC to help you find the most appropriate English language equivalent for the context in question.

Identify other problematic expressions in the translation above. Search the BNC or a similar resource in order to establish whether it might have helped the translator to select more appropriate modes of expression.

6.3.ii   Semantic prosodies (connotations through association)

The notion of semantic prosodies derives most recently from the work of John Sinclair (1991) and Bill Louw (1993, 1997). A semantic prosody arises when one word or expression collocates very regularly with one or a set of other words or expressions which share certain connotations. These connotations come to 'infect' the node terms through this regular concomitance. For example, Sinclair (1991) demonstrates that the phrasal verb 'set in', which, in isolation, looks fairly free of either positive or negative connotations, in fact tends to be reserved for use in collocation with terms like 'rigor mortis', 'rot', 'winter' and others that are generally understood to have negative connotations. This can mean that an expression like 'the current economic recovery set in last year' may appear slightly odd, and such oddities are usually best avoided in translation. Hunches about semantic prosodies can easily be checked in corpora. For example, a search for 'handsome', an adjective commonly associated with maleness and gravitas conducted on 8 October 2003 using the then free Collins COBUILD corpus sampler provided the following forty examples of the term:

Abasio was tall, and strong, and	handsome.	Abasio was a prince
at least you can add a	handsome	accessory to your wardrobe
own home/car, wants black male,	handsome,	affluent, fit, into Roots
fen villages – indeed, it's rather	handsome.	And The Kings is a
Life! formula. He was so clever and	handsome	and such a quick thinker that
He was suddenly so	handsome	and resigned that Kate knew
in Victorian style, but including	handsome	bathrooms, air-conditioning,
falls in love with	handsome	boy;
	handsome	boy's head is turned by other
setting beside Colmore Row, stands	handsome,	but admittedly modest,
The dining room is high and	handsome –	candle-lit by fine chandeliers,
the Volkswagen Corrado. Here was a	handsome	coupe which could provide a
Mae began asking me about this	handsome	crimebuster type
had grown older not too well, still	handsome	enough behind that footlights
when she was six, showed Jane's	handsome	father escorting her
Barrett House, an imposingly large,	handsome,	Federal-style mansion,
Good colour schemes and	handsome	furnishings would make them
Special presentable	handsome	Indian male graduate, 26, 6'2
Write to Box 8852a. [p]	HANDSOME,	loving, humorous, brown
clinic and was promised a fine,	handsome	male nose. Just before the
The oncologist was a very	handsome	man. When he asked if I had
and John Tilbury was a	handsome	man. They met and soon fell
Me: 39, 5'11 75kg,	handsome,	masculine and intelligent
Cute's not the word.	Handsome.	Mega-handsome. Cover-guy

Circe [p] COSMOLINE: A tall, dark,	handsome	pay rise? If you want to hear	
Oh it is a	handsome	place, green lawns and tall	
her Texan dude. [p] Originally,	handsome	playboy Steve was to have	
foursomes event, was relying on a	handsome	prize that week to pay some	
the business provided a	handsome	return on the Trust's	
from sustainable Canadian Maple, a	handsome,	richly grained wood, the	
medium built, very-fair complexion,	handsome,	seeks attractive, single girl	
male, 38, 5'7 intelligent, sincere,	handsome,	seeks younger, pretty, sexy,	
Above Smooth stainless steel is a	handsome	serviceable material which	
[p] BLACK male, friend sought by	handsome,	sincere, white guy, late	
BIRMINGHAM, tall, dark,	handsome	student, 21, easy-going,	
With his bright blue eyes,	handsome	tanned face and ever-ready	
will also bring you as many as five	handsome	wall maps in selected issues	
who had red hair, flashed a	handsome,	winning smile and	
and came out again with a tall,	handsome	woman of middle-age,	
is easy to install and comprises a	handsome	wrought iron pull which	
Merlin, in the guise of a	handsome	young student, found his	

6.3.iii Practice and discussion

Practice

What connotations do you have for the terms, 'pretty', 'cause' and 'reason'?

Search a corpus to see the extent to which your hunches are confirmed by the search.

Select up to ten lines from each search, that represent the most frequent collocation pattern for each term and translate them into your other language. Discuss the relationships between the search terms and the terms you selected for use in your translations.

6.4 NOTES OF CAUTION

Before we leave the notions of the corpus and of collocation, we should take into consideration the limitations of corpora, in particular the following (Hunston 2002: 22–3): Corpora provide information about frequency, not about what is possible in language. So the fact that we did not find in the BNC the odd expressions used in the translation from Italian into English that we looked at above is no guarantee that the expression is impossible in English. Nevertheless, in cases of uncertainty, frequency of occurrence in a corpus of specific combinations is a good guide to what is likely to seem normal in the language being translated into.

A corpus cannot show anything except what has been put into it, and representativeness is a big issue in corpus linguistics. It is very difficult to be certain that any corpus is truly representative of a language or of a text type since the sheer mass of text in circulation will, in the case of almost every genre and certainly in the case of general corpora, always outstrip the volume of text available in the corpus. Furthermore, as stressed in Chapter 3, and as suggested in the preceding paragraph, a corpus can *never* show the future, only a part of what has happened in the past. A corpus can therefore never be proscriptive (it cannot forbid behaviour) or prescriptive (it cannot demand behaviour), only descriptive (it can describe past behaviour).

As suggested by the practices in section 6.2.iii above, where we compared dictionary information with information derived from a corpus, 'a corpus can offer evidence but cannot give information' (Hunston 2002: 23). For information, it is usually necessary to turn to a dictionary or encyclopedia; what a corpus excels at is showing examples of use.

Hunston goes on to point out that 'a corpus presents language out of its context'. This is of course true. However, it is true of any piece of linguistic data captured for analysis that it is thereby removed from its immediate context – and it would be a quick-witted analyst indeed who could analyse language at its moment of live expression. An advantage of many corpora as far as translators' research purposes are concerned is that it is usually possible to retrieve sufficient information about the text from which an example derives to locate the full text, and, if necessary, to research its original projected audience and function. Besides, as pointed out in Chapter 3, a corpus is usually superior as a source of information about language use to individuals' introspection. It provides in any event information about language that has been used for a specific purpose.

Finally, in Chapter 2, we saw that Catford employs the notion of collocation to explain what might otherwise be thought of as cultural incompatibilities. According to Catford, whenever an expression seems incompatible with cultural expectations, it is equally possible to consider that the expression is incompatible with collocational expectations; in other words, cultural incompatibility is always reflected in the languages of the two cultures in question, presumably because all of culture, in Catford's view, is reflected linguistically.

Whether or not it is the case that all cultural facts are, or can be made to be, reflected in language, the study of collocation shows particularly clearly that it is manifestly not the case that every linguistic fact is a reflection of some cultural reality. Why should the rings mentioned in the Bertinoro text not be hung 'to' the column? Why should 'offer' be used with 'hospitality' as its object more frequently than 'give'? Certainly, some collocational tendencies can be explained with reference to how things are in the world, that is, a semantic explanation can be found for some collocational tendencies. For example, if 'whale' rarely appears close to 'egg', or appears there less frequently than 'chicken' does, then this might not be unrelated to the fact that whale eggs do not exist whereas chicken eggs do. If 'pleasure' does not often appear in texts close to for example 'exam', it may well be because few people take pleasure in exams, and so on. However, there are plenty of examples of collocational tendencies that are not so easily explained with reference to semantics. For example, the fact that the term 'blond' is restricted to describing the colour of hair and therefore to co-occurrence with 'hair' and a few related words like 'tresses' and 'wig' has little to do with cultural reality. What is at issue here is not what the world is like, but what language is like: reasons for circumstances such as that we call hair, but not cars, blond and that we can say of brains and eggs that they are addled, whereas we have to say of butter and bacon that they are rancid, must be sought within the history of languages.

Chapter 7

From words to texts

7.1 INTRODUCTION

In Chapters 5 and 6, we saw how words are dealt with by theorists and how they are presented in dictionaries and in machine readable corpora. We looked at ways of using such word stores resourcefully when translating. But translating is essentially concerned with the production of text, and it is to the phenomenon of text that we turn in this chapter. We shall begin, in section 7.2 by looking at the notion of texture (Halliday and Hasan 1976: 2), explicated in section 7.2.i and 7.2.ii in terms of the notions of cohesion and coherence. In section 7.3, we shall consider the related notion of implicature, and in section 7.4, the notions of speech acts and text functions before, finally, in section 7.5 turning to the notion of text genre.

7.2 TEXTURE

By texture (Halliday and Hasan 1976: 2) is meant the qualities that cause a stretch of language to be read as a text rather than as an unordered and unorganised jumble of linguistic items – or even as an ordered or principled list of items like those that constitute parts of, for example, phone books, dictionaries, shopping lists, inventories, lists of examples in phrase books, and so on. Clearly, a text is something different from these: a text is an entity somehow beyond the sum of its parts; it is an entity that allows for telling, for rephrasing and for summarising to produce gist. It is in large part because of texture that text can only rarely be successfully translated expression for expression, whereas a shopping list or an inventory might very well be successfully translated in that way (even if that might sometimes require lengthy explicitation). Texture is usually considered to be created by the two phenomena, cohesion and coherence, which interact closely.

Markers of cohesive relationships can generally, though not always, be identified in text, whereas coherence is created by the interplay of text – including the markers of cohesive relations found in it – and the reader or listener. Readers and listeners bring to text a host of skills and knowledge without which a text would simply appear to them as a sequence of unconnected linguistic items, clauses or sentences.

7.2.i Cohesion

Cohesion is created by patterns at every level of a text, including the types of sound pattern we examined in Chapter 4, as well as patterns made by lexical items, grammatical structures and speech acts (see below, section 7.4), so the notion of cohesion meets versification (see Chapter 4) at one of its limits and the notion of intertextuality at the other.

By 'intertextuality' is meant similarities between texts, which readers may recognise (Belsey 1980: 21) and which arise inevitably during the writing process (Kristeva 1969/1980/1986: 37; Barthes 1977: 146):

> the writer can only imitate a gesture that is always anterior, never original. His only power is to mix writings, to counter the ones with the others, in such a way as never to rest on any of them.

Intertextuality is an important stabilising factor in the flow of unique meaning relationships we discussed in Chapter 3, section 3.5.ii, and some especially regular intertextual repetition of linguistic items and structures very often characterises texts belonging to the same genre. Consider, for instance, the following set of thirteen texts taken from the web site: http://www.wineloverspage.com/:

Cabernet Sauvignon
2001 Castillo De Molina, Cabernet Sauvignon, Reserve, Molina, Chile, $9. Aromas of dark wood, ripe red cherries and berries flow from this deep ruby wine. Full-bodied, lush and silky, this is a great sub-$10 wine, loaded with blackberries, black cherries, and sweet vanilla; 87/89.

2000 Dry Creek, Cabernet Sauvignon, Sonoma County, California, $21, 22,000 cases. This dark ruby Cab gives off complex scents of cherries, blueberries, cigar leaf and vanilla. Medium to full-bodied, the flavors echo the nose. The tannins demand a few years of aging but the fruit is up to it; 87/89.

2001 Echelon, Cabernet Sauvignon, California, $12, 11,682 cases. Deeply hued, the wine gives off aromas and flavors of black cherries, mint and oak barrel notes. Tannins are pretty astringent and needs a hardy dish to pair with; 83/83.

2000 Hess Estate, Cabernet Sauvignon, Napa Valley, California, $20. This wine is richly colored with a delightful mix of black cherries, cedar and vanilla on the nose. Elegant, balanced, with chewy tannins, the fruit here delivers adequate pleasure; 87/87.

2000 Kenwood, Cabernet Sauvignon, Sonoma County, California, $16, 51,000 cases. Always a good value, this one maintains the standard. The nose display currants, black cherries and cedar that continue on the palate, with added berry fruit. Rounded tannins carry through on the lengthy finish; 86/88.

1999 Lyeth, Red Meritage, Sonoma County, California, $13. Ruby red in color, the nose of this blend is filled with plums, berries, cedar and dried herbs. The wine is very polished on the entry, with the fruit mirroring the aromas. Zippy acidity ties it all together. Match with beef or game; 86/88.

2002 McWilliam's Cabernet Sauvignon, Hanwood Estate, South Eastern Australia, $12. Medium-bodied, crisp, with bold tannins, this youthfully colored Cab has aromas of blackberries, herbs and cedar. Dark fruit, chocolate and cedary notes linger in the mouth; 83/84.

2000 Peachy Canyon, Cabernet Sauvignon, Paso Robles, California, $25, 1,478 cases. Aromas of cassis and cedar emanate from this deeply hued wine. Medium-bodied, with ripe tannins and integrated oak, the layers of black fruit should complex nicely with bottle age; 87/88.

2000 Peachy Canyon, Cabernet Sauvignon, DeVine, Paso Robles, California, $50, 477 cases. Dark ruby in the glass with aromas of black currants, dried cherries and mixed oak. Tannins are bold, but ripe, and should soften with time. Flavors mimic the nose; 87/86.

2000 Peachy Canyon, Bordeaux Blend, Para Siempre, Paso Robles, California, $38, 511 cases. This ruby red wine gives off a lovely perfume of mixed berries and cedar shakes. Full, lush and well-structured, the tannins definitely need cellar time. The lengthy aftertaste reveals red and black fruit, tobacco leaf, and cedar notes; 87/87.

2001 Turning Leaf, Cabernet Sauvignon, Coastal Reserve, Central Coast, California, $12. Purple-red in color, this value priced Cab has aromas of black cherries, currants, and wood, with threshold sweetness noted. Chalky mineral flavors adds to the fruit; 83/84.

1999 William Hill, Cabernet Sauvignon, Reserve, Napa Valley, California, $38, 3,948 cases. This is an elegant wine, with lovely aromas of cassis, cedar and vanilla. Rich fruit is highlighted by tobacco, leather, and mint. Tannins are obvious but rounded, making an ageworthy wine; 90/90.

2000 Woodbridge, Cabernet Sauvignon, Red Dirt Ridge, California, $11. You'll find a pretty nice nose of blackberries, spice and cocoa. Blackberry and cola flavors prevail on the palate of this middleweight. Good value; 85/87.

Each of these thirteen texts describes a wine. Each begins with a statement of the date of production of the wine, its name, its type, its region, its country and its price. There follows a brief description of the aroma and taste of the wine, sometimes followed by an indication of the kind of food for which it is especially suited. The lexis in these descriptive sentences is highly repetitive and displays some degree of specialisation of terminology; for instance, the term 'nose' is used to refer to the smell of the wine in six of the texts and the adjective '-bodied' (full/medium-) is used of the wine on eight occasions. The smells and tastes themselves are described using fruit, wood, spice and colour terms in frequent repetition across the texts. This type of inter-textual cohesion is, then, usually referred to as intertextuality, whereas the term cohesion is usually reserved for use of the intratextual phenomenon.

Since repetition is fundamental to cohesion within and also to a certain extent across texts, some linguists (for example Traugott and Pratt 1980: 21) consider that Jakobson's work on textual parallelism created by patterning and repetition in text (1960) is the earliest exposition of the notion of cohesion. However, the best known work on cohesion in English is without a doubt Halliday and Hasan's work of that name (1976). In his preface to the book, Halliday defines cohesion as follows:

> Cohesive relations are relations between two or more elements in a text that are independent of the structure; for example between a personal pronoun and an antecedent proper name, such as John … he. A semantic relation of this kind may be set up either within a sentence or between sentences; with the consequence that, when it crosses a sentence boundary, it has the effect of making the two sentences cohere with one another.

When a proper name or noun and a pronoun are used in this way to refer to one and the same person or object, they are said to co-refer;[1] and the relationship between the items themselves is called a cohesive 'tie' (Halliday and Hasan 1976: 3). Cohesive ties can also be established by means of ellipsis, conjunction, and lexical organisation. Most ties are established when an item is used to denote or refer to something that an item earlier in the text has already been used to denote or refer to. For example, in 'Wash and core six cooking apples. Put them into a fireproof dish' (Halliday and Hasan 1976: 2), we understand that 'them' in the second sentence co-refers with 'six cooking apples' from the first sentence. This type of tie, which is recognised at the mention of the second of two co-referential expressions and may therefore be thought to 'work backwards' in the text, is called an anaphoric tie. In addition, there are uses of certain expressions that signal that a cohesive tie is about to be created. For example, when we read, 'This is how to get the best results' (Halliday and Hasan 1976: 17), we expect to see a following stretch of text which will co-refer with 'this' (in this case it is 'You let the berries dry in the sun, till all the moisture has gone out of them. Then you gather them up and chop them up very fine' – quite a long explicitation of 'this'). This type of tie, which is recognised at the mention of the first term involved, and may therefore be thought to 'work forwards' in the text, is called a cataphoric tie. As Halliday and Hasan (1976: 17) point out, cataphora is sometimes signalled by a colon after the sentence that contains the cataphoric term (in this case, 'this').

Terms other than pronouns and determiners can be used to co-refer with nouns and verbs, namely terms such as 'one', 'some', 'do' and 'have. In 'There is a box of chocolates on the table. Help yourself to some', 'some' co-refers with 'chocolates'. Other examples include (Halliday and Hasan 1976: 89): 'My axe is too blunt. I must get a sharper one', where 'one' substitutes for 'axe', and 'You think Joan already knows? – I think everybody does', where 'does' substitutes for 'knows'. Halliday and Hasan refer to this phenomenon as 'substitution' between linguistic items, and they believe it differs from co-reference in being a purely linguistic relationship.[2]

Cohesive ties may also obtain between exactly repeated items or between different forms of the same lemma (see Chapter 5, section 5.1.i) and between expressions that stand in the kinds of sense relationships to one another that were discussed in Chapter 5, section 5.3. Finally, well established relationships of collocation (see Chapter 6, section 6.3) between terms can create textual cohesion.

Ellipsis works anaphorically by leaving out reference to something that has been mentioned earlier, when the context allows this to happen, or, indeed, when linguistic or discourse conventions are such that ellipsis is the norm. In English, for example, a grammatical object can often be omitted when the item in question can be retrieved from the context. For example, in 'There is a box of chocolates on the table. Help yourself', convention and the first sentence together make it clear that what is meant is that the addressee may help themselves to chocolate. Some languages allow for more ellipsis than others, and languages allow for different kinds of ellipsis. For example, in Spanish and a number of other languages, known as 'pro-drop languages', it is uncommon and generally inappropriate to mention a pronoun in response to questions like 'Where is John?'. The natural Spanish equivalent for a sequence like, 'Where is John?' – 'He went shopping' is '¿Donde está Juan?' – 'Salió de compras' ('went shopping') (McCabe 2001). It can, however, be argued that the third person masculine ending on 'Salió' has the same cohesive effect in Spanish as 'he' has in English in this context.

Cohesive ties between nouns and pronouns, and between nouns or verbs and substitution or ellipsis, tend to be confined to relatively short stretches of text, whereas ties established by repetition, collocation and sense relationships may extend throughout a text.

Other important cohesive ties in text are signalled by devices which express how segments of text relate to one another, as, for example, expressions of cause and consequence, temporal relations, counter-factuality, reason and result, and so on. These signals of conjunction are called conjunctive elements by Halliday and Hasan (1976: Ch. 5). De Beaugrande and Dressler (1981: 71–3) call the relationships 'junctions', and the devices signalling them 'junctive expressions'.

According to Halliday and Hasan (1976: 242–3), there are four main types of conjunctive relation: Additive, adversative, causal, and temporal. Signals of additive relations (or conjunction) include 'and', 'moreover', 'also', 'in addition', 'besides', 'furthermore', and so on. In English, signals of adversative relations (or contra-junctions) include 'but', 'however', 'yet', 'nevertheless'. Signals of disjunction include 'or', 'either/or', 'whether or not'. Signals of causal relations and subordination include 'because', 'since', 'as', 'thus', 'while', 'therefore', 'on the grounds that', 'then', 'next', 'before', 'after', 'since', 'whenever', 'while', 'during', 'if'. Finally, signals of temporal relations include 'then', 'next', 'at the same time', 'before that', and so on. Halliday and Hasan (1976: 242–3) provide a comprehensive table of these and a number of other English terms matched to the kinds of relationship they are used to signal.

7.2.ii Practice and discussion

Practice

Consider the following text extract (from Hospers, John 1967, *An Introduction to Philosophical Analysis, Second edition* [first edition 1956], London and Henley: Routledge and Kegan Paul, Chapter 1, section 1, 'Meaning and Definition' (p. 1):

> At the beginning of any systematic discussion one is expected to define terms, and our principal term is 'philosophy'. But the term 'philosophy' cannot be defined as easily as 'chemistry,' 'biology,' or 'sociology.' For one thing, people working in the field they call philosophy have offered very different, even conflicting, definitions of the term; and if we presented a definition at the outset, we would be running the great risk of making a premature judgment on a matter that should first be weighed as carefully as possible. It will be preferable to show, in the course of our investigations, *why* scholars in the field have suggested different definitions – and this will take time. Second, and more important, are special difficulties about the definition, which we shall not be in a position to understand until we have examined some problems about definition in general, and that is one of the things we shall endeavour to do in this chapter.

Copy the extract and indicate cohesive ties by numbers or lines. Translate the text into your other language. Are the cohesive patterns the same as in the English original?

Discussion

The philosophy text signals cohesive and junctive relationships very clearly. It is, however, characteristic of junctive relationships in English and a number of other languages that they do not need to be signalled explicitly. For example, in the philosophy text above, there is no junctive expression between the third and fourth sentence.

Below is the philosophy text with all those junctive markers that can be removed replaced by appropriate punctuation marks:

> At the beginning of any systematic discussion one is expected to define terms. Our principal term is 'philosophy'. The term 'philosophy' cannot be defined as easily as 'chemistry,' 'biology,' or 'sociology.' People working in the field they call philosophy have offered very different, even conflicting, definitions of the term. If we presented a definition at the outset, we would be running the great risk of making a premature judgment on a matter that should first be weighed as carefully as possible. It will be preferable to show, in the course of our investigations, *why* scholars in the field have suggested different definitions. This will take time. More important are special difficulties about the definition, which we shall not be in a position to understand until we have examined some problems about definition in general. That is one of the things we shall endeavour to do in this chapter.

It is still perfectly possible to make sense of the text, even though it is now up to the reader to work out relationships between sentences for themselves. The only junctive expression that had to be retained in the text was 'If' at the beginning of sentence four. In some languages, for example Chinese, it would be possible to remove that too.

Practice

Is it possible, in your translation of the original text, to remove the junctive relations and still make sense of the text?

Note the cohesive relationships in the following text:

Brussels City Tour
We start our visit at the Central Station and see the beautiful St.-Michael's cathedral. We drive further to the Heyseldistrict with the worldfamous Atomium. We marvel at the sight of the Chinese Pavilion and the Japanese tower. Passing the Royal Residence we return into the citycentre and see the Sablan district with countless antique dealer shops. We drive in front of the magnificent Palace of Justice and see the fashionable Louise Square. Passing the stately Royal Square, the Royal Palace and the Houses of Parliament we arrive in the Cinquantenaire district. The Triumphal Arch, exceptional museums and splendid Art Nouveau houses are the highlights of this part of Brussels. Here, we are also at the very heart of the European Union; we drive in front of the imposing EU buildings housing the Commission, the European Parliament and the Council of Ministers.

Discussion

Most noun phrases in this text refer to extratextual items which are to be seen on the tour mentioned in the heading. However, there is regular, cohesive repetition of the plural pronoun, 'we'. The fact so many noun phrases refer to buildings is itself a repetition phenomenon which contributes to establishing cohesion – as well as being a characteristic of the genre that this text belongs to (see section. 7.5 below).

Practice

Consider the contribution which verbs and conjunctive expressions make to cohesion in the text.

Compare the cohesive patterns in the English text with those established in one or more of the texts below.

Bruxelles Tour de Ville
Nous commençons notre tour de ville à la gare centrale et découvrons la capitale. Tout d'abord la majestueuse Cathédrale St-Michel, la Colonne du Congrès et nous atteignons les faubourgs du Heizel. La plateau du Heizel est plein de surprises. En effet, vous y découvrirez une molécule de fer géante; L'Atomium; le

Pavillon Chinois, ou encore la Tour Japonaise! Avant de revenir vers le centre de la ville, nous passons devant le Château Royal de Laeken. Et nous voici dans l'élégant quartier du Sablon et des antiquaires. A l'ombre du monumental Palais de Justice, voici la Place Louise, haut lieu de la mode, et ensuite, la place Royale, le Palais Royal et le Palais de la Nation, actuel siège de notre Parlement. Nous atteignons enfin le Parc du Cinquantenaire dominé par l'Arc Triomphal et les vastes musées. Dans cet élégant quartier subsistent quelques belles résidences de style Art Nouveau. A deux pas d'ici bat le coeur de l'Europe … la Commission, le Conseil des Ministres et le Parlement sont les organes essentiels de l'Union Européenne.

Brussel Stadtrundfahrt
Wir beginnen unseren Besuch am Zentralbannhof. Sie bewundern die einmalige Sankt Michaelskathedrale, die Kongresssäule und den Heyselbezirk mit dem Atomium, dem Wahrzeichen von Brüssel. Sie staunen vor dem merkwürdigen chinesischen Pavillon und dem japanischen Turm. Wir fahren entlang Schloss Laeken, der königlichen Residenz, weiter zur Stadtmitte. Wir sehen dem Sablon-bezirk, der internationalen Ruf hat durch die Zahllosen Antikgeschäfte. Die Fahrt geht weiter und jetzt sehen Sie den eindrucksvollen Justizpalast un den eleganten Luisenplatz. Weiter kommen noch der Königsplatz, der Königspalast und das Parlament. Im Cinquantenairebezirk mit eindrucksvollem Triumphbogen und Museen gibt es auch einige ausgefallene Jugendstilhäuser. In unmittelbarer Nähe gibt es das Herz der EU: die Gebäude von der europäischen Kommission, vom Europarlament und vom Ministerrat.

Bruselas visita de la Ciudad
Empezamos nuestra visita a la estación central. Vemos la magnifica Catedral San Miguel, la Columna del Congreso, el barrio del Heysel con el curioso Atomium, el Pabellón Chino y la Pagoda Japonesa. Regresamos al centro hasta la Plaza Sablon y sus anticuarios. Pasamos después el impresionante Palacio de Justica, la elegante plaza Louisa, la Plaza Real, el Palacio Real, y el antiguo Palacio de la Nación, sede actual del Parlamento.
En el barrio del Parque del Cincuentenario pasamos el impresionante Arco de Triunfo y sus famosos museos asi como varios ejemplos de casas de estilo Arte Nuevo. Cerca palpita el corazon de Europa: los edificios de la Comisión, del Consejo de Ministros y del Parlamento Europeo organas más importantes de la Unión Europea.

Bruxelles giro della citta
Il nostro giro di città incomincia de la stazione centrale e passiamo davanti alla grandiosa cattedrale di St-Michele, la colona del Congresso e raggiungiamo il parco del Heyzel, nei saborghi, il Atomium, una molecola di ferro gigante. Nel parco vediamo pure due gioielli d'arte orientale: il palazzo cinese e la torre giaponese. Tornando nel centro città vediamo il castello reale di Laeken e arriviamo al Sablon, centro per definizione dell'antiquariato. All'ombra dell'im-ponente palazzo di giustizia troviamo i negozi piu esclusivi della capitale: la piazza

Louisa. Piazza reale, palazzo reale e palazzo della nazione, sede dell'attuale Parlamento nazionale, si succedono lungo alla strada che porta al parco del Cinquantenario. Al centro del parco si levano 2 vasti edifici classicheggianti dove trovano sede vari musei ricchissimi, uniti da un arco di trionfo. A due passi del parco palpita il cuore dell'Unione Europea ... la Commissione, il Consiglio dei Ministri e il Parlamento sono gli organi essenziali delle instituzioni Europee. In questa parte della citta sopravivono tuttora alcune splendide dimore di stile 'Liberty'.

7.2.iii Coherence

We noted above that it is often possible for readers and listeners to understand the logical relationships that hold between text parts even when these are not signalled by junctive expressions. In inferring such unsignalled relationships, readers rely on their background knowledge of the world as well as of discourse conventions to establish what is generally known as coherence.

Interest in the notion of coherence grew in the early 1980s, when British linguistics began to take what may be called a cognitive turn away from what had until then been a primary interest in texts as physical entities more or less straightforwardly available for empirical analysis aimed at laying bare their structure, towards a primary interest in how mental representations arise and develop in the comprehending mind as a result of processing which involves interactive exploitation of the information derived from text and information already available to the comprehending mind. Some linguists with these cognitively oriented interests pointed to a number of shortcomings of Halliday's and Hasan's view of texture. For example, Brown and Yule (1983) consider that the notion of cohesion developed by Halliday and Hasan is neither necessary nor sufficient to explain texture. They provide the following examples (Brown and Yule 1983: 196):

A: There's the doorbell.
B: I'm in the bath

Just to test the water, I made one telephone call yesterday to a leading British publisher with offices in New York. There was immediate interest in Clear Speech. *(Letter from a literary agent)*

Both of these texts lack cohesive devices between the sentences that constitute them; yet they make sense as texts. In contrast, the following example (from Brown and Yule 1983: 197, drawing on Enkvist 1978: 110) is full of what might be thought to function as cohesive devices; yet it does not make sense as a text:

I bought a Ford. A car in which President Wilson rode down the Champs Elysées was black. Black English has been widely discussed. The discussions between the presidents ended last week. A week has seven days. Every day I feed my cat. Cats have four legs. The cat is on the mat. Mat has three letters.

In addition, Brown and Yule (1983: 200 and ff.) point out that text comprehension involves more than – in fact does not usually involve – remembering a chain of co-referring expressions. Rather, it involves the construction of mental images of characters and events in a setting – the construction, in Werth's (1999) terms, of a 'text world' in which things change and of which our knowledge grows as the discourse progresses. Brown and Yule (1983: 201–2) illustrate this with reference to the recipe quoted by Halliday and Hasan (see above): six cooking apples which form the basis of an apple pie have clearly changed in the reader's mind by the time the recipe tells them to remove the pie from the oven – they are now a well cooked mush encased in pastry, rather than the six individual raw apples the recipe mentions first. Similarly, the representation in the reader's mind of a plump chicken which has to be cut into smaller pieces to become part of a casserole is not the same chicken-representation as that which will have formed by the time the recipe instructs readers to eat the casserole piping hot with red wine and French bread.

The background knowledge that readers and listeners draw on in constructing text worlds may be of individual instances of a phenomenon or of types of phenomenon. Two people can have quite an involved conversation/correspondence about a place or person they know well without being especially explicit in what they actually say; and even if two people are conversing/corresponding about a place or person they do not know well, they are often able to assume a great deal of shared knowledge about the *type* of place or person in question. For example, as Brown and Yule (1983: 236) point out, if a restaurant is being discussed, then, unless explicitly told otherwise, interactants can assume that they all know that the restaurant will have in it tables and chairs, that there will be menus, cutlery and crockery available, and that waiters will take diners' orders and bring the food to their tables, and so on. But it is not always possible to assume sharedness of either individual or type knowledge across linguistic and cultural boundaries, so translators have to be especially alert to cases in which amplification of various kinds may be required if a text is to be comprehensible to its target readership. This need tends to be especially acute in texts that make regular reference to aspects of landscape, culturally specific phenomena and local history, such as texts intended for tourists.

7.2.iv Practice and discussion

Practice

Below you will find the initial paragraphs of Clémentine Perrin-Chattard's *Les crêpes et galettes* (1999 Éditions Gisserot: 2) and the adaption into English by Thibault Perrin-Chattard.

DES CREPES ET DES GALETTES

Les crêpes et galettes de sarrasin doivent leur nom à l'élégante céréale fleurie, rapportée du Moyen-Orient, au XIIᵉ siècle, par les croisés et cultivée avec succès sur les landes arides et acides de Bretagne.

Le nom générique est "crêpe". Ne dit-on pas "crêperie" et non "galetterie".

A l'origine, ces deux spécialités étaient, non seulement de facture différente, mais encore d'origine territoriale diverse.

La "galette" de sarrasin issue semble-t-il de Haute-Bretagne, se cuisait à la poêle …

ABOUT *CRÊPES* AND *GALETTES*

Buckwheat is the core ingredient of *crêpes* and *galettes* in Brittany. Introduced there in the 12th century by crusaders, riding back from the Middle East, it thrived on the desolate and rocky Breton moors and is still often referred to as "saracen".

If the generic name for *galettes* and *crêpes* is nowadays *crêpes* – one says a "crêperie" and not a "galetterie" when referring to a restaurant serving both specialities, these two dishes used to be very different in their making as well as in their geographic origin.

On the one hand, buckwheat *galettes*, which are thought to come from Upper Brittany (today's French departments of Ille et Vilaine, Loire Atlantique and the eastern halves of Côtes d'Armor and Morbihan), used to be cooked in a frying pan …

What information has been added to the translation which is not in the French source text?

Discussion

The English text tells us that the crusaders had been to the Middle East, that a crêperie is a restaurant serving both crêpes and galettes, and that Upper Brittany comprises the regions now known as Ille et Vilaine, Loire Atlantique and the eastern halves of Côtes d'Armor and Morbihan. Interestingly, it does not explain what a 'French department' is in this context, which leaves some room for confusion.

Practice

Compare with the Brussels city tour texts we looked at above. Does each of the language versions to which you have access make identical provision for potential gaps in readers' background knowledge?

Discussion

The English and Spanish texts both mention the Atomium without any explanation. The German text explains that the Atomium is a Brussels landmark ('*Wahrzeichen*'). However, the Italian and French texts both explain that the Atomium is a giant metal molecule (respectively 'una molecola di ferro gigante' and 'une molécule de fer géante'). All of the texts appear on facing pages of a small leaflet which is adorned with photographs of some of the attractions mentioned, among them the Atomium. The Spanish and Italian texts are printed below the picture of the Atomium, whereas the English, French and German texts are on the page facing, so there is clearly no regular relationship to be established between explicitation and text position relative to the photograph.

7.3 IMPLICATURE

As we saw in section 7.2.iii above, background knowledge is an essential component in language comprehension. We met the notion of background knowledge earlier in the book, in Chapter 3, section 3.6, where we discussed the translation of Danish discourse particles into English. There, we suggested that these particles, which are monosyllabic and unstressed in speech, unobtrusively but conventionally mark information as mutually shared between utterer and audience. What was at issue there was not so much whether a specific piece of knowledge was mutually shared, but rather an acknowledgement or suggestion that whatever information was in focus was mutually available.

We also noted that the conventions for marking information as mutually shared differed between Danish and English. In English, where the sharing of information is marked by 'heavier', stressed items, sometimes of several syllables such as 'of course' and 'well', explicit marking is less frequent than it is in Danish. We found that it is only necessary and perhaps even appropriate to translate the discourse particles into English when they have an additional function to that of marking knowledge as shared, namely to indicate aspects of the structure of an argument. So even where a feature of language comprehension and use must be presumed to be universal, such as the need to draw on background knowledge, we should not expect that different languages will deal identically with the feature.

We noted, finally, in Chapter 3, section 3.6, regularities in the relationships between (a) intratextual relationships between text parts, and (b) the translator's selections of translation equivalents for the discourse particles. It is possible that the translator was not fully conscious of following any explicit rule in her selections of translation equivalents for the discourse particles. Rather, we might say that she was obeying a set of principles, unwritten and unspoken, but open to formulation *a posteriori*, in light of analyses of phenomena that are claimed to be their effects. In translation studies, such principles are known as norms (see Chapter 1, section 1.5 and Chapter 2, section 2.3.ii).

In this section, we shall look at a set of similarly implicit principles and their potential for exploitation for meaning generation, namely Grice's (1975) principle of conversational cooperation and the associated notion of implicature. As in the case of translation norms, what is at issue here is not so much general world knowledge, but, rather, the knowledge of certain principles, in this case of conversation, and, in addition, knowledge of the general consequences of the 'exploitation' of these principles.

7.3.i Logic and conversation

The theory of conversational implicature was first presented by H. Paul Grice in a series of William James lectures he delivered at Harvard University in 1967. The notion is developed in the course of explaining why it is that the formal logical sentence forming operators, ¬, &, v, →, ∀, and ∃, seem not to be straightforwardly translatable into their natural-language counterparts, the junctive expressions 'not', 'and', 'or', 'if-then', 'all', and 'some'. If no such translation equivalence can be established, then logic, the science of valid argument, would not be able to function as a yard stick for natural language reasoning, or as the source for definitions of the various relationships between clauses as set out, for example, in part of Halliday and Hasan's (1976: 242–3) table of conjunctive relations.

To show that translatability does in fact obtain between the logical sentence-forming operators and junctive relations, Grice draws a distinction between what expressions mean and what they conventionally implicate. He claims that the natural language terms mean exactly what logical terms mean, but that the natural language terms are conventionally considered to imply certain things in addition to what they mean. This kind of implication Grice calls conventional implicature. For example, it is conventional in natural language only to link two clauses with 'and', if the order of events matches the order of telling. So if someone says 'James and Wilhelmina had a child and got married', it will be assumed that the child was born before its parents' marriage. But this cannot be part of the meaning of 'and', strictly speaking, because it is possible to cancel the assumption out by adding for example, 'but not in that order'. Real meaning cannot be cancelled in that way. The real meaning of 'and' is simply conjunction or 'bothness', and this cannot be cancelled from 'and'.

While conventional implicature is tied to linguistic expressions, other forms of implicature, which Grice calls non-conventional implicature, are completely dependent on the non-linguistic circumstances surrounding a speech event. Grice (1975: 43) gives the following example:

> A and B are talking about a mutual friend, C, who is now working in a bank. A asks B how C is getting on in his job, and B replies, *Oh quite well I think; he likes his colleagues, and he hasn't been to prison yet.*

Whatever is implicated here obviously depends on a multitude of non-linguistic facts pertaining to the life histories of A, B and C, and would be expected to vary if we varied the participants.

But between the extremes of complete conventionality and total contingency on non-linguistic circumstances lies a type of implicature which Grice refers to as conversational. This does not arise from individual terms, but from the combination of several utterances. Like cohesion and coherence, it is essential to most cases in which several utterances or several text parts are understood to constitute text.

We assume, according to Grice, that conversation is governed by one overriding principle called the co-operative principle: make your contribution such as is required, at the stage at which it occurs, by the accepted purpose or direction of the talk exchange in which you are engaged. This demand can be broken down into several sub-principles called maxims. Maxims of quantity urge speakers to make their contribution to the discourse as informative as is required for the current purposes of the exchange, and not to make it more informative than is required. Maxims of quality urges speakers to try to be truthful, which means not to say what they believe to be false and not to say something they do not have sufficient evidence for. There is also a maxim of relation, which simply tells speakers to ensure that what they say is relevant, and a number of maxims of manner, which regulate how what is said is formulated. These include the super-maxim, 'be perspicuous', which, more specifically, means that a cooperative speaker normally strives to avoid obscurity and ambiguity, and to be brief and orderly in what they say.

Now, it is very obvious that conversations do not, in fact, proceed along such tidy lines always or even regularly. But Grice's point is exactly that the co-operative principle and its maxims offer speakers opportunities to generate implicatures in cases where it is, on the one hand, clear that the co-operative principle is being followed, while, on the other hand, individual maxims are being flouted. When this happens, listeners will supply whatever information is required to re-instate the maxim that has been flouted, and the maxim has been exploited. For example, say that A has sent B out to buy carrots and potatoes. B gets back, and A asks, 'did you get them?' If B replies, 'I got some carrots', A will assume that B did not get any potatoes, because B is either saying too much ('yes' would have sufficed) or not enough (if more than 'yes' is said, it ought to be something like 'yes, I got both carrots and potatoes'). Speakers are able to exploit maxims because they assume that everyone involved shares an understanding of the conventional meaning of the words used, knows the referents of referring expressions, is familiar with the co-operative principle and its maxims, has access to the co-text and context for the speech event, and shares relevant background knowledge.

Obviously, the degree to which it can be assumed that the participants in a speech event are fully qualified on the parameters relevant to the generation of implicatures will vary according to how close, metaphorically and physically, the persons involved are to one another, and in many cases involving translation, they will be further apart than those involved in the original event. Therefore, it is sometimes necessary to provide extra clues to implicature generation in translation, or to provide different clues to those offered by the original text.

It is important to note that the need to preserve a text's implicature generative potential is different from the need to ensure cohesion and coherence in translation. If cohesion and coherence cannot be established, texture itself is at risk, and a translation may be judged to be nonsense. Losing implicatures is less drastic, though it does mean that readers of the translation will not have access to all of the information on offer to suitably skilled readers of the original. Some implicature may of course be lost deliberately.

Conversational implicatures arise from the place and role of what is said within the entire speech situation; that is, from the speech act (see below, section 7.4). Furthermore, implicature is often indeterminate: several possible implicatures may be generated from a flouting of a maxim, though the types of data mentioned above will, of course, help hearers determine the most likely implicature.

7.3.ii Practice and discussion

Practice

Playwrights often play with implicature generation. Consider the following extract from the Norwegian playwright, Henrik Ibsen's, play, *Gengangere* (1881), translated by William Archer (1907–8) as *Ghosts*. The exchange occurs very early in Act I. Regine, who has grown up in the upper class Alving household, is talking to her father, Engstrand, who is a carpenter and has a misshapen leg. Engstrand has come to see if he can persuade her to come away to work with him in an entertainment establishment for sailors which he intends to set up with money he has saved.

Original
Engstrand: Jeg var ute på en rangel i går kveld –
Regine: Det tror jeg gjerne

Translation
Engstrand: I was out on the loose last night –
Regina: I can quite believe that

What is the implicature of Regine's reply to her father's remark?

Discussion

Engstrand is supplying information to Regine, namely that he has been out on the town the night before. The maxim of quality encourages speakers to speak the truth, and a natural response to information is simply to acknowledge it. So in explicitly saying that she believes her father's remark, Regine is doing more than is necessary, and listeners will begin to generate implicatures along the lines that Engstrand is a frequent night time reveller. Engstrand's next remark shows that he, too, understands Regine's implicature – indeed, that he understands it as a reproach. Effectively, he offers an explanation:

Original
Engstrand: Ja, for vi mennesker er skrøbelige, barnet mitt –
(yes because we humans are delicate, child of mine)

The translation (below), too, shows that Engstrand generates an implicature on the basis of Regine's response, though the expression, 'we poor mortals' is likely to cause listeners to understand him to be offering an excuse rather than an explanation. It may present him as a slightly weaker character than he appears in the original:

Translation
Engstrand: Yes, we're weak vessels, we poor mortals, my girl

This play presents the translator with the question of what to do with text in foreign languages. Regine peppers her remarks with French phrases, for example:

Regine: Ja, ja, kom deg nu bara av sted. Jeg vil ikke stå her og ha rendez-vous'er med dig.

(Yes, yes, just get going. I don't want to be having rendez-vous [+ PLURAL] with you)
Engstrand: Hva vil du ikke ha for noe?
(What don't you want to be having?)
Regina: Jeg vil ikke ha at noen skal treffe deg her. Se så; gå så din vej.
(I do not want anyone to meet you here. Look; go on your way now.)

Practice

Discuss the implicatures generated by this small exchange and use the gloss-translation provided in brackets to translate the exchange into your other language.

The translation into English reads as follows:

Regina: Very well; only be off now. I won't stop here and have *rendezvous* with you.
Engstrand: What is it you won't have?
Regina: I won't have anyone find you here; so just you go about your business.

There is a note to explain that terms in French are in French in the original. Compare the implicatures in the original, in your own translation and in the published English translation.

A little further in, the following exchange occurs:

Regine: (*vender sig bort, halvhøyt*). Uff – ! Og så det benet.
((*turning away, quietly*). Argh —! And then that leg)
Engstrand: Hva sier du, barnet mitt?
(What did you say, child of mine?)
Regine: Pied de mouton.
Engstrand: Er det engelsk, det?
(Is that English?)
Regine: Ja
(Yes)

What is the implicature of Regine's use of French? What implicatures arise on the basis of her lies (she deliberately mistranslates and she claims that 'Pied de mouton' is English)?

The published English translation is as follows:

Regina [*turns away; half aloud*]. Ugh! And that leg too!
Engstrand: What do you say, girl?
Regina: *Pied de mouton.*
Engstrand: Is that English, eh?
Regina: Yes.

Do you think that the translation will generate the same kinds of implicature as the original?

Discussion

Arguably, an English speaking Engstrand inquiring whether a remark in French is English may seem either a lot less intelligent than a Norwegian speaking Engstrand making the same enquiry. But it is also possible that the English speaking Engstrand will be understood to be speaking sarcastically at this point, mocking his daughter. In either case, to understand the implicatures generated by the use of French at all, it is necessary to know that the ability to use French was a sign of sophistication and learning in Scandinavia at the time when Ibsen wrote. This implicature transfers to the English context relatively unproblematically, but it may not transfer to every context. And how might the play be translated into French?

7.4 HOW TO DO THINGS WITH WORDS

Article 6 of the Treaty on European Union says that 'The Union shall respect the national identities of its Member States' (see Wagner, Bech and Martínez 2002: 1). In normal circumstances, if someone tells you outright that they will respect you, it is difficult not to generate the implicature that they believe that you believe that they will not respect you just as a matter of course. This can raise a doubt in your mind, where none existed before, about whether it is really obvious that the person will respect you. The wording of the provision is also rather odd: 'The Union shall' sounds more like an order than a promise. But who is issuing an order to whom? The Union to itself?

In fact, what we have here is a provision within a treaty, and its formulation is characteristic of that particular text genre. What is at issue is really neither an order nor a promise, but a rule by which the members of the Union volunteer to abide by signing up to the treaty. Promises, orders and commitments are examples of speech acts, and in this section we shall discuss this notion.

The theory of speech as action was developed by the Oxford philosopher J. L. Austin in the 1930s, but the theory first became widely known with the publication in 1962 of his book, *How To Do Things With Words*, based on a series of twelve lectures which Austin delivered at Harvard University in 1955. The theory is the first large-scale exposition in English of the so-called natural language philosophy which came to form one of the pillars of the discipline of linguistic pragmatics.

Like Grice, later, Austin wants to find a way of dealing with those parts of natural language that take it beyond logic; but his target is not relations between clauses so much as the relationship between language and the world. The prevailing view of this relationship at the time when Austin developed his theory of speech acts was that the meaning of sentences depends in large part on their truth conditions; that is, the meaning of a sentence can be worked out if we know the circumstances in which the sentence would be true and the circumstances in which it would be false. In Chapter 3, section 3.5.ii, we met a much more recent truth-based theory of meaning, but one in which the notion of truth as such was replaced by the notion of holding true, which was relativised to a time, a speaker and a set of circumstances. The theory of truth in operation at the time when Austin wrote was very different – a correspondence theory of truth, according to which sentences are or are not true because of how the world is. Sentences are true if they correspond to the facts.

This reliance on language-world correspondence in the theory of meaning had led, according to Austin, to general acceptance of what he terms the descriptive fallacy (1962: 3), the view that a declarative sentence is always used to describe a fact, or state of affairs, and that it must do so truly or falsely. Austin points out that the primary purpose of many declarative sentences is not, in fact, to describe a state of affairs, and that in the case of many it does not even make sense to ask whether they are true or false. For example (1962: 5) 'I do', as uttered as part of a marriage ceremony, 'I name this ship the Queen Elizabeth', as uttered by the appropriate person while smashing a bottle against the stem of the ship, 'I give and bequeath my watch to my brother', as written in a will, and 'I bet you sixpence it will rain tomorrow'. What is at issue here is not description of a state of affairs beyond the utterance itself, and the main purpose of the utterance is not this description, purely and simply, but something quite other, namely the performance of an action which no sane person would describe as merely saying something: taking someone as a spouse, naming a ship, leaving something to someone else to have after one's death, and betting. Austin calls such utterances 'performatives' or 'performative utterances' to distinguish them from utterances that are used primarily to describe; these, he calls 'constatives' or 'constative utterances', and the question of truth is only relevant to them. What is relevant when we judge performative utterances, in contrast, is whether the circumstances in which they are uttered are appropriate, and Austin uses the terms 'happy' and 'unhappy' to indicate whether this is so or not. The happiness of performative utterances obviously cannot depend on truth conditions; rather, they depend in Austin's terms on sets of 'felicity conditions', which are of four main types (1962: 14–15):

1. It must be a commonly accepted convention that the uttering of particular words by particular people in particular circumstances will produce a particular effect.
2. All participants in this conventional procedure must carry out the procedure correctly and completely.
3. If the convention is that the participants in the procedure must have certain thoughts, feelings, and intentions, then the participants must in fact have those thoughts, feeling, and intentions.
4. If the convention is that any participant in the procedure binds her/himself to behave subsequently in a certain way, then s/he must in fact behave subsequently in that way.

If any of these conditions does not obtain, the performative will be unhappy and either the act it is intended to perform is not performed at all, or it is performed insincerely. If an act is not achieved, Austin talks of a 'misfire'. Misfires arise if conditions 1 or 2 above are not fulfilled. If an act is performed insincerely, so that conditions 3 and 4 are unfulfilled, Austin talks of 'abuses'.

It is not necessary for a performative to contain within it a so-called speech act verb, which names the action being performed. Convention teaches us to recognise very brief utterances, such as, for example, 'fire', as a performative utterance, in this case a warning. But it is always possible to explicate these so-called 'implicit performatives' by expanding them into utterances that do contain the relevant speech act verb. In the case of 'fire', for example, we might say 'I warn you that there is a fire'; in the case of 'remain seated at all times' we might say 'passengers are advised to remain seated at all times'.

This opportunity for expanding any implicit speech act into an explicit speech act seems to give the theory considerable bite. Since any utterance can be prefaced with 'I state that', the way is clear to seeing all speech as action. However, the trick of expansion, by means of which every constative becomes an act of stating, may also be thought to show up a weakness in the approach: It gets us no further in the quest to explain the workings of those utterances which really are meant to connect to the world by description. For example, in the case of manuals that describe how something works, or of scientific theories intended to do the same, or of diagnoses of illnesses, and numerous other descriptive statements, we would not be content to know simply that so-and-so states that such-and-such; we want to know whether what the person proposes is likely to be accurate, because this has serious consequences for our ability to deal with our environment. Austin is explicit about this (1962: 148):

> We may well suspect that the theory of 'meaning' as equivalent to 'sense and reference' will certainly require some weeding-out and reformulating in terms of the distinction between locutionary and illocutionary acts ... [see below]. I admit that not enough has been done here: I have taken the old 'sense and reference' on the strength of current views.

Performatives can be divided into five broad classes according to their so-called 'illucutionary force'. Different illocutionary forces enable different 'illocutionary acts' to be performed, and the illocutionary act is distinguished from the 'locutionary act' and the 'perlocutionary act' which are performed simultaneously with the illocutionary act.

To perform a locutionary act is to say something in what Austin (1962: 94) calls 'the full normal sense', that is, using language *as* langauge, rather than as mere noises or graphic shapes, and using linguistic items to refer to things in the world conceived of in a certain way, that is, with a certain reference and sense.

Each time a person performs a locutionary act, he or she is also thereby performing some illocutionary act, such as stating, promising, warning, betting, apologising, and so on. If a hearer, through his or her knowledge of the conventions of the language, understands which action is being performed by the utterance, there is 'uptake' of the illocutionary force of the utterance. The utterance will then have a certain effect on the hearer or reader beyond their mere understanding of its sense and reference. The engendering of this effect is called the 'perlocutionary act'. Perlocutionary acts include, for example, persuading, deterring, surprising, misleading, or convincing.

Perlocutionary acts are performed *by* saying something rather than *in* saying it, and they differ from illocutionary acts in that the producer of an illocutionary act does not have full control of the perlocutionary act that is thereby performed. For example, it is misleading or unduly optimistic to say that 'Passengers are being reassured about the safety of rail travel after the Potters Bar accident (6 o'clock news, Radio 4, 12 May 2002), because there is no guarantee that whatever rail chiefs or anyone else may say to passengers in the hope that they will be reassured will, in fact, reassure passengers.

The classes of speech act that Austin (1962: Lecture 12) identifies are the following:

1. Verdictives: typified by the giving of a verdict, estimate, reckoning or appraisal; giving a finding.
2. Exersitives: the exercising of powers, rights or influence, exemplified by voting, ordering, urging, advising, warning, etc.
3. Commissives: typified by promising or otherwise undertaking (*op. cit.*: 151–2): 'they *commit* you to doing something, but include also declarations or announcements of intention, which are not promises, and also rather vague things which we might call espousals, as for example, siding with'.
4. Behavitives: which have to do with social behaviour and attitudes, for example apologising, congratulating, commending, condoling, cursing, and challenging.
5. Expositives: which make it clear how our utterances fit into the course of an argument or conversation. Examples are *I reply*; *I argue*; *I concede*; *I illustrate*; *I assume*; *I postulate*.

By means of this system, it becomes possible to solve the riddle of the mismatch between grammatical mood (declarative, interrogative and imperative) and speech action. Whereas in standard situations of language use declarative utterances are used to make statements, interrogative utterances to ask questions and imperative utterances to give orders, in many cases, these relationships between mood and function break down. For example, 'I will see you in my office at 2pm', which is a declarative sentence, can function as an order and 'is it a good idea to watch TV the day before your exam?' which is in the interrrogative mood, would tend to be understood as a declaration that it is not a good idea to watch TV the night before an exam. In such cases, according to Searle (1975), an 'indirect' speech act is being performed. This can happen when speakers exploit their hearers' knowledge about 'direct' speech act, by deliberately breaking one or more of the conventions for using that speech act. Speakers understand the indirect speech act, because they understand the felicity conditions for the direct speech act and notice that they do not all obtain, whereas some felicity conditions for the indirect speech act do. For example, someone who declares that they will see someone else later in a particular place must be certain that the other person will be there. If the addressee knows that no such arrangement has been made, they will realise that this felicity condition for statements does not obtain. But they will also know that a person who has power over someone else can order them to act in a certain way. If this felicity condition for ordering obtains, the declarative utterance will be understood to perform the action of ordering.

The evidence speakers rely on in working out indirect speech action includes, in addition to their knowledge of the felicity conditions for speech acts, general background knowledge and reasoning powers, knowledge of the co-operative principle and its maxims, genre conventions, and the principles that govern polite linguistic behaviour. Some linguistic politeness conventions for English are described in detail by Leech (1983), who emphasises that politeness concerns lie behind indirectness both in the form of indirect speech acts and in the form of the flouting of conversational maxims. A theory of politeness may be found in Brown and Levinson (1978), and some cross cultural differences in politeness conventions and their consequences for translation are discussed by House (1998).

7.4.i Practice and discussion

In the previous exercise involving Ibsen's *Gengangere* (1881), we noted the interplay between conversational maxims and speech acts. We noted that in the passage,

Original
Engstrand: Jeg var ute på en rangel i går kveld –
Regine: Det tror jeg gjerne
Engstrand: Ja, for vi mennesker er skrøbelige, barnet mitt –

Translation
Engstrand: I was out on the loose last night –
Regina: I can quite believe that
Engstrand: Yes, we're weak vessels, we poor mortals, my girl

Engstrand's second remark is most likely to be understood as an explanation in the original and as an excuse in the translation. We noted that the use of 'for' in the original in this remark is instrumental in producing this understanding of the original. A matching term that would signal explanation does not appear in the translation.

Consider the following passage from a little later on in Act I. A clergyman from the local town, Pastor Manders, has come to see Mrs Alving, and Regine is making him comfortable while he waits for her. What speech acts are Regine and Pastor Manders carrying out? How do you know? As the passage is long, the translation is printed below the original, remark for remark.

Pastor Manders: Deres far er ingen riktig sterk personlighet, jomfru Engstrand. Han trenger så inderlig til en ledende hånd.
   Your father is not a man of strong character, Miss Engstrand. He stands terribly in need of a guiding hand.

Regine: Å ja, det kan gjerne være, det.
Oh, yes; I daresay he does.

Pastor Manders: Han trenger til å ha noe om seg som han kan holde av, og hvis omdømme han kan legge vekt på. Han erkjente det selv så trohjertig da han sist var oppe hos meg.
He needs to have someone near him whom he cares for, and whose judgement he respects. He frankly admitted that when he last came to see me.

Regine: Ja, han har snakket til meg om noe slikt. Men jeg vet ikke om fru Alving vil være av med meg – helst nu da vi får det nye asylet å styre med. Og så ville jeg så gruelig nødig fra fru Alving også, for hun har da alltid vært så snill imot meg.
Yes, he mentioned something of the sort to me. But I don't know whether Mrs. Alving can spare me; especially now that we've got the new Orphanage to attend to. And then I should be so sorry to leave Mrs. Alving; she has always been so kind to me.

Pastor Manders: Men den datterlige pligt, min gode pike —. Naturligvis måtte vi først innhente Deres frues samtykke.
But a daughter's duty, my good girl – Of course we must first get your mistress's consent.

Regine: Men jeg vet ikke om det går an for meg, I min alder, å styre huset for en enslig mannsperson.
But I don't know whether it would be quite proper for me, at my age, to keep house for a single man.

Pastor Manders: Hva! Men kjære jomfru Engstrand, det er jo Deres egen far her er tale om!
What! My dear Miss Engstrand! When the man is your own father!

Regine: Ja, det kan så være, men allikevel –. Ja, hvis det var I et godt hus og hos en riktig reel herre –
Yes, that may be; but all the same – Now if it were in a thoroughly respectable house, and with a real gentleman –

Pastor Manders: Men, min kjære Regine –
But, my dear Regina –

Regine: – en som jeg kunne nære hengivenhet for og se opp til og være liksom I datters sted –
– one I could love and respect, and be a daughter to –

Pastor Manders: Ja, men mitt kjære gode barn –
Yes, but my dear, good child –

Regine: For så ville jeg nok gjerne inn til byen. Her ute er det svært ensomt, – og herr pastoren vet jo selv hva det vil si å stå ensom i verden. Og det tør jeg nok si at jeg er både flink og villig. Vet ikke herr pastoren noen slik plass for meg?

Then I should be glad to go to town. It's very lonely out here; you know yourself, sir, what it is to be alone in the world. And I can assure you I'm both quick and willing. Don't you know of any such place for me, sir?

Pastor Manders: Jeg? Nei tilforlatelig om jeg det vet.
  I? No, certainly not.

Discussion

In the passage above, the identification of individual speech acts seems to depend to a large extent on their place in the context of the entire passage. A number of scholars have questioned whether speech acts are really such discrete entities as Austin and Searle's treatment of them suggests (see for example Ferrara (1980 a and b).

The speech act as discussed by Austin and Searle, is very much a feature of the spoken language. It is possible to identify acts in written text[3] that resemble speech acts to some extent, for example the salutations found at the beginnings and ends of letters and the sections of acknowledgements and dedications often found in dissertations, theses and books. However, these phenomena are usually studied as part of genre, discourse and text analysis, where they tend to be described as 'moves' rather than 'acts' and to be linked closely to concepts like text function and the concept of genre itself. The final section of this chapter is dedicated to these notions.

7.5 TEXTS AND GENRES

7.5.i Genre analysis

There are a number of definitions of 'genre' in operation in the disciplines of linguistics and literary theory. For example, Abrams (1971: 67–8) gives the following definition:

> **GENRE**, a term taken from the French, is used in literary criticism to signify a literary species or, as we now often say, a "literary form."

Examples include tragedy, comedy, epic, satire, lyric, epigram, novel, essay, biography, and the definition is, as Abrams remarks, largely formal, although subject matter also plays a part. The definition limits itself to literary genres, but there are a number of non-literary genres in which form plays a significant role too. Consider, for example, the following extract from the British Housing Act of 1980, Section 24, subsection 5 (from Bhatia 1993: 32):

> Where the dwelling-house with respect to which the right to buy is exercised is a registered land, the Chief Land Registrar shall, if so requested by the Secretary of State, supply him (on payment of the appropriate fee) with an office copy of any document required by the Secretary of State for the purpose of executing a vesting order with respect to the dwelling-house and shall (notwithstanding section 112 of the Land Registration Act 1925) allow any person authorised by the Secretary of State to inspect and make copies of and extracts from any register or document

which is in the custody of the Chief Land Registrar and relates to the dwelling-house.

As Bhatia (1993: 33) points out, this text displays what he refers to as an 'Interactive move-structure': an interplay between legislating provisions and specifying conditions:

Legislating provisions	*Specifying conditions*
	Where the dwelling-house with respect to which the right to buy is exercised is a registered land,
the Chief Land Registrar shall	
	if so requested by the Secretary of State
supply him	
	on payment of an appropriate fee
with an office copy of any document required by the Secretary of State	
	for the purpose of executing a vesting order with respect to the dwelling-house
and shall	
	notwithstanding section 112 of the Land Registration Act 1925
allow any person authorised by the Secretary of State to inspect and make copies of and extracts from any register or document which is in the custody of the Chief Land Registrar and relates to the dwelling-house.	

However, not only formal features need to be taken into consideration in genre definitions. In Swales' (1990: 58) definition, the relationship between the genre and its users plays a prominent role:

> A genre comprises a class of communicative events, the members of which serve some set of communicative purposes. These purposes are recognized by the expert members of the parent discourse community, and thereby constitute the rationale for the genre. This rationale shapes the schematic structure of the discourse and influences and constrains choice of content and style.

Swales is primarily concerned with the genre of academic research articles, in the case of which there is considerable coincidence of consumers and producers of the genre, and a high level of sharing of expertise and interest: many people who read academic research articles also produce them, and almost everyone who wants to read a research article will have a certain level of expertise in its subject matter. This is not the case for many other genres, such as for example newspaper and magazine editorials and articles, promotional material, brochures and manuals of use, and so on, and these differences in the relationships between producer and consumer of the genre is to a certain extent reflected in generic structure and manner of formulation.

In the case of research articles, where co-incidence of interest and expertise is high and large numbers of members of the discourse community are interchangeably producers and consumers of members of the genre, it is possible to employ specialist terminology and phrasing, and it is not necessary to prioritise attention-attracting devises. In contrast, promotional material and texts which appear in publications that face strong competition in the market place, such as newspapers, need to employ strategies that ensure the widest possible appeal and distribution, including the use of terminology and phrasing that can be widely understood, and the use of catchy titles and headlines.

Within the research article introduction, Swales establishes the following three moves with a number of potential steps in each:

Move 1	**Establishing a Territory**
Step 1	Claiming Centrality
	and/or
Step 2	Making topic generalisations
	and/or
Step 3	Reviewing items of previous research
Move 2	**Establishing a Niche**
Step 1A	Counter-claiming
	or
Step 1B	Indicating a Gap
	or
Step 1C	Question Raising
	or
Step 1D	Continuing a Tradition
Move 3	**Occupying a Niche**
Step 1A	Outlining purposes
	or
Step 1B	Announcing present research
Step 2	Announcing principal findings
Step 3	Indicating research article structure

It is very obvious from this model, known as the CARS (Creating A Research Space) model, that each step in a move performs a function or action which could, without stretching the notion too far, be considered a written text version of the speech act – a text act, perhaps. The presentation of moves in genres in such terms is very common indeed. For example, Bhatia (1993: 45–75) identifies the following moves in two types of business letter (adapted from Dudley-Evans 2002; for actual examples of business letters, see Bhatia 1993[4]):

	Sales Promotion Letter	*Job Application Letter*
Move 0	Opening salutation	Opening salutation
Move 1	Establishing credentials	Establishing credentials
Move 2	Introducing the offer	Introducing the candidature
	(i) Offering the product/candidature	
	(ii) Essential details of the offer/candidature	
	(iii) Indicating value of the offer/candidature	
Move 3	Offering incentives (common)	Offering incentives (rare)
Move 4	Soliciting response	Soliciting response
Move 5	Ending politely	Ending politely
Move 00	Final salutation	Final salutation

As we can see, the main difference between the two letter types is that it is rare for candidates applying for jobs to offer their prospective employers incentives to take them on; the power relationships between the two parties hardly permits such a move, and most job applicants would not be in a position to offer any such incentives. In the sales promotion letter, on the other hand, this move is extremely common.

Each of the moves listed is carried out in a way that is characteristic of the genre in question and each has a particular function. In sales promotion letters, credentials may be established by means of claims to expertise and long practice and to understanding the potential customer or client's needs. The second move is devoted to product detailing, and the third to trying to persuade the customer to order by offering incentives such as reductions in the standard price for specific customer groups, discounts on large orders, gifts, and so on. The function of the fourth move is to encourage the letter recipient in some way to act on or respond to the letter by providing them with the means to do so, for example an order form or registration documents or with information enabling them to do so, such as contact details. The final move, ending politely, allows the letter writer to flatter the recipient in various ways, for example by mentioning how much they hope to hear or look forward to hearing from and/or being of service to the recipient.

A very interesting feature of genres is that they seem to be adopted and adapted by what Dudley-Evans (2002: 208) refers to as 'local' discourse communities to meet their own specific needs and to suit their general outlook on life. Consider, for example, the sales promotion e-mail of 5 October 2003 below[5] (telephone contact details removed):

Dudes & Dudettes,
    Once again, we've been busy here at wicked HQ so we thought we'd send out a mail to let you all know what's going on.
Firstly, our V.I.P. Promotion has been so successful, we're about to close applications.

Over the next week we'll be updating our site & at some point the application page will vanish, anyone who's signed up by then has until the end of the month to make purchases to be eligible for a Gold Card and V.I.P. status with all that comes with it.

All V.I.P.'s who've already ordered and have received their V.I.P. packs & membership number are already on the list to receive their gold cards which will be sent out next month.

Everyone who's signed up for the V.I.P. Card but not ordered will be added to our new mail out list which will be coming shortly (more details to follow).

Secondly, We've opened our new store in Sheffield for people in that area. It's stocked with all our Molotow Belton Premiums & loads of Burners & Coversalls. Get in touch with Oscar on xxxxx xxx xxx for more info.

Those of you who've had the pleasure of dealing with Becky over the summer will be sad to hear that she's left & gone to Manchester, she'll be back, and we now have the wonderful Emily taking her place.

For all questions & queries regarding paint, orders, membership & relationship problems you can reach her at emily@wickedpaint.com.

Finally, if any of you haven't checked out the web site recently, We're now selling Burner Chrome 600ml for £3.00. And remember, V.I.P.'s get V.A.T free prices as soon as they sign up.

So check out http://www.wickedpaint.com & put some colour in your life.

Peace
Tom
Wicked

7.5.ii Practice and discussion

Practice

To what extent is it possible to analyse this e-mail using the adaptation of Bahtia's model for the business promotion letter?

Discussion

The promotional e-mail begins with an opening salutation, 'Dudes & Dudettes' and ends with a closing salutation, 'Peace'. Credentials are established (or, perhaps, maintained or strengthened, as this is not a first-contact e-mail) through the mention of how busy the sender's organisation has been recently and of the need to close the V.I.P. promotion because of the success it has met with. Next, the V.I.P. promotion is offered to the recipient as available until the end of the following week only (applying pressure tactics), and the benefits and value of the offer are detailed. The incentive to take up the offer of becoming a V.I.P. is not explicitly mentioned, beyond the promised receipt of a gold card, V.I.P. status or, for those who make no purchase, being added to a new mailing list. However, as most recipients of this e-mail have already signed up, they know that incentives to do so included a number of free items which they have already received when they made their first purchase.

The letter moves on apparently to offer information about a new store, though this is accompanied by the introduction of a new offer (of 'Molotow Belton Premiums & loads of Burners & Coversalls') along with instructions on how to obtain more information. Again, the announcement that Becky has left to be replaced by Emily is followed immediately with a paragraph detailing Emily's contact details and status as a person with whom orders can be lodged. Similarly the final paragraphs encourage readers to respond along with providing some product detail. There is an ending, which again includes the solicitation of a reponse, 'check out http … & put some colour in your life'. This is not formally polite, but it is friendly and serves to reinforce the sense of group or sub-culture membership which is evident in many features of this text: Product details, apart form details of the V.I.P. promotion, are limited to prices because customers are assumed to understand what is on sale; the ampersand, '&', is used instead of 'and'; contractions of pronoun and verb are common, and so on.

Practice

Below are two further e-mails from the same company. Examine them to see whether they display the same structural and linguistic features as the e-mail promotion we have just looked at:

(15 November 2003)
Ok guys so the V.I.P. membership has now closed.
83 of you have signed up & purchased from us & will have their membership cards sent out to them soon.
Unfortunately, no one sent in any card designs so we'll use one of our own.

We've opened a new office in Hoxton, London, as of next week we'll be offering same day delivery in London & all V.I.P.'s can come & choose their colours whenever they like.

Also, in our quest for global domination, we're opening up in Belfast & will be covering the whole of Northern & Southern Ireland.

We'll have a contact number for you next week & more details will be up on our web site soon.

Next week sees the launch of the new 'Coversall 2 Black Top' available in 600 & 400ml cans.
As all users of Coversall know it's already the best out there but the Black Top comes out Faster & thicker. People who've tried it call it 'Liquid Tar'!
Wicked Paint is going to be the first company in the UK to have them in stock &

we're giving our V.I.P.'s the opportunity to pre-order Black Tops for the same price as Coversall 2, that's £3.00 for 600ml & £2.50 for 400ml.

Orders will be sent out the same day we receive them direct from the factory so you'll be the first in the UK to have the new cans.

This offer applies to V.I.P.'s only and only applies to orders received by Friday 21st of November.

We've got more Nice Hot irons in the fire so watch this space.

Peace
Tom
Wicked
www.wickedpaint.com

e-mail of 10 February 2004
Dudes & Dudettes,

It's time for another Wicked update from your friendly spray paint team here at http://www.wickedpaint.com.
And firstly we have to start with some sad news...

Graphotism is closing down it's shop in Clapham, we know, it's tragic, but they don't seem too bothered, for the news from the horses mouth check out http://www.graphotism.com/benchDetails.asp?bid=260

To help people with the grieving process we thought that this was a good time to remind everyone that our office in Hoxton is open 6 days a week from Morning to Night, & even Sunday this week, stocked full of the finest Belton, Coversall 1,2 & now 3, Burners, caps, masks, T-shirts & other goodies.
Now that we've got our CC TV cameras installed, you can come down & collect any time you like.

We've got a selection of Belton Premium which have got water damaged labels so anyone coming to the Hoxton store can get their hands on them for £2.00 each.

Montana Spain & Molotow have put their heads together & come up with Bombers Best, It's a sick new bombing paint in 46 thick, fast flowing colours, the Tin looks cool, it costs £2.25 per 400ml can & will be in stock next week.
Colour charts will go up on site over the next few days but check out http://www.bombersbest.com for info & colours.

We're constantly updating our site http://www.wickedpaint.com & in case you haven't visited us for a while ... you should!
We've Lowered our prices by ruthlessly cutting the VAT so our prices are now as follows:

Bombers Best 400ml   £2.25
Belton Premium 400ml   £2.50

Devil Colours 500ml	£3.00
Burner Chrome 600ml	£3.00
Coversall II 600ml	£3.00

We can deliver anywhere in the UK & Ireland within 24 hours. Check the site for full details of delivery charges & our stock including mixed bags of caps, clothing & masks.

So, peace, love & happy painting to you all.
Tom
http://www.wickedpaint.com
Stepping up the pace

Discussion

You will have noted similarities as well as differences between the three e-mails. A number of the differences arise from the fact that the e-mails form a sequence clearly marked out as such. For example, one e-mail will refer to offers that were the topic of another, so, like the texts about wine used in Chapter 6 above, this e-mail sequence displays clear markers of intertextuality.

Practice

Produce translations of the three e-mails as if they were to be addressed to members of the relevant subculture (hip-hop and graffiti) in the country where your other language is spoken.

7.5.iii Newspapers

No promotional material can function unless it attracts the attention of the intended consumer, and intended consumer groups who do not share a language are not often as culturally homogenous as the hip-hop culture can be assumed to be. It is therefore very common to find that cultural adaptation is necessary in the translation of text parts that function to attract attention, and in the final sections of this chapter we shall look briefly at some genres in which attention capture is especially important, namely newspapers and advertising material.

Newspapers host some of the most thoroughly analysed English language genres outside literature, namely editorials and news reportage. These are of special interest to text typologists because their structure tends to be fairly regular, and to scholars interested in the representation in language of ideology, because they tend to display ideological slants on the topics they deal with in fairly clearly perceptible ways, which may be predictable in light of their proprietors' acknowledged political allegiances. Of course, they also host advertising text, another much discussed and analysed text genre, which we shall look at briefly in section 7.5.iv below.

The United Kingdom is unusual compared to many other countries in having a press which is relatively clearly divisible into what is popularly known as the quality press and the gutter press, or, more temperately, broadsheet newspapers and tabloids. This terminology is based on the size of the pages of the newspapers, which, of course, has no direct influence on the nature and quality of content of the papers; it just happens that the so-called quality newspapers used to be printed on large sheets and the rest on smaller sheets. In the early years of the twenty-first century, the distinction that was previously so clear was muddied when *The Times* and *The European* began to produce tabloid sized editions in order to make the page turning process easier for commuters on trains and others struggling to control the vast paper expanses on which their daily news was printed. The lists below (based on Reah 1998: 1–2) is relevant to the time before this change was instituted:

UK newspaper types	*Examples*
Broadsheets	*The Telegraph*; *The Independent*; *The Times*; *The Guardian*
Regional broadsheets	*The Yorkshire Post*; *The Scotsman*; *The Herald* (Glasgow); *The Western Mail* (Cardiff)
Middle-range tabloids	*The Express*; *The Daily Mail*; *The Sun*; *The Mirror*; *The Star*
Middle-range local tabloids	*The Daily Record* (Scotland); *The Evening Standard* (London); *The Cambridge Evening News*
Clearly politically aligned	*The Socialist Worker*
Special Interest Groups	*The Times Higher Education Supplement*; *The London Review of Books*

It is clearly more likely that copy that appears in a broadsheet will be translated than it is for local news in a local paper to be translated.

The types of newspaper exemplified above differ in the proportion of local versus foreign news they contain and also in the proportion of space they devote to, e.g., news, sport, entertainment and advertising. For example, Reah (1998: 3) provides the following figures for *The Sun* and *The Guardian*:

	The Sun	*The Guardian*
No. of pages	60	34
News	13.5 (28%)	14 (41%)
Advertising	17 (35%)	8 (24%)
Sport and entertainment	14 (29%)	6 (18%)

Practice

Is it possible to draw similar distinctions between the newspapers available in the country or countries which use your other language or languages?

Obtain one or more newspapers written in your other language or languages and compare Reah's figures with what you find there.

In addition to these text types, newspapers can also include feature articles, letters to the editor, reviews of arts and literature, weather reports, fashion columns (Bhatia 1993: 157) and obituaries.

The function of an editorial in a British newspaper is, according to Reah (1998: 6–7) to comment on, give opinions about and draw conclusions from events in a context in which the newspaper addresses its (implied) readership directly. Bhatia (1993: 164–5) suggests the following move structure for editorials:

1. Presenting the case
2. Offering the argument
3. Reaching the verdict
4. Recommending action

Practice

Choose a UK editorial and an editorial published in a newspaper written in your other language (most well established newspapers have a strong web presence, and you will probably find an electronic version of the paper of your choice by entering its name in a search engine like Google). Does Bhatia's suggested structure match what you find in the English language editorial? And in the editorial in your other language?

Newspapers operate in a highly competitive market place in which they vie with each other for sales and their headlines are important devices for attracting the attention of potential buyers. The headlines are in large print and they often employ rhyme, alliteration, allusion (to well known features of a culture) ambiguity, polysemy and punning. On 4 June 2004, for example, *The Sun* headed a story about the possibility that petrol tax might rise with the caption, '2p or not 2p'[6] above a picture of the chancellor of the exchequer. In English, newspaper headlines also characteristically leave out non-content words such as articles, auxiliaries and people's titles, which has the dual effect of saving word space so that the type face can be large and of sometimes leaving relationships between those phenomena that are mentioned unclear. The words that are in the headline need to be focal to the story to come, so they tend to denote events, people involved, location and manner. Time is only mentioned if it is especially relevant since news is by its nature otherwise assumed to report what has happened very recently.

Headlines are rarely written by the reporter who wrote the story. A translator may or may not get to compose their own headline, and they may (probably rarely) be asked to compose headlines for copy translated by somebody else.

Practice

Compare one day's headlines in one UK paper and one paper published in your other language.

7.5.iv Advertising

According to Goddard (1998: 8), the purpose of advertising is to promote branded products or to enhance the images of people, groups and/or organisations. To achieve this, they must appeal and attract the attention of their intended audience, which they can do linguistically using similar strategies to those found in headlines, but also by means of images, graphology, exploitation of genre conventions (for example an advertisement may be in the form of a letter, news story, or scientific report) or by encouraging interaction with the text (for example there may be coupons to cut out, tokens to save, reservations to make, surfaces to scratch) (Goddard 1998: 19). Like sales promotion letters, advertisements often form sequences in which later advertisements for one product draw on the audience's familiarity with earlier advertisements for the same product; that is, they display intertextuality (see section 7.2.i). Occasionally, advertisements appear in the form of other text genres. In 2003 and 2004 for instance, new mini cars were advertised in a series of 'mini adventures', brief sequences simulating adventure films (on TV) or narratives (in other media) with minimal story lines.

Advertisements may employ the register (see Chapter 3) typical of specific target groups, and employ narrative, description or dialogue form (Goddard 1998: 23 ff.). They often use slogans (for example 'pure genius' for Guinness, 'probably the best lager in the world' for Carlsberg, or 'Hello Moto' for Motorola) and exploit stereotypes. Some advertisements, like some sales promotion letters, promise their audience that they will solve a particular problem such as bad breath, smelly toilets, bored children and so on (see Goddard 1998: 75).

Practice

Examine a selection of advertisements, preferably for the same or the same kind of product, in English and in another language. How do they make their appeal? How can you tell what their target audience is? Are there consistent differences between the advertisements in the two languages?

NOTES

1. Please note that the use of the term 'refer' by Halliday and Hasan is less precise than the use of the term in philosophical discourse, where 'reference' denotes the relation that holds between a referring expression and the item in the world that it refers to (Frege 1892; Evans 1982). Referring expressions are names and definite descriptions. Halliday and Hasan use the term 'reference' to stand for relationships both between linguistic items and non-linguistic items and between one linguistic item and another. They do not distinguish, either, between what philosphers tend to refer to as 'extension' (the set of items in the world that a given term can be used to refer to in a referring expression) and reference, or between sense/intension (the mental representation evoked by an expression) and reference.

2. In light of Halliday and Hasan's non-adherence to the distinctions mentioned in note 1 above, the distinction they wish to draw here between co-reference to things in the world and

purely interlinguistic relationships does not stand up. In 'Wash and core six cooking apples. Put them into a fireproof dish', 'six cooking apples' is not a referring expression in the philosophical sense – nor indeed in a common sense sense, since no specific set of six apples in the world can be in question (or the recipe would only work once); obviously *any* six apples would do. Irrespective, therefore, of the understanding of relationships between expressions and the world which readers may rely on in recognising a cohesive tie, the tie itself obtains between expressions in the text.

3. Note that these are not to be confused with text acts in the sense developed by Horner (1975) who, according to Hatim (1998: 73) 'suggests that the act of writing a "composition" as an academic exercise is a special kind of pragmatic act (which she calls a "text-act")'.

4. Bhatia does not include the two salutation moves. These are numbered 0 and 00 here because they are not functional in the sense that the other moves are functional. Salutations in letters, although they are of course important, are usually highly formulaic (though see the e-mail messages used in the exercise following). In addition, Bhatia includes two moves which are not included here. His fourth move is 'enclosing documents' and his sixth move is 'using pressure tactics'. But although many business letters do enclose document and do use pressure tactics, neither the enclosing of documents nor the use of pressure tactics is itself a move in the text-act sense of a unit of structure within which certain functions are fulfilled. Mentioning that documents are enclosed could of course be called a move within which it is mentioned that documents are enclosed. But there seems little justification for doing this other than that such a mention regularly occurs in this type of letter; and we do not want to make a move out of every regular mention. Using pressure tactics, in turn, is something that a writer of this kind of text may do within any move; it is not a move in itself.

5. Of course a discourse community that can communicate via e-mail need not be local in any geographical sense; as in the case of the kind of discourse community Swales (1990) refers to, what unites the intended readership of the e-mail sales promotion letter is their common interests and expertise.

6. '2p' was written on a coin face. The pun is that '2p' sounds like 'to pee' (urinate) and the allusion is to Shakespeare's Hamlet's famous 'to be or not to be' soliloquy.

Chapter 8

Perspectives and reflections in clauses and texts in translation

8.1 INTRODUCTION

In Chapter 7, we introduced the notion of language as action. We looked at Austin's theory of speech acts and at the analysis of genre in terms of so-called moves, units of structure which may be sequenced in orders that are characteristic of specific genres and within which a number of text acts can be performed. We noted that neither speech acts nor moves necessarily coincide with any unit of linguistic structure (such as a word, phrase/group, clause or sentence) and that along with implicatures, they are interpreted on the basis of the interplay of text, co-text, context, and interactants' background knowledge.

In this chapter, we concentrate mainly on a unit of structure that is clearly linguistic, namely the clause. We shall take a so-called 'functional' approach to this unit (Halliday 1985), which understands it as the locus for three types of action performed by the manipulation of three linguistic system, carried by it, namely the systems of mood, theme and rheme, and transitivity. Each of these systems enables the realisation of a clause function: the clause as exchange, as message and as representation, and each of these functions, in turn, relates to one of the three metafunctions of language that we met in Chapter 3: the interpersonal, the textual and the ideational. Recalling that these functions determine selections among linguistic units to reflect the three aspects of context theorised as tenor, mode and field, we shall, by the end of this chapter, have introduced a view of language that may be represented as in figures 8.1 and 8.2 below.

8.2 THE CLAUSE SYMPHONY

As mentioned above, the clause in English is the locus for the three linguistic systems which enable three functions to be realised at clause level. The three systems operate together to produce a whole, rather as the different parts of an orchestra work together to produce one symphony (cf. Halliday 1978: 31), and, just as it is possible to concentrate in musical description on, for example, the strings at one point, then on the brass and then on the woodwind, it is possible to describe each of the linguistic systems that operate at clause level, and the functions which they realise,

CLAUSE FUNCTION	LINGUISTIC SYSTEM	CONTEXT	METAFUNCTION
Clause as exchange (grammar)	MOOD	TENOR	INTERPERSONAL
Clause as message (psychology)	THEME and RHEME	MODE	TEXTUAL
Clause as representation (semantics/logic)	TRANSITIVITY	FIELD	IDEATIONAL

Figure 8.1   Clause functions in relation to non-linguistic context and to the metafunctions of the human meaning potential.

Aspect of situation	Metafunction	Linguistic systems and classes
FIELD	IDEATIONAL	Lexis: nouns, verbs, adjectives, prepositions, adverbs Clause: tense, aspect, transitivity
TENOR	INTERPERSONAL	Lexis: pronouns Clause: mood, modality
MODE	TEXTUAL	Genre and style Clause: theme/rheme, voice Texture: cohesion

Figure 8.2   The relationship between context, metafunctions and selections among options offered within linguistic systems.

individually. In the section below, we begin with the structure and function of the mood system (section 8.2.i), then we turn to thematic structure (section 8.2.ii) and finally to the representation of roles, participants and relationships through the transitivity system (section 8.2.iii).

8.2.i The clause as exchange: grammatical mood

The clause enable its users provide one another with information, to ask for or demand information and to ask or demand that non-linguistic acts be performed and it functions, in this sense, as a locus for the exchange of goods and services. In straightforward situations, speakers recognise whether another person is providing information, asking for information or demanding information or some non-linguistic service because they understand the clause mood. Mood is realised through choices among components of clause structure, which will be familiar to most readers of this book. In the functional grammar we shall use here (Halliday 1985), five functions are recognised at the level of clause grammar, conveniently enumerated in the mnemonic, 'SPOCA', which stands for 'Subject', 'Predicator', 'Object', 'Complement' and 'Adjunct'. These functions of the elements of clause structure are usually realised by elements from the following classes of phrase (or group):

Subject: Noun Phrase/Nominal Group
Predicator: Verb Phrase/Verbal Group
Object: Noun Phrase/Nominal Group
Complement: Noun Phrase/Nominal Group or Adjective Phrase/Adjectival
                Group
Adjunct: Adverb Phrase/Adverbial Group or Adjective Phrase/Adjectival
                Group or Prepositional Phrase/Prepositional Group

The grammatical subject of a clause in English can be identified as the element which is picked up in a tag question, and this element will stand for the thing with reference to which the proposition is affirmed or denied. The subject will stand in person and number concord with the verb, though as Halliday points out, 'apart from the verb *be*, the only manifestation [in Modern English] of person and number in the verb is the *-s* on the third person singular present tense' (Halliday 1985: 73). In the case of 'This translation was made by Sergio' the tag would be 'wasn't it?' (not 'wasn't he?'), so the grammatical subject is realised by 'This translation'. In the case of 'Aissata made that translation', the tag would be 'didn't she?' (not 'didn't it?'), so the grammatical subject is realised by 'Aissata'. In the case of 'Mr Prodi commissioned that translation from Kheira', the tag would be 'didn't he?' (not 'didn't it?' or 'didn't she'), so the grammatical subject is realised by 'Mr Prodi'.

The Object is something which could function as a subject in the clause but does not. If the clause is put into the passive voice, then the object becomes the subject:

Ori made *the translation* – *the translation* was made by Ori
         OBJECT   SUBJECT

The Complement says something about the subject or about the object; it cannot become a subject even if the clause is put into passive voice:

The translation is *well made* — *well made is been by the translation
SUBJECT   COMPLEMENT

The translators made their client *happy/a happy woman* – * (A) Happy
            (Indirect) OBJECT COMPLEMENT
(woman) was made by the translators of their client

The adjunct is generally whatever is left.

Below is a basic analysis of the first six clauses of the economics text printed at the end of Chapter 5:

Three years after the shock of the Suq al Manakh crash (A) Kuwait's economy (S) is (P) now (A) at a crossroads (A).

For years (A) the state's economy (S) has been [largely (A)] based (P) on three factors – the trickle down effect of large government budgets, and the boom in values in the share market and in local property and land (A).

Now (A) all three of these principal sources of wealth in Kuwait (S) are (P) in jeopardy (A).

The government (S) has [itself] been hit (P) by the decline in world oil demand (A), and [linker] production (S) [?in the last four years (A)?] has been halved (P).

Yet [linker], as a producer of medium heavy crude oil (A), Kuwait's oil output (S) has suffered (P) less than those states producing light crudes (A).

and [linker] unlike other states in the Gulf (A), Kuwait (S) has [at least (A)] managed to maintain (P) production (O) at the levels set by OPEC (A).

Mood is indicated in English through the position relative to one another of the subject and predicator in the clause, and three moods are generally recognised in English, declarative, interrogative and imperative.

In the declarative mood, the subject precedes the predicator, as in the case of each of the clauses above.

In the interrogative mood, the predicator usually precedes the subject or the subject is enclosed within the predicator, when the predicator is realised through a verbal group that includes an auxilliary verb like 'is', 'did', 'can' and 'have':

Are (P) all three of these principal sources of wealth in Kuwait (S) now (A) in jeopardy (A)?

Has [The government itself (S)] been hit (P) by the decline in world oil demand (A), and [linker] has [production (S) [?in the last four years (A)?] been halved (P)?

In the imperative mood, there is usually no subject present in a clause:

Halve (P) production (O)
Maintain (P) production (O) at the levels set by OPEC (A).

As we noted in Chapter 7, section 7.4, there is no one-to-one relationship between mood and speech action. Mood is completely dependent on grammatical structure, and clearly identifiable, whereas speech action depends to a great extent on context. Consider the following examples;

Is that your coat on the floor (Mood: Interrogative; Speech act: question, rebuke or command)
Did you eat the cake (Mood: Interrogative; Speech act: question, rebuke or, unlikely but possible – see below – command)
Did you eat all your greens (Mood: Interrogative; Speech act: question, rebuke or command)
Would you like a sandwich (Mood: Interrogative; Speech act: question or offer)
Take a seat (Mood: Imperative; Speech act: offer)
Have a chocolate (Mood: Imperative; Speech act: offer)
I apologise (Mood: Declarative; Speech act: apology)
I am not satisfied with this watch (Mood: Declarative; Speech act: complaint)
I promise to be there (Mood: Declarative; Speech act: promise)

Languages can be classified into types according to the standard order in which the elements of clause structure are placed in declarative sentences. In English, the standard order of elements is (where the more common term 'V' for 'verb' is used instead of the term 'P' for 'predicator', which is peculiar to functional grammars): SVO/C (Quirk *et al.* 1972: 36). This, according to Tomlin (1986: 3), is one of the two most frequent word orders displayed by the world's languages; the other is SOV. The next most frequent word order is VSO, followed by VOS, OVS, and finally OSV.

Tomlin explains this with reference to interaction of three principles: the Theme First Principle, the Verb–Object Bonding Principle, and the Animated First Principle, which are in turn explained with reference to the psychology of perception. The Theme First Principle (TFP) says that thematic information – information which is particularly salient to the development of discourse – is likely to come first in simple main clauses. The Verb–Object Bonding (VOB) principle says that in general the object in a transitive clause is more tightly bound to the predicator than to the subject, and the Animated First Principle (AFP) states that in basic transitive clauses, the noun phrase which stands for the most animated phenomenon will precede others.

According to these principles, we should expect the subject of a sentence to be whichever item stands for the most animated thing spoken about, and we should expect this to be put first, at least in English, which is an SVO language. Of the following four sentences, therefore, we should expect the first to be the most likely to occur:

1. The Lady Anna Gordon came to Morton Hall as a bride of just over twenty.
2. As a bride of just over twenty the Lady Anna Gordon came to Morton Hall.
3. To Morton Hall came the Lady Anna Gordon as a bride of just over twenty.
4. ?Came the Lady Anna Gordon to Morton Hall as a bride of just over twenty.

Obviously, the other three clauses are not ungrammatical, though the fourth is a little odd, perhaps poetical. The subject in each is realised by the same lexical items, 'the Lady Anna Gordon'.

In fact, of the three clauses, the third is probably the only one that has actually been used as part of a published text, namely the novel *The Well of Loneliness* (1928) by Radclyffe Hall (1893–1943), which begins:

> Not very far from Upton-on-Severn – between it, in fact, and the Malvern Hills – stands the country seat of the Gordons of Bramley; well-timbered, well-cottaged, well-fenced and well-watered, having, in this latter respect, a stream that forks in exactly the right position to feed two large lakes in the grounds.
>
> The house itself is of Georgian red brick, with charming circular windows near the roof. It has dignity without arrogance, repose without inertia; and a gentle aloofness that, to those who know its spirit, but adds to its value as a home. It is indeed like certain lovely women who, now old, belong to a bygone generation – women who in youth were passionate but seemly; difficult to win but when won all-fulfilling. They are passing away, but their homesteads remain, and such an homestead is Morton.

Our clause is the first in the next paragraph:

To Morton Hall came the Lady Anna Gordon as a bride of just over twenty.

In this context, we would probably not be at all surprised at the ordering of elements in this clause. Morton Hall has been thoroughly described in the preceding paragraphs, so it is uppermost in our minds when we come to the third paragraph, where, incidentally, the tense changes from present to past, to indicate that the narrative proper begins here.

The notion of something being uppermost in the reader's mind can be considered to constitute thematicity in a rather pre-theoretical, common sense way. In the following section, however, we will consider its use as a theoretical concept in functional grammar.

8.2.ii The clause as message: theme and rheme

The system of theme and rheme is used to structure the message carried by the clause to show which part of the message is expected to be already present in the minds of those involved in the language event, and which part is considered to be newly introduced. The part that is assumed to be present already in the minds of all participants is the theme, which is sometimes called the 'psychological subject' of the clause. The remainder of the clause, which typically contains what is considered new information for the recipient of the message is called the rheme. In English, according to Halliday (1985: 38) 'we signal that an item has thematic status by putting it first'.[1] Other languages do not necessarily use positioning in the clause to indicate theme; Japanese, for example, uses the postposition, '-wa' on the thematic element.

In English, when the theme is an element of clause structure other than the grammatical subject, the grammatical subject and the theme, or psychological subject, come apart:

To Morton Hall	came	the lady Anna Gordon	as a bride of just over twenty
A	P	S	A
THEME	RHEME		

As it happens, the coming to Morton Hall from the outside of a stranger is important in this novel, not only because it is in an important sense the beginning of the story – hence the change of tense – but also because the fate of Anna is to be contrasted with that of her daughter later. The daughter does not come to Morton Hall as a stranger since she is born there. But whereas Anna is accepted at Morton in spite of her foreignness because she conforms to the expectations people have of her as a woman, the daughter later becomes an outcast from both Morton and from her mother's affections because in spite of her resemblance to her forebears, she does not conform to the norms for womanly behaviour.

However, thematicity is not only important in literary texts – it is fundamental to the progression of texts of all types. Speakers of English are primed to attach prominence to the first element of the clause. They understand it to indicate what the message is about, or to be the point of departure for the rest of the message. Consider:

1. The school is to the left of the post-office
2. The post-office is to the right of the school
3. To the right of the school is the post-office
4. To the left of the post-office is the school

In (1) the focus is on the school; this clause might be uttered in response to an enquiry about what is to the left of the post office, which is the school, or about where the school is; in (2) the focus is on the post office, and the clause might be uttered in response to an enquiry about what is to the right of the school, which is the post office, or about where the post office is; in (3) and (4), the focus is on the position of x relative to y, and these clauses might be uttered by someone trying to help someone else to create a mental map of a place.

Of course the actual positioning in the world (fictional or real) of two buildings remains stable however speakers deal with them; it is only the interactants' perspectives on the situation that differ in the four cases. But perspective in language can be as important as it is in painting and photography, and can be exploited in many ways by writers. It can be important, but sometimes difficult, to maintain an original's thematic structure in a translation.

8.2.iii Practice and discussion

Practice

Identify the clause themes in the following text, from *Soccer Star* (Football Association in association with Coca-Cola, ISBN 0 00 196196-9 HB, p. 8):

(Header) Running with the ball
(1) Running with the ball is the first technique that youngsters learn – (2) they kick and then chase after the ball. (3) Running with the ball is not the same as dribbling. (4) Dribbling involves beating players (5) whereas running with the ball involves moving the ball across areas that do not contain defenders. (6) To be able to cover the ground quickly with the ball under control is a very important and valuable technique.

Translate the passage into your other language, trying to retain the thematic structure. Is it possible to do so? If not, why not? If so, do you need to make choices of lexis and expression that you would not necessarily have made otherwise?

Discussion

The theme in clause 5 above is strictly speaking realised by 'whereas', which is a subordinator that shows the relationship between the two clauses it links. According to Halliday (1985: 51), since speakers have no choice in where in the clause to position subordinating or co-ordinating conjunctions, which must come first, and since these have no function as grammatical subject, adjunct, object or complement, 'when one of them is present it does not take up the whole of the thematic potential of the clause'. The remaining thematic potential, then, is taken up in this case by 'running with the ball'. This is also theme in clauses (1) and (3) and in the headline. In clause (1), running with the ball is said to be the first technique that youngsters learn, and these youngsters, which are now in the reader's mind, remain as theme in clause (2), which explains *how* youngsters learn to run with the ball. Running with the ball recurs as thematic in clause (3), which makes clear that it is not the same as dribbling. Dribbling, the last word in the rheme in clause (3) and therefore now clearly present in the reader's mind is thematic in the next clause, (4), where it is defined. In the following clause, (5), 'whereas' reminds readers that an issue of the difference between running with the ball and dribbling has been clearly signalled in clause (3). Running with the ball, however, recurs in clause (5) to take up what according to Halliday remains as the thematic potential in the clause. The rheme here further specifies what is involved in running with the ball. Finally, clause (6) makes thematic the reason why it is worth spending so much energy and so many words on the concept of running with the ball.

Opinions vary about whether theme in Spanish is indicated by first position in the clause, because Spanish, as we noted in Chapter 7, is a pro-drop language, so some phenomena that might be expected to be selected as thematic may not in fact be explicitly mentioned in Spanish clauses. In Spanish, instead, the verb often occurs in first position. Recall the following example from McCabe (2001) also used in Chapter 7:

> *¿Donde está Juan?* (Where is Juan?)
> *Salió de compras* (Went shopping)

McCabe maintains that *salió* is theme, even though the agency of Juan is implied by the third person, singular, masculine ending, *-ó*.

In Spanish, many clauses also show subject–verb inversions, as in the following examples from McCabe (1991):

Faltaba	*evidentement*	*un modo*	*diferente de hacer historia*
was missing	evidently	a way	different of doing history
emigran	*los habitantes*	*de paises*	*superpoblados*
emigrate	the inhabitants	of countries	overpopulated

This means that it is more common in Spanish than in English to find predicators in theme position. If the theory that items in theme position are psychologically salient is correct, this may indicate that Spanish speakers focus more on the process parts of events than on the participants in them. Notice, however, that in the soccer text above, the process of running with the ball is regularly made thematic. This is made possible through the technique of grammatical metaphor which enables what is basically a tense-less clause to function in a clause position (subject) where a name, noun or noun phrase would usually occur.

Practice

Below is the first paragraph of Joseph Conrad's (1902; Penguin edition 1973: 5) *Heart of Darkness* and of Amado Diéguez Rodríguez's translation *El corazón de las tinieblas* (2001, Madrid, Santillana Ediciones Generales, S.L., notes not included):

> The *Nellie*, a cruising yawl, swung to her anchor without a flutter of the sails, and was at rest. The flood had made, the wind was nearly calm, and being bound down the river, the only thing for it was to come to and wait for the turn of the tide.

> La *Nellie*, una yola de crucero, giró sobre el ancla sin el menor movimiento de las velas y quedó inmóvil. Había subido la marea, apenas soplaba el viento y, puesto que se dirigía río abajo, sólo le quedaba fondear y esperar al cambio de la marea.

Underline the themes in the two texts and notice the phenomenon of theme positioned processes in the Spanish text.

Do the same for the two extracts about crêpes and galettes we examined in Chapter 7, and notice instances of thematisation of a process in the English language text which do not rely on the device of grammatical metaphor.

Discussion

In English, the Adjunct is a very mobile unit of clause structure, which means that it is possible to thematise temporal progression, as in the introductory clauses of the economics text printed at the end of Chapter 5:

Theme	*Rheme*
Three years after the shock of the Suq al Manakh crash	Kuwait's economy is now at a crossroads
For years	the state's economy has been largely based ...
Now	all three of these principal sources of wealth in Kuwait are in jeopardy.

Practice

Identify the themes in the rest of the economics text and consider how themes are used to structure the message or messages conveyed in this text. Can this message structure be retained in a translation of the text into your other language?

8.2.iv The clause as representation: transitivity

As mentioned in the discussion above of the relative positioning of a church and a post office, their actual position in the world (even if that is a fictional world only) remains stable whatever linguistic perspective we decide to impose on them. The clause also enables speakers and writers to represent this stability, not necessarily – not even very often, perhaps – purely factually, but in light of particular modes of seeing and understanding the processes and events that surround them. In the following section, we turn our attention to the system that facilitates this representation of interpretations of both fictional and actual reality.

Through the transitivity system, the clause represents an interpretation of reality. The world, as represented in human consciousness, can be considered to be made up of processes each of which consists of potentially three components (Halliday 1985: 101): the process itself, the participants in the process and the circumstances associated with the process. Processes are typically realised by verb phrases, participants by noun phrases and circumstances by adverbial or prepositional phrases.

Halliday (1985: Ch. 5) identifies three main types of process: material, mental and relational.

Material processes, or processes of doing, have an obligatory actor, sometimes known as the 'logical subject' (someone who does something) and an optional goal, to whom the process 'is extended' (1985: 103). Clauses in which both the actor and the goal are present are called 'transitive' and clauses in which only the actor is present are called 'intransitive':

They	kick and then chase after	the ball
ACTOR	MATERIAL PROCESS	GOAL

Tom	sang	beautifully
ACTOR	MATERIAL PROCESS	CIRCUMSTANCE OF MANNER

Mental processes of feeling, thinking, sensing and perceiving have an obligatory 'senser' and an obligatory 'phenomenon' which may, however, remain implicit and not be mentioned explicitly in the clause.

Amy	heard	the song
SENSER	MENTAL PROCESS	PHENOMENON

Nils	was worried
SENSER	MENTAL PROCESS

Relational processes are processes of being. 'The central meaning of clauses of this type is that something is' (Halliday 1985: 112):

> But every language accommodates, in its grammar, a number of distinct ways of being, expressed as different types of relational process in the clause. Those of English may be summarised as follows:

(1) intensive   'x is a'
(2) circumstantial   'x is at a'
(3) possessive   'x has a'

Each of these comes in two modes:

(i) attributive   'a is an attribute of x'
(ii) identifying   'a is the identity of x'

Identifying processes are reversible; attributive processes are not:

Running with the ball   is   the first technique that youngsters learn
IDENTIFIED   PROCESS   IDENTIFIER

The first technique that youngsters learn   is   running with the ball
IDENTIFIED   PROCESS   IDENTIFIER

These galettes   are   very tender
CARRIER   PROCESS   ATTRIBUTE

See Halliday (1985, Ch. 5) for further subdivisions of process and participant types.

The main types of circumstantial element of clauses in English are (Halliday 1985: 137): 'Extent and Location in time and space, including abstract space; manner (means, quality and comparison); cause (reason, purpose and behalf); accompaniment; matter, role'. Again, these can be further subdivided.

In the standard English declarative clause in the active voice, the actor, or logical subject, will coincide with the theme, or psychological subject, and also with the grammatical subject:

They   kick and then chase after   the ball
ACTOR   MATERIAL PROCESS   GOAL
THEME
SUBJECT

In clauses in the passive voice, the actor, if the actor is mentioned, departs from the position occupied by the theme and the grammatical subject:

The government has [itself] been hit by the decline in world oil demand
                                                          ACTOR
THEME
SUBJECT

Production in the last four years has been halved
THEME
SUBJECT

If the theme in such clauses is a circumstantial element, then all three subjects come apart:

Recently, the government has been hit by the decline in world oil demand
                                                          ACTOR
THEME
          SUBJECT

To see how analyses of the transitivity system and the system of theme and rheme can be used in stylistic analyses of literature, consult for example Burton (1982), Halliday (1971), or Knowles and Malmkjær (1996). Here, we shall concentrate on its use in non-literary texts.

8.2.v Practice and discussion

Practice

Compare the following text (from http://www.carsdirect.com/research/audi/a4/ 2004/18t) with the Brussels City Tour passage we met in Chapter 7. The English language version of the latter is repeated here for convenience. Identify grammatical subjects, themes and actors in both texts:

> Audi aims for its A4 to be the benchmark for sports sedans. The A4 might well be THE benchmark if it wasn't for the existence of the BMW 3 Series. In spite of the big shadow cast by rear-wheel-drive BMW, the Audi A4 is a fantastic sports sedan and certainly a leader among front-drive sedans. The A4 is unquestionably a standard against which sport sedans can be measured, and that fits the definition of a benchmark.
>
> A4 delivers crisp handling, a firm ride, and a well-controlled suspension that make for a precise, high-quality driving experience. A4 feels like it's on rails around fast sweepers, especially when equipped with the Quattro all-wheel-drive system. The 3.0 V6 engine is wonderfully smooth and quite strong, while the turbocharged 1.8T delivers spry performance when paired with the manual gearbox. A host of active safety features help keep drivers on the road. A4's beautifully finished interior exudes quality and ergonomic excellence. A4 was completely redesigned for 2002 and introduced with a new 3.0-liter V6. A new model, the 2003 A4 Cabriolet, brings top-down motoring to the line, and Avant (wagon) models have joined the new generation. Minor interior upgrades are available for 2003.
>
> **Brussels City Tour**
> We start our visit at the Central Station and see the beautiful St.-Michael's cathedral. We drive further to the Heyseldistrict with the worldfamous Atomium. We marvel at the sight of the Chinese Pavilion and the Japanese tower. Passing the Royal Residence we return into the citycentre and see the Sablan district with countless antique dealer shops. We drive in front of the magnificent Palace of Justice and see the fashionable Louise Square. Passing the stately Royal Square, the Royal Palace and the Houses of Parliament we arrive in the Cinquantenaire district. The Triumphal Arch, exceptional museums and splendid Art Nouveau houses are the highlights of this part of Brussels. Here, we are also at the very heart

of the European Union; we drive in front of the imposing EU buildings housing the Commission, the European Parliament and the Council of Ministers.

Discussion

Each text displays remarkable regularity in its selections of realisations of grammatical and thematic functions and transitivity roles. And the two texts contrast very markedly in the kinds of item referred to by the lexical items and structures that realise these functions. In the Audi text, 'Audi' is subject, theme and actor in one case, an Audi model is subject, theme and actor/identified/carrier in seven cases, subject and actor in one case and subject and theme once. Components of an Audi model is subject, theme and actor/carrier in three cases and 'Minor interior upgrades' functions as subject and theme on one occasion. There is one problematic case: 'A4 feels like it's on rails …'. The difficulty is that while the structure here is like that of, for example, 'Peter feels like he's on rails', background knowledge tells us that the A4 is not a kind of phenomenon capable of engaging in the mental process of feeling. So while the senser in 'Peter feels like he's on rails' is Peter, the senser in 'A4 feels like it's on rails …' must be a person driving the A4. This clause is the clearest example of the almost total absence in this text of direct reference to any human actors. The drivers who are helped to stay on the road constitute the one exception to this rule, however, they are not cast in the actor's role, but in the role of goal. Where the car is said to deliver crisp handling, spry performance and so on, we understand that this is 'delivered' to drivers, but in these cases, the drivers remain implicit, to be inferred by the reader. Again, when we read what Audi aims for in the first clause, we are left to infer that Audi is metonymic for the people in charge of the company. By these means, the focus remains clearly on the product being advertised which is presented as inherently dynamic and powerful, and the use of the metaphorical 'generation' implies the kind of biological propagation which is actually only a feature of living organisms. So a property of natural kinds is here ascribed to a manufactured kind (see Chapter 5).

In the text about Brussels, in contrast, every actor role is ascribed to the group of persons referred to by means of the first person plural pronoun, 'we', which includes both writer and reader. This actor/senser solidarity between reader and writer is also a feature of the texts in Spanish and Italian, whereas in the text in French, the reader/writer solidarity is broken in one instance when the pronoun is the second person plural, *vous* and in another when *voici* is used in a clause in the imperative mood so that the speech act is, if not exactly a command, then at least a suggestion on the part of the writer that the reader should observe something. In the text in German, the first person alternates even more regularly with the second person (three instances of each).

In the text in English, the theme position is occupied either by 'we' or by 'passing x' or by reference to objects to be admired, or to a position, 'here'. In other words, the text thematises people moving past, and to and from sights, as one would expect given the header. Similar selections are made in the texts in the other languages.

Both of the texts we have discussed above are promotional. Their thematic and transitivity structures are easily related to the nature of the product they are intended to promote. Their writers have obviously made quite deliberate choices in the three linguistic systems offered by the clause, which are likely to be motivated mainly by the wish to promote a product of a particular type.

In the case of other text types, however, writer motivation is less straighforwardly relatable to text topic and text genre. News reports, for example, are intended to convey news, but while the news to be conveyed may be the same in different texts, the writers have considerable freedom in selecting a particular perspective on the events in question. Consider, for example, the selections below of passages from three newspapers in different languages reporting on the same event. The papers and the story headlines are:

> *El Mundo* 28 March 2004, 'Abrogado francés defenderá a Hussain'
> *The Observer* 28 March 2004, 'French lawyer to defend Saddam'
> *Le Monde* 27 March 2004, 'Me Jacques Vergès devrait assurer la défense de Saddam Hussein'

Practice

Consider the different ways in which the three papers present essentially the same information, paying particular attention to the interplay of themes and transitivity role assignments. The paragraphs present essentially the same information, but not necessarily in the same order in the three papers:

> El abogado francés Jacques Verges asumirá la defensa de Saddam Hussein, tras recibir una petición de un familiar del ex dictador iraquí, reveló ayer la prensa francesa. (para 1)

> 'El sobrino de Saddam Hussein acaba de nombrarme' defensor de su tío, afirma Verges en la grabación de un programa televisivo que será difundido el próximo martes y a la que tuvo acceso el diario 'Le Parisien'. (para 2)

> The world's most controversial lawyer, Jacques Vergès, who has built his reputation on defending despots, Nazis and terrorists, has been asked by the family of Saddam Hussein to represent the deposed Iraqui dictator. (para 1)

> The French advocate yesterday told a radio station that he had received a letter from one of Saddam's relatives confirming his role as legal representative for the former Iraqui leader, whom he described as a 'vanquished hero'. 'I was ready to defend him and then I received a letter from his nephew', Vergès said. He read out a section of the letter on air: 'In my capacity as nephew of President Saddam Hussein, I commission you officially by this letter to assure the defence of my uncle,' Vergès told the national radio station *France Inter*. The nephew is believed to be Ali Barzan al-Tikriti. (para 2)

> L'avocat Jacques Vergès a annoncé qu'il défendrait Saddam Hussein avec l'appui

de douze autre avocats français, écrit samedi 27 mars *Le Parisien*. L'avocat aurait confié, lors de l'enregistrement d'une émission de télévision qui doit être diffusée mardi, avoir été désigné par un proche de l'ex-dictateur irakien. '*Le neveu de Saddam Hussein vient de me désigner*,' aurait-il lâché. (para 2)

Me Vergès a confirmé cette information à l'AFP samedi matin. Il a précisé qu'il avait reçu une lettre du neveu de Saddam Hussein lui demandant d'assurer la défense de son oncle, sans donner plus de détails. (para 3)

Discussion

The texts we have examined in this section illustrate clearly the remarkable opportunities language offers its users to highlight and hide aspects of processes, events and objects. Since the 1970s, there has been considerable interest in this phenomenon within linguistics, and this interest is shared by many members of the community of translation scholars. Within linguistics, the phenomenon is usually discussed under the headings 'critical linguistics', coined by Fowler *et al.* (1979), 'critical discourse analysis' (Fairclough 2002: 102), 'language and ideology' (see, for example, Stephens 1992), 'language and power' (see, for example, Fairclough 1989) or 'language and control' (see, for example, Knowles and Malmkjær 1996). Translation scholars tend to employ the term 'ideology' (see, for example, Puurtinen 2000 and Calzada-Perez 2003). In the final section of this chapter we shall look briefly at the relationship between language, ideology and translation.

8.3 LANGUAGE, IDEOLOGY AND TRANSLATION

In this section, we begin by outlining a view of how language can be used to serve ideological ends before moving on to a brief discussion of the relationship between translation and indicators of ideology.

8.3.i Language and ideology

According to Thompson (1990: 56) 'to study ideology is to study the ways in which meaning serves to establish and sustain relations of domination'. By 'relations of domination' Thompson means systematically asymmetrical relations of power such as those which obtain or have obtained between, for example, men and women, adults and children, masters and slaves, coloniser and colonised, masters and servants, managers and secretaries, rich and poor, rich countries and poor countries, different classes and races, and so on.

Language can be mobilised in a variety of ways to sustain these relations. For example, 'stories' (Thompson 1990: 59–67) of various kinds, such as myths, legends, tales of past battles, but also novels, poems, plays and news stories can be told in which these relationships are presented as being natural, as always having obtained, as being universal phenomena, as being other than they actually are – for example, as being beneficial to the oppressed.

Linguistic strategies for creating these impressions are various, but among the most obvious are careful lexical selection (for example, 'freedom fighter' versus 'terrorist', 'famous' versus 'infamous', 'claims' versus 'demonstrates'), and manipulation of thematicity and transitivity roles, often involving, for example, nominalisation of processes, which can give an impression of permanency, and passivatisation, which can hide agency and highlight those affected by an action.

Of course, it is also possible to express an ideological stance straightforwardly (as in 'Vote Labour'), and it is important to distinguish various levels of realisation of ideological stances in text. Hollindale (1988 in Hunt 1992: 27–34) mentions the levels of intended surface ideology, implicit, possibly subconscious assumptions and fixed limits of expression. The latter phenomenon is referred to by Chomsky (1979: 38–9), who claims that a democracy fixes the limits of possible thought: 'supporters of official doctrine at one end, and the critics … at the other' (see Chilton 1982: 94).

It is obvious that translation, which involves writing anew, can result in texts that express different ideologies than those expressed in the texts with which they originate, or which serve assymmetrical power relationships which were not present in the culture of the recipient group for the original. For example, Millán-Varela (2000) shows how the translation into Galician in 1926 of fragments of Joyce's *Ulysses* were used to promote the interests of Galician nationalism by means of careful selection of lexis (2000: 288):

> Otero the translator does not choose the expected literal translation which would have coincided in form both with the Latin forms of the ST and the Spanish language. Instead, he opts for an alternative solution: translate the meaning into 'pure' Galician forms, free of any influences.

For example, the purely Galician forms *xantar* ('diet'), *calzós* ('trousers'), *abó* ('ascendant') and *choque* ('impact') are chosen in preference to forms that Galician shares with Spanish: *dieta, pantalón, ancestro* and *impacto*.

Whereas the case of the Galician Joyce illustrates how a minority culture can use translation in order to promote their own cause vis-à-vis a majority culture, wa Goro (2004) shows how a majority culture can employ similar means in order to further cement its dominance. She discusses the way in which Biblical names were carefully given Gikuyu forms that were based on the original Hebrew names, even though names for Gikuyu deities could have been used, in order that Gikuyu mythology should not be given prominence. 'Adam' and 'Eve' were translated as *Adamu* and *Hawa*, instead of being rendered by means of the Gikuyu terms *Mundu* and *Mumbi*.

Finally, Nitsa Ben-Ari (2002) shows how an ideology[2] which permeates a text to be translated, but which may seem inappropriate in the context of a translation of that text, can be effectively filtered out during the translation process. She discusses eight translations into Hebrew of Lew Wallace's novel *Ben-Hur: A Tale of the Christ* (1880) as examples of this strategy, which she describes as 'double conversion': 'elimination of "undesirable" Christian elements and conversion of the translated text to a more "desirable" model' (2002: 272). In the case of *Ben-Hur*, it amounts to the conversion of 'Ben-Hur (the person) back to the Jewish faith and that of the novel to a "Jews against Romans" model'. In all the translations, the most common strategy for achieving these aims are large scale omissions, mainly of Christian elements (2002: 281), including, in each of the translations the omission of the subtitle, 'A Tale of the Christ' (2002: 282). Six of the translations also omit 'Book first', which provided the Christian background to the story, and of those which retain it, one omits the chapter describing the birth of Christ and provides a new chapter that provides a Hebrew historical background (2002: 283). Smaller scale, more directly linguistic filters, include, for example, the omission of the name of the village of Nazareth, which in the translation is 'a village in Galilee' (2002: 287) and the provision of chapter headings instead of the original's numbering system; Ben-Ari (2002: 292) mentions the heading, 'A Jew and a Roman'.

The study by Malmkjær (2003) of Dulcken's treatment of Hans Christian Andersen's stories mentioned in Chapter 3 might perhaps fall into the category of ideologically slanted translation, though since it is not clear that what is at issue here is a power struggle between two special interest groups, to include it and similar studies in this category would be to run the risk of watering down the notion of ideology to an extent that might render it meaningless.

NOTES

1. As Quirk *et al.* (1972: 945) point out, however, it is possible for the first element in the clause to carry both given and new information, as in: '[Who gave you that magazine?] BILL gave it to me.'

2. In this case, more correctly, a religion, but Ben-Ari (2002: 262) explains that 'due to its [*Ben-Hur*'s] predominantly Christian character, it can serve as an illuminating case study both for the subversion of Christian elements and for the more "creative" conversion into the "Few against Many" or "Jewish bravura against the Roman Empire" model'.

Conclusion

This book is based on the fundamental assumption that translation, like all linguistic activity, is inherently forward looking. Meaning is seen as relational and momentary, as a function which maps a constellation of utterances, circumstances and interactants onto interpretations. Language use must therefore be deferential to future users, and although past usage constitutes a monumental corpus that guides and informs future usage, it can neither determine nor reflect future usage. Seen in this light, translating is a display of creativeness, and translations display their equivalence with their originals. Language has been presented (see particularly Chapter 3, section 3.3.i and Chapter 7) as a meaning potential which functions in three main ways for its speakers: enabling them to interact with each other, to reflect on the world and to adopt particular perspectives on it. Linguistic interaction has been presented as fundamentally translational (see in particular Chapter 3, sections 3.5.i and 3.5.ii): Language really *is* the language of translation, and we have drawn on descriptive and theoretical notions from linguistics to describe and work with the language of and in translations and translating (Chapters 4–8). It has not been possible to cover all the concepts and notions available and it has not been possible to address the related activity of interpreting. However, students and teachers will perhaps be able to use the models provided here as a basis for their own investigations of how linguistic notions and concepts may be set to work in the study of the language of translation.

References

Abelin, Åse (n.d.), 'Phonesthemes in Swedish', http://www.ling.gu.se/~abelin/phonest.html

Abrams, M. H. (1971), *A Glossary of Literary Terms: Third Edition* (1st edition by Dan S. Norton and Peters Rushton, 1941, second edition by M. H. Abrams, 1957), New York: Holt, Rinehart and Winston, Inc.

Aichison, Jean [1987] (1994), *Words in the Mind: An Introduction to the Mental Lexicon*, Oxford: Basil Blackwell.

Allan, R., P. Holmes and T. Lundskær-Nielsen (1995), *Danish: A Comprehensive Grammar*, London and New York: Routledge.

Allen, Ward (ed.) (1969), *Translating for King James*, Nashville: Vanderbilt University Press.

Austin, J. L. (1962), *How to do Things with Words*, Oxford: Oxford University Press.

Axelsen, Jens (ed.) (1984), *The Standard Danish–English English Danish Dictionary; Dansk-Engelsk Engelsk-Dansk Ordbog*, Copenhagen: Gyldendalske Boghandel, Nordisk Forlag A/S.

Baker, Mona (1993), 'Corpus linguistics and translation studies – Implications and applications', in Mona Baker, Gill Francis and Elena Tognini-Bonelli (eds), *Text and Technology: In Honour of John Sinclair*, Philadelphia and Amsterdam: John Benjamins, pp. 213–50.

Baker, Mona (1995), 'Corpora in translation studies: An overview and suggestions for future research', *Target* 7(2): 223–43.

Baker, Mona (1998), *Routledge Encyclopedia of Translation Studies*, London and New York: Routledge.

Baker, Mona (1999), 'The Role of Corpora in Investigating the Linguistic Behaviour of Professional Translators', *International Journal of Corpus Linguistics* 4(2): 281–98.

Bakhtin, Mikhail (1965), *Rabelais and His World*. Translated by Helene Iswolsky, Cambridge, MA: The MIT Press.

Bakhtin, Mikhail (1973), *Problems of Dostoevsky's Poetics*. Translated by R. W. Rotsel, Ann Arbor, MI: Ardis.

Bartelink, G. J. M. (ed.) (1980), *Liber de optimo genere interpretandi (Epistula 57)*, Leiden: Brill.

Barthes, Roland (1977), *Image-Music-Text* (tr. Stephen Heath), London: Fontana.

Bassnett-McGuire, Susan [1980] (1991), *Translation Studies: Revised Edition,* London and New York: Methuen/Routledge.

Bassnett, Susan and André Lefevere (eds) (1990), *Translation, History and Culture*, London and New York: Pinter Publishers.

Bassnett, Susan and Harish Trivedi (eds) (1999), *Post-Colonial Translation: Theory and Practice*, London and New York: Routledge.

Beaugrande Robert de and Wolfgang Dressler (1981), *Introduction to Text Linguistics*, London and New York: Longman.

Begley, Sharon (2002), 'New ABCs of Branding: Product Names Pack Punch One Letter at a

Time; StrawBerry Is No BlackBerry', *Wall Street Journal*, 26 August. http://online.wsj.com/article/0,,SB10303107301794 74675.djm,00.html

Béjoint, Henri (1994), *Modern Lexicography: An Introduction*, Oxford: Oxford University Press.

Bell, Roger T. (1991), *Translation and Translating: Theory and Practice*, London and New York: Longman.

Belsey, Catherine (1980), *Critical Practice*, London and New York: Methuen.

Ben-Ari, Nitsa (2002), 'The double conversion of *Ben-Hur*: A case of manipulative Translation', *Target* 14(2): 263–301.

Berlin, B. and P. Kay (1969), *Basic Color Terms*, Berkeley and Los Angeles: University of California Press.

Bhatia, Vijay K. (1993), *Analysing Genre: Language Use in Professional Settings*, Harlow: Longman.

Black, Max (1979), 'More about Metaphor', in Andrew Ortony (ed.), *Metaphor and Thought*, Cambridge: Cambridge University Press, pp. 19–45.

Boas, Franz (1911), *Handbook of American Indian Languages*, Washington, DC: Smithsonian Institution.

Bowerman, Melissa (1996), 'The origins of children's spatial semantic categories: Cognitive versus linguistic determinants', in John J. Gumperz and Stephen C. Levinson (eds), *Rethinking Linguistic Relativity*, Cambridge: Cambridge University Press, pp. 145–76.

Bredsdorff, Elias (1954), *H. C. Andersen og England*, Copenhagen: Rosenkilde og Baggers Forlag.

Brower, Ruben A. (ed.) (1959), *On Translation*, Cambridge, MA: Harvard University Press.

Brown, Gillian and George Yule (1983), *Discourse Analysis*, Cambridge: Cambridge University Press.

Brown, Penelope and Stephen C. Levinson (1978), *Politeness: Some Universals in Language Usage*, Cambridge: Cambridge University Press.

Bühler, Karl (1933), 'Die Axiomatik der Sprachwissenschaft, *Kant-Studien* 38: 19–20.

Burton, Deirdre (1982), 'Through glass darkly: Through dark glasses', in Ronald Carter (ed.), *Language and Literature: An Introductory Reader in Stylistics*, London: George Allen and Unwin.

Calzada-Perez, Maria (ed.) (2003), *A Propos of Ideology*, Manchester: St Jerome Publishing.

Cambridge International Dictionary of English (CIDE) (1995), Cambridge: Cambridge University Pres.

Carroll, John B. (ed.) (1956), *Language, Thought and Reality: Selected Writings of Benjamin Lee Whorf*, Cambridge, MA: The MIT Press.

Catford, J. C. (1965), *A Linguistic Theory of Translation: An Essay in Applied Linguistics*, Oxford: Oxford University Press.

Chilton, Paul (1982), 'Nukespeak: Nuclear language, culture and propaganda', in Crispin Aubrey (ed.), *Nukespeak: The Media and the Bomb*, London: Comedia.

Chomsky, Noam (1957), *Syntactic Structures*, The Hague: Mouton.

Chomsky, Noam (1979), *Language and Responsibility*, Brighton: Harvester Press.

Collins-COBUILD English Language Dictionary (1987), London: Collins.

Craig, Ian (1998), 'Translation and the authoritarian regime: *William* and the *Caudillo*', in Peter Bush and Kirsten Malmkjær (eds), *Rimbaud's Rainbow: Literary Translation in Higher Education*, Amsterdam and Philadelphia: John Benjamins, pp. 157–69.

Dagut, Menachem (1981), '"Semantic Voids" as a problem in the translation process', *Poetics Today* 2(4): 61–71.

Davidsen-Nielsen, Niels (1992), 'Discourse particles in Danish', *PEO* 69: 1–34.

Davidson, Donald (1967), 'Truth and Meaning', *Synthese* 17: 304–23.

Davidson, Donald (1973), 'Radical interpretation', *Dialectica* 27: 313–28. Reprinted in (1984), *Enquiries into Truth and Interpretation*, Oxford: Clarendon Press.

Davidson, Donald (1974), 'On the very idea of a conceptual scheme', reprinted from *Proceedings and Addresses of the American Philosophical Association*, 47, in (1984), *Inquiries into Truth and Interpretation*, Oxford: Clarendon Press, pp. 183–98.

Davidson, Donald (1984), *Inquiries into Truth and Interpretation*, Oxford: Clarendon Press.

Davidson, Donald (1986), 'A Nice Derangement of Epitaphs', in Ernest LePore (ed.), *Truth and Interpretation: Perspectives on the Philosophy of Donald Davidson*, Oxford: Basil Blackwell, pp. 433–46. Also in R. E. Grandy and R. Warner (eds) (1986), *Philosophical Grounds of Rationality: Intentions, Categories, Ends*, Oxford: Clarendon Press, pp. 157–74.

Denofsky, Murray (n.d.), 'Johnny and the sound CL-', http://www/conknet.com/~mmagnus/SSArticles/Denofcl.html

Dinneen, F. P. (1967), *An Introduction to General Linguistics*, New York: Holt, Rinehart and Winston.

Dorsch, T. S. (ed.) (1965), *Aristotle/Horace/Longinus: Classical Literary Criticism*, Harmondsworth: Penguin.

Dudley-Evans, Anthony (2002), 'Genre analysis', in Kirsten Malmkjær (ed.), *The Linguistics Encyclopedia: Second Edition*, London and New York: Routledge, pp. 205–8.

Ellis, Roger and Liz Oakley-Brown (1998), 'British Tradition', in Mona Baker (ed.), *Routledge Encyclopedia of Translation Studies*, London: Routledge, pp. 333–47.

Empson, William (1947), *Seven Types of Ambiguity*, 2nd edition, London: Chatto and Windus.

Enkvist, Nils Erik (1978), 'Coherence, pseudo-coherence, and non-coherence', in Jan-Ola Östman (ed.), *Cohesion and Semantics*, Åbo: Åbo Akademi Foundation.

Evans, Gareth (1982), *The Varieties of Reference* (ed. John McDowell), Oxford: Clarendon Press and New York: Oxford University Press.

Even-Zohar, Itamar (1971), 'Mavo le-te'orya šel ha-tirgum ha-sifruti [Introduction to a Theory of Literary Translation], Tel Aviv: Tel Aviv University [Unpublished PhD Thesis. English summary: I–XX].

Even-Zohar, Itamar (1978), 'The position of translated literature within the literary polysystem', in James S. Holmes, José Lambert and Raymond van den Broek (eds), *Literature and Translation: New Perspectives in Literary Studies*, pp. 117–27, Leuven: acco.

Even-Zohar, Itamar (1990), *Polysystem Studies*, Tel Aviv: The Porter Institute for Poetics and Semiotics, Tel Aviv University. [= *Poetics Today* 11:1].

Fairclough, Norman (1989), *Language and Power*, Harlow: Longman.

Fairclough, Norman (2002), 'Critical linguistics/critical discourse analysis', in Kirsten Malmkjær (ed.), *The Linguistics Encyclopedia: Second Edition*, London and New York: Routledge, pp. 102–7.

Ferrara, A. (1980a), 'An extended theory of speech acts: Conditions for subordinate acts in sequences', *Journal of Pragmatics* 4: 233–52.

Ferrara, A. (1980b), 'Appropriateness conditions for entire sequences of speech acts', *Journal of Pragmatics* 4: 321–49.

Firth, J. R. (1930), *The Tongues of Men and Speech*, London: Oxford University Press.

Firth, J. R. (1957), *Papers in Linguistics 1934–1951*, London: Oxford University Press.

Fowler, Norman, Robert Hodge, Gunter Kress and Tony Trew (1979), *Language and Control*, London: Routledge and Kegan Paul.

Frege, Gottlob [1892] (1977), 'On sense and reference', in Peter Geach and Max Black (eds), *Translations from the Philosophical Writings of Gottlob Frege*, Oxford: Basil Blackwell, pp. 56–78

Gallie, W. (1955–6) 'Essentially contested concepts', *Proceedings of the Aristotelian Society* LVI: 167–98.

Gardner, Martin (ed.) [1960] (1970), *The Annotated Alice*, Harmondsworth: Penguin Books.

Gimson, A. C. [1962] (1980), *An Introduction to the Pronunciation of English: Third Edition*, London: Edward Arnold.

Goddard, Angela (1998), *The Language of Advertising: Second Edition*, London and New York: Routledge.

Grice, H. Paul (1975), 'Logic and conversation', in P. Cole and J. L. Morgan (eds), *Syntax and Semantics 3: Speech Acts*, New York: Academic Press, pp. 41–58.

Gumperz, John J. and Stephen C. Levinson (eds) (1996), *Rethinking Linguistic Relativity*, Cambridge: Cambridge University Press.

Gutt, Ernst-August (1991), *Translation and Relevance: Cognition and Context*, Oxford: Basil Blackwell.

Halliday, Michael Alexander Kirkwood (1961), 'Categories of the theory of grammar', *Word* 17(3): 241–92.

Halliday, Michael Alexander Kirkwood (1970), 'Language structure and language function', in John Lyons (ed.), *New Horizons in Linguistics*, Harmondsworth: Penguin.

Halliday, Michael Alexander Kirkwood (1971), 'Linguistic function and literary style: An inquiry into the language of William Golding's *The Inheritors*', in Seymore Chatman (ed.), *Literary Style: A Symposium*, Oxford: Oxford University Press. Reprinted in Michael Alexander Kirkwood Halliday (1973), *Explorations in the Functions of Language*, London: Edward Arnold, pp. 103–44.

Halliday, Michael Alexander Kirkwood (1978), *Language as Social Semiotic*, London: Edward Arnold.

Halliday, Michael Alexander Kirkwood (1985), *An Introduction to Functional Grammar*, London: Edward Arnold.

Halliday, Michael Alexander Kirkwood and Hasan Ruqaiya (1976), *Cohesion in English*, London: Longman.

Harvey, Keith (1998), 'Translating camp talk: Gay identity and cultural transfer', *The Translator* 4(2): 295–320.

Hatch, Elvin (1985), 'Culture', in Adam Kuper and Jessica Kuper (eds), *The Social Science Encyclopedia*, London, Boston and Henley: Routledge and Kegan Paul, pp. 178–9.

Hatim, Basil (1998), 'Text politeness: A semiotic regime for a more interactive pragmatics', in Leo Hickey (ed.), *The Pragmatics of Translation*, Clevedon: Multilingual Matters, pp. 72–102.

Haugaard, Erik (1974), *Hans Andersen: Fairy Tales and Stories. The Complete Collection Translated by Erik Haugaard*, London: Victor Gollancz Ltd.

Heaney, Seamus (tr) (1999), *Beowulf: A New Translation*, London: Faber and Faber.

Hinton, L., J. Nichols and J. J. Ohala (eds), *Sound Symbolism*, Cambridge: Cambridge University Press.

Hjelmslev, Louis (1953), *Prolegomena to a Theory of Language* (tr. F. J. Whitfield), *International Journal of American Linguistics* 1(1): Memoir no. 7, Madison: University of Wisconsin Press.

Hjørnager Pedersen, Viggo (2004), *Ugly Ducklings? Studies in the English Translations of Hans Christian Andersen's Tales and Stories*, Odense: University Press of Southern Denmark.

Ho, George (2003), 'Brand names and translation: The Economic Value of Translation', Paper presented at the 10th International Conference on translation and Interpreting: 'Translation Targets', Charles University, Prague, 12 September. MS.

Hockett, Charles F. (1958), *A Course in Modern Linguistics*, New York: Macmillan.

Hofland, Knutt and Stig Johansson (1998), 'The translation corpus aligner: A program for automatic alignment of parallel texts', in Stig Johansson and Signe Oksefjell (eds), *Corpora and Cross-linguistic Research: Theory, Method and Case Studies*, Amsterdam and Atlanta, GA: Rodopi, pp. 87–100.

Hollindale, P. (1988), 'Ideology and the children's book', *Signal* 55: 3–22. Reprinted in Peter Hunt (ed.) (1992), *Literature for Children: Contemporary Criticism*, London and New York: Routledge, pp. 19–40.

Holmes, James S. [1972] (1988), 'The name and nature of translation studies'. Paper presented in the translation section of the Third International Congress of Applied Linguistics, Copenhagen, 21–26 August 1972, in *Translated! Papers on Literary Translation and Translation Studies*, Amsterdam: Rodopi, pp. 66–80.

Holz-Mänttäri, Justa (1984), *Translatorisches Handlen: Theorie und Methode* (Annales Academiae Scientiarum Fennicae B 226), Helsinki: Suomalainen Tiedeakatemia.

Hookway, Christopher (1988), *Quine: Language, Experience and Reality*, Cambridge: Polity Press.

Horner, W. B. (1975), *Text act theory: A study of non-fiction texts*. Unpublished PhD thesis, University of Michigan.

House, Juliane (1998), 'Politeness and Translation', in Leo Hickey (ed.), *The Pragmatics of Translation*, Clevedon: Multilingual Matters Ltd.

Hung, Eva and David Pollard (1998), 'Chinese tradition', in Mona Baker (ed.), *Routledge Encyclopedia of Translation Studies*, London and New York: Routledge, pp. 365–74.

Hunston, Susan (2002), *Corpora in Applied Linguistics*, Cambridge: Cambridge University Press.

Hunt, Peter (1992), *Literature for Children: Contemporary Criticism*, London and New York: Routledge.

Ilson, Robert (1991), 'Lexicography', in Kirsten Malmkjær (ed.), *The Linguistics Encyclopeadia*, London and New York: Routledge.

Ingarden, Roman [1931] (1973), *The Literary Work of Art: An Investigation on the Borderlines of Ontology, Logic, and Theory of Literature. With an Appendix on the Functions of Language in the Theatre*. Translated by George G. Grabowicz from the third edition of *Das literarische Kunstwerk*, copyright 1965 by Max Niemeyer Verlag, Tübingen, first published by Niemeyer in 1931. Evanston: Northwestern University Press.

Ingarden, Roman [1937] (1973), *The Cognition of the Literary Work of Art*. Translated by Ruth Ann Cowlcy and Kenneth R. Olson from *Vom Erkennen des literarischen Kunstwerks*, copyright 1968 by Max Niemeyer Verlag, Tübingen. First published in 1937 in Polish as *O poznawaniu dziela literackiego*. Lvov: Ossolineum. Evanston: Northwestern University Press.

Ireland, Jeanette (1989), 'Ideology, myth and the maintenance of cultural identity', *ELR Journal (new series)* 3: 95–136 (School of English; Birmingham University).

Isenberg, Arnold (1953), 'Some problems of interpretation', in Arthur Wright (ed.), *Studies in Chinese Thought*, Chicago: University of Chicago Press, pp. 232–46.

Jakobson, Roman (1959), 'On linguistic aspects of translation', in Reuben A. Brower (ed.), *On Translation*, Cambridge, MA: Harvard University Press, pp. 232–9. Reprinted in Roman Jakobson (1987), *Language in Literature*, ed. Krystyna Pomorska and Stephen Rudy, Cambridge, MA and London, England: The Belknap Press of Harvard University Press, pp. 428–35.

Jakobson, Roman (1960), 'Closing statement: Linguistics and poetics', in Thomas A. Sebeok (ed.), *Style in Language*, Cambridge, MA: The MIT Press. Reprinted in Roman Jakobson (1987), *Language in Literature*, ed. Krystyna Pomorska and Stephen Rudy, Cambridge, MA and London, England: The Belknap Press of Harvard University Press, pp. 62–93.

Jarvella, R. J. (1971), 'Syntactic Processing of Connected Speech', *Journal of Verbal Learning and Verbal Behaviour* 10: 409–16.

Jerome (Saint) (1980), *Liber de optime genere interpretandi* (Epistula 57), ed. G. J. M. Bartelink, Leiden: Brill.

Jespersen, Otto (1922), *Language, its Nature, Development and Origin*, London: George Allen and Unwin.

Johansson, Stig and Signe Oksefjell (eds) (1998), *Corpora and Cross-linguistic Research: Theory, Method and Case Studies*, Amsterdam and Atlanta, GA: Rodopi.

Keenaghan, Eric (1998), 'Jack Spicer's pricks and cocksuckers: Translating homosexuality into visibility', *The Translator* 4(2): 273–94.

Kelly, Louis (1998), 'Latin tradition', in Mona Baker (ed.), *Routledge Encyclopedia of Translation Studies*, London and New York: Routledge, pp. 495–503.

Kempson, Ruth (1977), *Semantic Theory*, Cambridge: Cambridge University Press.

Knowles, Murray and Kirsten Malmkjær (1996), *Language and Control in Children's Literature*, London and New York: Routledge.

Köhler, Wolfgang (1947), *Gestalt Psychology: An Introduction to New Concepts in Modern Psychology*, New York: Liveright.

Krishnamurthy, Ramesh (1998), 'Indian tradition', in Mona Baker (ed.), *Routledge Encyclopedia of Translation Studies*, London and New York: Routledge, pp. 464–73.

Kristeva, Julia (1969), 'Word, Dialogue and Novel', *Séméiotiké*, tr. Alice Jardine, Thomas Gora and Léon S. Roudiez in 1980, *Desire in Language: A Semiotic Approach to Literature and Art*, Oxford: Basil Blackwell. Reprinted in Toril Moi (ed.), 1986, *The Kristeva Reader*, Oxford: Basil Blackwell.

Lakoff, George and Mark Johnson (1980), *Metaphors We Live By*, Chicago and London: The University of Chicago Press.

Langacker, R. W. (1987), *Foundations of Cognitive Grammar*, Stanford, CA: Stanford University Press.

Langacker, R. W. (1991), *Concept, Image, and Symbol: The Cognitive Basis of Grammar*, Berlin: Mouton.

Langacker, R. W. (1999), *Grammar and Conceptualization*, Berlin: Mouton.

Laviosa, Sara (1997), 'How comparable can comparable corpora be?', *Target* 9(2): 289–319.

Laviosa, Sara (1998), 'Core patterns of lexical use in a comparable corpus of English Narrative Prose', *Meta* 43(4): 557–70.

Lederer, Marianne (1994), *La traduction aujourd'hui – Le modèle interprétatif*, Paris: Hachette.

Leech, Geoffrey N. (1969), *A Linguistic Guide to English Poetry*, London: Longman.

Leech, Geoffrey N. (1983), *Principles of Pragmatics*, London and New York: Longman.

Lefevere, André (1990), 'Translation: Its genealogy in the West', in Susan Bassnet and André Lefevere (eds), *Translation, History and Culture*, London and New York: Pinter Publishers, pp. 14–28.

Leppihalme, Ritva (1997), *Culture Bumps: An Empirical Approach to the Translation of Allusions*, Clevedon: Multilingual Matters.

Levinson, Stephen C. (1996), 'Relativity in Spatial Conception and Description', in John J. Gumperz and Stephen C. Levinson (eds), *Rethinking Linguistic Relativity*, Cambridge: Cambridge University Press, pp. 177–202.

Lewis, David (1983), *Philosophical Papers Volume I*, New York and Oxford: Oxford University Press.

Locke, John [1690] (1977), *An Essay Concerning Human Understanding*, Glasgow: Fontana Collins.

Lombardi, L. and M. C. Potter (1992), 'The regeneration of syntax in short term memory', *Journal of Memory and Language* 31: 713–33.

Louw, Bill (1993), 'Irony in the text or insincerity in the writer? – the diagnostic potential of semantic prosodies', in Mona Baker, Gillian Francis and Elena Tognini-Bonelli (eds), *Text and Technology: In Honour of John Sinclair*, Amsterdam and Philadelphia: John Benjamins, pp. 157–76.

Louw, Bill (1997), 'The role of corpora in critical literary appreciation', in A. Wichmann, S. Fligelstone, Tony McEnery and G. Knowles (eds), *Teaching and Langauge Corpora*, London: Longman, pp. 140–251.

Low, Peter (2003), 'Translating poetic song: An attempt at a functional account of strategies', *Target* 15(1): 91–110.

Lyons, John (1963), *Structural Semantics*, Oxford: Basil Blackwell.

Lyons, John (1968), *Introduction to Theoretical Linguistics*, Cambridge: Cambridge University Press.

Lyons, John (1996), 'On competence and performance and related notions', in Gillian Brown, Kirsten Malmkjær and John N. Williams (eds), *Performance and Competence in Second Language Acquisition*, Cambridge: Cambridge University Press, pp. 9–32.

McCabe, Anne (Thursday, 31 May 2001 21:39:01 + 0200), contribution to the discussion list *[Sys-func] Theme in Spanish* on http://listserve.uts.edu.au/archives/sys-func/Week-of-Mon-20010528/000089.html

McCarthy, Michael (1991), 'Morphology', in Kirsten Malmkjær (ed.), *The Linguistics Encyclopedia*, London and New York: Routledge, pp. 314–23.

McGowan, James (1993), *The Flowers of Evil*, Oxford: Oxford University Press.

Malinowski, Bronislaw [1923] (1953), 'The problem of meaning in primitive languages'. Supplement to C. K. Ogden and I. A. Richards, *The Meaning of Meaning*, London: Routledge and Kegan Paul.

Malinowski, Bronislaw (1935), *Coral Gardens and their Magic*, London: Allen and Unwin.

Malmkjær, Kirsten (1993), 'Underpinning translation theory', *Target* 5(2): 133–48.

Malmkjær, Kirsten, (1996), 'Who walked in the emperor's garden: The translation of pronouns in Hans Christian Andersen's introductory passages', in Gunilla Anderman and C. Banér (eds), *Proceedings of the Tenth Biennial Conference of the British Association of Scandinavian Studies*. The University of Surrey, Department of Linguistics and International Studies.

Malmkjær, Kirsten (1999a), 'Translation and linguistics: What does the future hold?', *Textus* XII: 213–24.

Malmkjær, Kirsten (1999b), *Descriptive Linguistics and Translation Studies: Interface and Difference*, Platform Papers on Translation Studies 1, Utrecht: Platform Vertalen & Vertaalwetenschap.

Malmkjær, Kirsten (2003), 'What happened to God and the angels: An Exercise in Translational Stylistics', *Target* 15(1): 39–62.

Malmkjær, Kirsten (2004), 'Censorship or error: Mary Howitt and a problem in descriptive TS', in Gyde Hansen, Kirsten Malmkjær and Daniel Gile (eds), *Translation Studies: Claims, Changes and Challenges. Selected papers from the EST Congress, Copenhagen 2001*, Amsterdam and Philadelphia: John Benjamins, pp. 141–55.

Mandelbaum, David G. (ed.) (1949), *Edward Sapir, Culture, Language, Personality: Selected Essays*, Berkeley, Los Angeles and London: University of California Press.

Meta 43 (4) 1998.

Meyer, Charles F. (2002), *English Corpus Linguistics: An Introduction*, Cambridge: Cambridge University Press.

Millán-Varela, Carmen (2000), 'Translation, Normalisation And Identity In Galicia', *Target* 12(2): 267–82

Nabokov, Vladimir (1955), 'Problems of translation: *Onegin* in English', *Partisan Review* 22: 496–512. Reprinted in Lawrence Venuti (ed.) (2000), *The Translation Studies Reader*, London and New York: Routledge, pp. 71–83.

Newmark, Peter (1981), *Approaches to Translation*, Oxford: Pergamon Press.

Newmark, Peter (1988), *A Textbook of Translation*, New York: Prentice Hall.

Nida, Eugene A. (1964), *Toward a Science of Translating: With Special Reference to Principles and Procedures Involved in Bible Translating*, Leiden: E. J. Brill.

Nida, Eugene A. (1998), 'Bible translation', in Mona Baker (ed.), *Routledge Encyclopedia of Translation Studies*, London: Routledge, pp. 22–8.

Nord, Christiane (1995), 'Text-Functions in translation: Titles and Headings as a Case in Point', *Target* 7(2): 261–85.

Palmer, F. R. [1976] (1981), *Semantics: Second Edition*, Cambridge: Cambridge University Press.

Pöchhacker, Franz and Miriam Shlesinger (eds), *The Interpreting Studies Reader*, London and New York: Routledge.

Potter, M. C. and L. Lombardi (1990), 'Regeneration in the short-term recall of sentences', *Journal of Memory and Language* 29: 633–54.

Putnam, Hilary (1970), 'Is semantics possible?', in H. Kiefer and M. Munitz (eds), *Languages, Belief and Metaphysics*, New York: State University of New York Press.

Putnam, Hilary (1978), *Meaning and the Moral Sciences*, London, Henley and Boston: Routledge and Kegan Paul.

Puurtinen, Tiina (2000), 'Translating linguistic markers of ideology', in Andrew Chesterman, Natividad Gallaro San Salvador and Yves Gambier (eds), *Translation in Context*, Amsterdam and Philadelphia: John Benjamins, pp. 177–86.

Qvale, Per (1998), *Fra Hieronymus til hypertext: Oversettelse i teori og praksis*, Oslo: H. Aschehoug & Co.

Qvale, Per (2003), *From St. Jerome to Hypertext: Translation in Theory and Practice* (tr. Norman R. Spencer), Manchester, UK and Northampton, MA: St Jerome Publishing.

Quine, Willard van Orman (1959), 'Meaning and translation', in Reuben A. Brower (ed.), *On Translation*, Cambridge, MA: Harvard University Press.

Quine, Willard van Orman (1960), *Word and Object*, Cambridge, MA: The MIT Press.

Quirk, Randolph, Sidney Greenbaum, Geoffrey Leech and Jan Svartvik (1972), *A Grammar of Contemporary English*, Harlow, Essex: Longman.

Reah, Danuta (1998), *The Language of Newspapers: Second edition*, London and New York: Routledge.

Reiss, Katharina [1971] (2000), *Translation Criticism – The Potentials and Limitations: Categories and Criteria for Translation Quality Assessment.* Translated by Erroll F. Rhodes from *Möglichkeiten und Grenzen der Übersetzungskritik* (Max Hueber Verlag), Manchester: St Jerome Publishing, and New York: American Bible Society.

Reiss, Katharina and Hans Josef Vermeer [1984] (1991), *Grundlegung einer allgemeine Translationstheorie.* Second edition, Tübingen: Niemeyer.

Richards, I. A. (1936), 'Metaphor', in I. A. Richards, *The Philosophy of Rhetoric*, London: Oxford University Press.

Rieu, E. V. and J. B. Phillips (1954), 'Translating the Gospels', *Concordia Theological Monthly* 25: 754–65.

Robins, R. H. [1964] (1989), *General Linguistics: An Introductory Survey*, London and New York: Longman.

Robinson, Douglas (ed.) (1997), *Western Translation Theory: From Herodotus to Nietzsche*, Manchester: St Jerome Publishing.

Rosch, Eleanor (1973), 'Natural categories', *Cognitive Pychology* 4: 328–50.

Rosch, Eleanor (1977), 'Human categorisation', in N. Warren (ed.), *Studies in Cross-Cultural Psychology*, Volume 1. London: Academic Press.

Rosch, Eleanor (1978), 'Principles of categorization', in Eleanor Rosch and B. B. Lloyd (eds), *Cognition and Categorization*, Hillsdale, NJ: Lawrence Erlbaum Associates.

Sampson, Geoffrey (1980), *Schools of Linguistics: Competition and Evolution*, London: Hutchinson.

Sapir, Edward (1921), *Language: An Introduction to the Study of Speech*, New York: Harcourt Brace.

Sapir, Edward (1929), 'The status of linguistics as a science'. *Language* 5. Reprinted in Mandelbaum, David G. (ed.) (1949), *Edward Sapir, Culture, Language, Personality: Selected Essays*, Berkeley, Los Angeles and London: University of California Press, pp. 65–77.

Schäffner, Christina (1998), 'Skopos theory', in Mona Baker (ed.), *Routledge Encyclopedia of Translation Studies*, London and New York: Routledge, pp. 3–5.

Schulte, Rainer and John Biguenet (eds) (1992), *Theories of Translation: An Anthology of Essays from Dryden to Derrida*, Chicago and London: The University of Chicago Press.

Scruton, Roger (1974), *Art and Imagination: A Study on the Philosophy of Mind*, London: Methuen.

Searle, John R. (1975), 'Indirect Speech Acts', in P. Cole and J. Morgan (eds), *Syntax and Semantics*, vol. 3, *Speech Acts*, New York: Academic Press.

Seleskovitch, Danica (1975), *Langage, langues et mémoire. Étude de la prise de notes en interprétation consécutive*, Paris: Minard Lettres Modernes.

Seleskovitch, Danica, and Marianne Lederer (1989), *Pédagogie raisonnée de l'interprétation*, Paris: Didier Érudition.

Shisler, Benjamin K. (1997), 'The Influence of Phonasthesia on the English Language', http://www.geocities.com/SoHo/Studios/9783/phonpap1.html

Simon, Sherry (1996), *Gender in Translation: Cultural Identity and the Politics of Transmission*, London and New York: Routledge.

Sinclair, John McHardy (1991), *Corpus, Concordance, Collocation*, Oxford: Oxford University Press.

Smith, Norman Kemp (tr.) (1933), *Immanuel Kant's Critique of Pure Reason. Second Impression with Corrections*, London and Basingstoke: The Macmillan Press Ltd.

Snell-Hornby, Mary [1988] (1995), *Translation Studies: An Integrated Approach*, Amsterdam and Philadelphia: John Benjamins Publishing Company.

Sperber, Dan and Deirdre Wilson (1986), *Relevance: Communication and Cognition*, Oxford: Basil Blackwell.

Steiner, George [1975] (1992), *After Babel: Aspects of Language and Translation*, Oxford and New York: Oxford University Press.

Stephens, John (1992), *Language and Ideology in Children's Fiction*, London and New York: Longman.

Swales, John M. (1990), *Genre Analysis: English in Academic and Research Settings*, Cambridge: Cambridge University Press.

Tarski, Alfred (1956), 'The concept of truth in formalised languages', in *Logic, Semantics, Mathematics*, Oxford: Oxford University Press.

Thompson, John B. (1990), *Ideology and Modern Culture: Critical and Social Theory in the Era of Mass Communication*, Cambridge: Polity Press.

Tomlin, R. S. (1986), *Basic Word Order: Functional Principles*, London: Croom Helm.

Toury, Gideon (1978), 'The nature and role of norms in literary translation', in James Holmes, Jose Lambert and Raymond van den Broeck (eds), *Literature and Translation: New Perspectives in Literary Studies*, Leuven: Acco. 83–100.

Toury, Gideon (1980), 'Translated literature: System, norm, performance: Toward a TT-oriented approach to literary translation', in *In Search of a Theory of Translation*, Tel Aviv, Tel Aviv University, The Porter Institute for Poetics and Semiotics, pp. 35–50. Reprinted in *Poetics Today* (1981), 2:4, 9–27.

Toury, Gideon (1981), 'Contrastive linguistics and translation studies: Toward a tripartite model', in Wolfgang Kühlwein, Gisela Thome and Wolfram Wilss (eds), *Konstrastive Lingvistik und Übersetzungswissenschaft: Akten des Internationalen Kolloqviums Trier/Saarbrücken 25.-30.9.1978*, Munich: Wilhelm Fink, pp. 251–61.

Toury, Gideon (1995), *Descriptive Translation Studies and Beyond*, Amsterdam and Philadelphia: John Benjamins Publishing Company.

Traugott, Elizabeth Closs and Mary Louise Pratt (1980), *Linguistics for Students of Literature*, San Diego: Harcourt Brace Jovanovich.

Venuti, Lawrence (1995), *The Translator's Invisibility: A History of Translation*, London and New York: Routledge.

Venuti, Lawrence (ed.) (2000), *The Translation Studies Reader*, London and New York: Routledge.

Vermeer, Hans Josef [1978] (1983), 'Ein Rahmen für eine allgemeine Translationstheorie', *Lebende Sprachen* 23: 99–102. Also in *Aufsätze zur Translationstheorie*, Heidelberg: Vermeer, pp. 48–61.

Viberg, Åke (1996), 'Cross-linguistic lexicology. The case of English *go* and Swedish *gå*', in

Karin Aijmer, Bengt Altenberg and Mats Johansson (eds), *Languages in Contrast: Papers from a symposium on text-based cross-linguistic studies, Lund 4–5 March 1994*, Lund: Lund University Press.

Wagner, Emma, Svend Bech and Jesús Martínez (2002), *Translating for the European Institutions*, Manchester, UK and Northampton, MA: St Jerome Publishing.

wa Goro, Wangui (2004), Hectorosexism in Translation: A Comparative Study of *Devil on the Cross* and *Matigari*. PhD, Middlesex University.

Wang, William S.-Y. (1982), *Human Communication*, New York: W. H. Freeman.

Wang, William S.-Y. [1991] (2002), 'Tone Languages', in Kirsten Malmkjær (ed.), *The Linguistics Encyclopedia*, second edition, London and New York: Routledge, pp. 552–8.

Werth, Paul (1999), *Text Worlds: Representing Conceptual Space in Discourse*, London: Longman.

Whorf, B. L. (1940), 'Science and linguistics', *Technol. Rev.* 42(6): 229–31 and 247–8. Reprinted in John B. Carroll (ed.) (1956), *Language, Thought and Reality: Selected Writings of Benjamin Lee Whorf*, Cambridge, MA: The MIT Press, pp. 207–19.

Whorf, B. L. (1941), 'The relation of habitual thought and behavior to language', in L. Spier (ed.), *Language, Culture and Personality: Essays in Memory of Edward Sapir*, Menasha, WI: Sapir Memorial Publication Fund, pp. 75–93. Reprinted in John B. Carroll (ed.) (1956), *Language, Thought and Reality: Selected Writings of Benjamin Lee Whorf*, Cambridge, MA: The MIT Press, pp. 134–59.

Whorf, B. L. (1950), 'An American Indian model of the universe'. *International Journal of American Linguistics* 16: 67–72. Reprinted in John B. Carroll (ed.) (1956), *Language, Thought and Reality: Selected Writings of Benjamin Lee Whorf*, Cambridge, MA: The MIT Press, pp. 57–64.

Williams, John N. (2002) 'Psycholinguistics', in Kirsten Malmkjær (ed.), *The Linguistics Encyclopedia, Second Edition*, London and New York: Routledge, pp. 432–48.

Wierzbicka, Anna (1972), *Semantic Primitives*. Linguistische Forschungen No. 22, Frankfurt: Athenäum.

Wierzbicka, Anna (1996), *Semantics: Primes and Universals*, Oxford and New York: Oxford University Press.

Zanettin, Federico, Silvia Bernardini and Dominic Stewart (eds) (2003), *Corpora in Translator Education*, Manchester, UK and Northampton, MA: St Jerome Publishing.

PRIMARY SOURCES

Hans Christian Andersen

H. C. Andersens Eventyr: Kritisk udgivet efter de originale Eventyrhæfter med Varianter ved Erik Dal og Kommentar ved Erling Nielsen. I:1835–42, 1963; *II:1843–55*, 1964. Copenhagen: Hans Reitzels Forlag.

Märschen und Erzählungen für Kinder. Translated by G. F. von Jenssen, Braunschweig: Vieweg und Sohn, 1939ff.

Wonderful Stories for Children. By Hans Christian Anderson [sic], *Author of 'The Improvisatore' etc.* 1846 Mary Howitt, London: Chapman and Hall.

A Danish Story-Book. Tr. By Charles Boner. With numerous illustrations by the Count Pocci, London: Joseph Cundall, 1846.

Danish Fairy Legends and Tales (tr. Caroline Peachey), London: Addey & Co., 1846.

Tales and Fairy Stories. Madame de Chatelain, London: Routledge & Co., 1852.

Hans Christian Andersen's Stories for the Household. H. W. Dulcken, London: Routledge, 1866. Re-issued as *The Complete Illustrated Works of Hans Christian Andersen*. London: Chancellor Press, 1983.

Andersen's Tales for Children. Alfred Wehnert. London: Bell and Daldy, 1869.

The Complete Andersen: All of the 168 Stories by Hans Christian Andersen. Jean Hersholt. New York: Limited Editions Club 1942–47. Available in electronic form on MAGNUS, from CD-Danmark A/S, Palægade 4, PO Box 9026, DK-1022 Copenhagen K, Denmark.

Eighty Fairy Tales. Translated by R. P. Keigwin. Odense: Skandinavisk Bogforlag. 1976. Translation first published by Flensted, Denmark, in 1950.

Hans Andersen's Fairy Tales: A Selection. L. W. Kingsland. London: Oxford University Press, 1959.

Hans Christian Andersen. Fairy Tales and Stories. Translated, with an Introduction, by Reginald Spink. London, 1960. Republished in Everyman's Library Children's Classics, London, 1992.

Hans Christian Andersen: Fairy Tales. Marie-Louise Peulevé. Copenhagen: Skandinavisk Bogforlag, c. 1965.

The Complete Fairy Tales and Stories. Erik Christian Haugaard. London: Gollanz, 1974.

Tales from Hans Andersen. Stephen Corrin. London: Guild Publishing, 1978.

Hans Andersen's Fairy Tales. Naomi Lewis. Harmondsworth: Penguin, 1981.

The Faber Book of Favourite Fairy Tales. Sara and Stephen Corrin. London and Boston: Faber and Faber, 1988.

Hans Christian Andersen. Stories and Fairy Tales. Erik Blegvad. London: Heinemann, 1993.

Peter Høeg

Høeg, P. (1993), *De måske egnede.* Copenhagen. Rosinante. English translation by Barbara Haveland (1994), *Borderliners.* First published in the UK in 1995. London: Harvill.

Index

Abrams, M. H., 156
Abuse, 151
Academic writing, 71
Acceptability, 64
Acknowledgement, 156
Act, 169
Actor, 177, 178, 179, 180
Adaptation, 163
Addition, 66
Addressee, 14
Addresser, 14
Adjective, 14, 91, 93, 169
Adjunct, 169, 170, 176
Adverb, 14, 91, 169
Adverbial phrase, 177
Advertising, 74, 75, 76, 163, 166
Advising, 153
Aeneid, 7
Aesthetic attitude, 69
Affricate, 73
African language, 74
Afterlife, 13
Agamemnon (Aeschylus), 11
Aichison, Jean, 87
Allan, Robin, 60
Alliteration, 14, 19, 74, 75, 77, 165
Allusion, 165
Ambiguity, 27, 107–8, 109, 165
    lexical, 107–8
    of sentences, 108
    structural, 108
    systematic, 108
Amerindian language, 74
'An American Indian model of the universe'
    (Whorf), 49
Anaphora, 137
Anaphoric tie, 137
Anapest, 78, 82
Anchor word, 59
Andersen, Hans Christian, 15–16, 64–5, 66

Animated First Principle (AFP), 172
Antonym, 106
Antonymy, 106
Apologising/Apology, 152, 153, 171
Appraisal, 153
Approaches to translation, 1, 20–41
    cultural, 20, 36–7
    descriptive, 15, 20, 32–5: function oriented,
        17–18, 35–6; process oriented, 17–18;
        product oriented, 17–18
    functional, 20, 30, 35–6
    linguistic, 20, 21–32
    philosophical, 52–8
    source text oriented, 32
    target text oriented, 32
Archer, William, 148–50
Arnold, Matthew, 12
Ars poetica, 1–2, 3, 87
Article, 90, 91, 93, 165
Aspect, 169
Assonance, 75
Assumptions, 183
Attitude, 14
Attribute, 178
Audience, 12, 30
Aufgabe des Übersetzers, die (Benjamin), 12–13
Austin, John L., 150–4, 154, 168
Auxiliary, 165, 171
Axelsen, Jens, 60, 62

Bank of English, 116, 120–2, 130–1
Barthes, Roland, 135
Base form, 86
Bassnett, Susan, 36
Batteux, Charles, 5, 6, 7
Background knowledge, 142, 143, 144, 145,
    147, 154, 168
Baudelaire, Charles, 71–2
Beat, 78
Beaugrande, Robert de, 138

Begley, Sharon, 75
Behabitive, 153
Béjoint, Henri, 115–16
Bell, Roger T., 88–9
Ben-Ari, Nitsa, 183–4
Benjamin, Walter Bendix Schoenfliess, 6, 10,
    12–13
Beowulf (Heaney tr.), 12
Berlin, B., 50–1
Betting, 152
Bhatia, Vijay K., 156–7, 158, 165
Bible
    Authorised Version *see* King James
    King James, 4–5
    Wycliffite, 4, 5
Bible translation, 3, 28, 31
Bible translators, 3–5
Blütenstaub (Novalis), 10
Black, Max, 112
Boas, Franz, 48
Bowerman, Melissa, 42–3, 51
Brand naming, 76
Bredsdorff, Elias, 66
British National Corpus (BNC), 116, 120,
    123–30, 131
Brown, Gillian, 142–3
Brown, Penelope, 154
Bühler, Karl, 14, 35

Cambridge International Dictionary of English,
    118–210
Carrier, 178, 180
Carroll, Lewis, 92–102
Cataphora, 137
Cataphoric tie, 137
Category, 102
Catford, J. C., 21–8, 29, 32, 33, 55, 60, 69, 132
Causal relations, 138
Censorship, 36
Challenging, 153
Chapman, George, 5, 6
Chemnitz corpus, 117
Chiming, 75
China, 2, 109
Chinese, 47, 73, 74, 76, 140
Choices, 64
Chomsky, Noam, 108, 183
Cicero, Marcus Tullius, 1, 2, 87
Circumlocution, 91
Circumstance, 177–82
Classification, 102–4
Clause, 88, 91, 93, 168–82
    functionalist approach to, 168–9
    in Spanish, 175
    intransitive, 177

main, 172
    transitive, 172, 177
Clause grammar, 169
Clause function, 168–82
Clause structure, 169, 173
Clause symphony, 168–9
Client, 35
COBUILD corpus *see* Bank of English
Code, 13, 14
Coherence, 134, 142–3, 146, 147
    in translation, 147
Cohesion, 134, 135–42, 146, 147, 169
    in translation, 147
    inter-textual, 136–7
Cohesive devices, 142
Cohesive relations, 134, 137, 140
    marker of, 134
Cohesive tie, 137–8
Cohyponym, 104
Collins Cobuild English Language Dictionary,
    118–20
Collocate, 121
Collocation, 23, 27, 115, 122–30, 132, 138
Collocational range, 23
Colour terminology, 50–1, 109
Combining form, 92
Command, 171, 180
Commending, 153
Commissive, 153
Commitment, 150
Communication, 14, 57
Communicative act, 29
Complaint, 171
Complement, 169, 170
Components of meaning *see* meaning
    components
Concept, 86–7, 115
Conceptual distinction, 88
Concord, 170
Concordance, Key Word in Context (KWIC),
    120–2
Concordance lines, 120–2
Concordance sampler, 120
Condition, specifying, 157
Condoling, 153
Conjunction, 91, 137, 138, 175
Conjunctive element, 138
Conjunctive relation, 138, 146
    additive, 138
    adversative, 138
    causal, 138
    temporal, 138
Congratulating, 153
Connotation, 115, 130–1
Conrad, Joseph, 176

Consonant, 70, 72–3
Constative *see* Utterance; constative
Contact, 14
Context, 14, 46, 147, 168–9, 171
Contradiction, 103
Contrajunction, 138
Convergence, 117
Conversation, 146, 147
Conversational implicature *see* Implicature,
    conversational
Converseness, 106
Convincing, 152
Co-occurrence, 115
Co-operative principle *see* Principle of
    conversational co-operation
Co-ordination test, 108
Co-reference, 137
Co-referring expressions, 143
Corpora, 18, 25–6, 59, 60, 115, 116–33
    comparable, 116–17
    English and German, 117
    English and Norwegian, 117
    general, 116, 131
    historical, 117
    learner, 117
    monitor, 117
    parallel, 117
    specialised, 116
Corpus *see* Corpora
Corpus linguistics, 131
Correspondence, 23
Correspondence theory of truth, 151
Corrin, Sarah, 65
Corrin, Stephen, 65
Co-text, 147, 168
Couturier, Maurice, 77–8
Cowley, Abraham, 6, 7, 8, 9
Creating a Research Space (CARS) Model, 158
Creativity, 3, 61, 112, 185
Critique of Pure Reason (Kant), 49
Cultural readiness, 10
Cultural turn, 36
Culture, 36, 42, 132, 183
Cursing, 153

Dactyl, 78
Dagut, Menachem, 6, 27
Danish, 16, 60, 63, 68, 145
Data, 32
Davidson, Donald, 54–7, 66
Davidsen-Nielsen, Niels, 60, 63
De interpretatione (Huet), 8
De l'esprit des traductions (Madame de Staël), 8
Dedication, 156
Decoding effort, 31

Defence of Poetry (Shelley), 7
Definiteness, 91, 93
Definition, 115
Deixis, 23–4, 42, 49, 65
Demonstrative, 90, 91
Denham, John, 6, 7
Description, 17, 152, 166
Descriptive fallacy, 151
Destruction of Troy (Virgil), 7
Determiner, 91
Deterring, 152
Dialect, 46
Dialogue, 166
Dictionary, 64, 92, 115–16, 122, 132
    bilingual, 60, 116
    English, 116
    general, 116
    monolingual, 116
    specialised, 116
Diphthong, 73
Discourse analysis, 156
    critical, 182
Discourse community, 157, 158, 159
Discourse particle, 60, 63, 145
Disjunction, 138
Dolet, Étienne, 5, 6
Domestication, 2, 9, 10
Dressler, Wolfgang, 138
Dryden, John, 6, 9
Dubbing, 73–4
Dudley-Evans, Anthony, 159

École Superieure d'Interprètes et de Traducteurs
    (ESIT), 88
Editorial, 163, 165
Einstellung, 14
Ellipsis, 137, 138
E-mail (sales promotion), 159–63
Emphasis, 14
Emotion, 14
Empson, William, 75
Ending politely, 159
English, 4, 63, 68, 78, 87, 88, 91, 105, 117, 137,
    138, 144, 145, 154, 163, 165, 168, 170,
    171–2, 173, 175, 176, 177–8, 180
English–Norwegian Parallel Corpus, 117
Enkvist, Nils Erik, 142
Enzenberger, Christian, 98–9
Equivalence, 3, 14, 15, 21, 22, 32, 55, 64–9,
    185
    conditions of, 32
    dynamic, 3, 30, 31, 32
    formal, 3, 30, 31
    functional, 26, 32
    of meaning, 54

of response, 31
total, 30
Equivalent, 24
Erasmus, Desiderius, 4, 16n
Error, 64–9
Error identification, 69
Establishing a Niche, 158
Establishing a Territory, 158
Establishing credentials, 159, 160
Estimate, 153
European languages, 76
Evans, Kathy, 112–14
Even-Zohar, Itamar, 41n
Exchange, 168–9
Exclamation, 91
Excuse, 148, 154
Explanation, 148, 154
Exploitation
    of maxims, 147
    of principles, 145
Expositive, 153
Extension, 107, 108
Eye-alliteration, 75
Eye-rhyme, 74, 75

Fact, 151
Factor, 14
    cultural, 27
    linguistic, 27
False friends, 68
Fashion column, 165
Felicity conditions, 151–2, 153–4
Field, 46, 168–9
Figure of speech, 109
Finding, 153
Finnish, 87
Firth, J. R., 22, 23, 122
Fitzgerald, Edward, 10
Fixed limits of expression, 183
Flexibility, 107–10
Flouting of maxims, 147, 154
Foot (metrical), 78
Footnote, 91
Foreignisation 2, 9, 10
France, 91
French, 77, 78, 94–6, 101, 105, 140–1, 143–4,
    148–9, 180, 181–2
Frequency, 122, 131
Fricative, 73
Function, 35, 46–7, 153
    appellative, 35
    cognitive, 14
    conative, 14
    denotative, 14
    distinctive, 35

expressive, 35
grammatical, 180
ideational, 46, 168–9
interpersonal, 46, 168–9
metalinguistic, 14
metatextual, 35
of moves, 159
phatic, 14, 35
poetic, 14
referential, 14
representative, 35
textual, 46, 168–9
thematic, 180
Function word, 90
Functionalism, 45
Functionally relevant features of situation, 26, 27,
    32

Galician, 183
Gardner, Martin, 94
Genre, 135, 156–66, 169
Genre analysis, 156–66, 168
Genre conventions, 154, 166
German, 4, 47, 68, 94, 97–9, 101, 117, 141,
    144, 180
Gikuyu, 183
Glossary, 88
Goal, 177, 180
Goddard, Angela, 166
Goethe, Johan Wolfgang von, 10
Gradability, 103–4
Grammar, 22, 60, 64, 168
    functional, 169, 173
    generative, 29
    systemic, 29
    systemic functional, 22
Grammatical information, 92
Grammatical relationship, 106
Grammatical structure, 135, 171
Graph, 70, 73
Grapheme, 87
Graphology, 166
Greek, 2, 3, 91
Grice, H. Paul, 34, 145–6, 150
Ground, 112
Group see Phrase
Gumperz, John, J., 43

Hall, Radclyffe, 172–4
Halliday, Michael Alexander Kirkwood, 22, 45,
    46, 55, 108, 137, 138, 142–3, 168, 169,
    170, 173, 175, 177, 178
Handbook of American Indian Languages (Boas),
    48
Happiness (of performative speech acts), 151

Hardy, Thomas, 79
Hasan, Ruqaiya, 137, 138, 142–3
Haugaard, Erik, 15–16
Haveland, Barbara, 60–1
Headline, 158, 165, 166
Heaney, Seamus, 12
Hearer, 147, 152, 153
Hebrew, 3, 4, 183–4
Herder, Johan Gottfried von, 6, 9, 10
Hjørnager Pedersen, Viggo, 65, 66
Ho, George, 76
Hofland, Knutt, 59
Holding true, 55, 56, 150
Hollindale, P., 183
Holmes, James S., 17–20
Holz-Mänttäri, Justa, 35
Homer, 9, 12
Homograph, 107
Homoioteleuton, 74
Homonymy, 107
Homophone, 107
Hopi, 49
Horace, 1, 2–3, 87
Hospers, John, 139
House, Juliane, 154
Howitt, Mary, 37, 66–9
Huet, Daniel, 6, 8
Humboldt, Wilhelm von, 6, 11
Hung, Eva, 2
Hunston, Susan, 87, 116–17, 122, 131, 132
Hyponym, 104, 106–7
Hyponymy, 104–5
   text-local, 106–7

Iamb, 78
Ibsen, Henrik, 148–50, 154
Identified, 178, 180
Ideology, 35, 36, 163, 182–4
Iliad (Homer), 9
Illocutionary act, 152, 153
Illocutionary force, 152
Ilson, Robert, 116
Image, 166
Imitation, 2, 9
Implicature, 34, 145–50, 168
   conventional, 146
   conversational, 34, 146–50
   non-conventional, 146
Implicature generation, 147, 148
   in translation, 147
Importation, 91
Incompatibility, 103
Indian subcontinent, 2
Infix, 92
Information, 169

new, 173
thematic, 172
Ingarden, Roman, 11, 13, 25, 27
Initiator, 35
Innovation, 2
Interjection, 14, 91
International Phonetic Alphabet (IPA), 70, 74
International Translators' Day, 3
Interpretation, 29
Interpreting, 88, 185
Interpreting studies, 88
Intertextuality, 135–7, 163, 166
Introducing candidature, 159
Introducing offer, 159, 161
Inuktitut, 87
Invention, 91
Irony, 109
Isenberg, Arnold, 29
Italian, 47, 123, 141–2, 144, 180

Jakobson, Roman, 6, 11, 13, 14, 25, 27, 28, 45,
   50, 59, 64, 65, 137
Japanese, 27, 73, 173
Johansson, Stig, 59
Johnson, Mark, 50, 51, 111, 112
Junction, 138
Junctive expression, 138, 142, 146

Kant, Immanuel, 49
Kay, P., 50–1
Kelly, Louis, 2
Kempson, Ruth, 108, 109
Kinds
   cultural, 102–3
   natural, 102–3, 180
   manufactured, 102–3, 180
   psychological, 102–3
Korean, 42–4
Krishnamurthy, Ramesh, 2
Kristensen, Tom, 80–4

L2, 122
La manière de bien traduire d'une langue en aultre
   (Dolet), 6
Lakoff, George, 50, 51, 111, 112
Langacker, R. W., 11
Language, 42, 46, 132, 152, 182, 185
   level of, 24
   literal, 111
   Mayan, 88
   natural, 150
   poetic, 78
   pro-drop, 138, 175
   pure, 13
   stress timed, 78

syllable timed, 78
Language (Sapir), 50
Language academy, 91
Language adjustment, 91
Language change, 90, 117
Language development, 91
Language function(s), 14
  emotive, 14
  expressive, 14
Language history, 132–3
Language system, 23
Language type, 171–2
Language unit, 91
Latin, 2, 3, 4, 91
Laviosa, Sara, 117
Laws, 34
Lederer, Marianne, 88
Leech, Geoffrey, 74, 75, 78, 79, 110, 154
Leibniz, Gottlieb Wilhelm, 6
Lemma, 86, 87, 125, 138
Les belles infidèles, 8
Letter, 156, 164–5, 166
  business, 158–9
  job application, 159
  sales promotion, 159, 166
Levinson, Stephen C., 43, 154
Lexeme, 86
Lexical density, 117
Lexical incompatibility, 42–3
Lexical item, 135
Lexical organisation, 137
Lexical selection, 183
Lexical semantics *see* semantics, lexical
Lexicography, 86, 116
  bilingual, 26
Lexis, 22, 169
Libellus de optimo genere oratorum (Cicero), 1–2,
  87
Liber de optime genere interpretandi (Jerome), 3
Linguistic act, orientation of, 14
Linguistic innovation, 91
Linguistic issue, 6
Linguistic level, 25
Linguistic relativity *see* Relativity, linguistic
Linguistic theory, 21, 22, 58–69
Linguistics, 58–69, 185
  British, 142
  cognitive, 11, 142
  contrastive, 59
  critical, 182
Lip rounding, 73
Lip spreading (unrounding), 73
Listener, 134, 142, 143, 147, 148
Literature, 163, 179
Localisation, 76–7

Locke, John, 75
Locutionary act), 152
Logic, 146, 147, 169
Logical relationship, 142
Longman Dictionary of the English Language,
  118–20
Louw, Bill, 130
Low, Peter, 71–2
Luther, Martin, 4
Lyons, John, 108

McCabe, Anne, 175
McGowan, James, 72
Machine translation, 18, 25, 28
Macpherson, James, 41n
Madame de Staël, 8
Malinowski, Bronislaw, 14, 35, 44–5, 46, 87
Malmberg, Carl, 80–4
Manipulation, 64–9, 183
Manual, 152
Maxim, 146–7, 154
  of manner, 147
  of quality, 147, 148
  of quantity, 146–7
  of relation, 147
Meaning, 22, 24, 29, 54, 56–7, 66, 75, 86–114,
  146, 150, 182, 185
  contextual, 22, 23, 24, 26
  emotive, 29
  equivalence of, 54
  formal, 22, 23, 24
  functional, 29
  guide to, 122
  linguistic, 29
  referential, 29
Meaning components, 51
  universal, 51
Meaning unit, 88
Ménage, Gilles, 8
Message, 14, 30, 168–9, 173–6
  equivalent, 13, 14
  universality of, 31
Metafunction, 46, 168–9
Metaphor, 37, 109–12
  constructivist views of, 111
  grammatical, 175–6
  interaction view of, 112
  non-constructivist views of, 111
  sentence level, 110–11
  underlying, 111, 112
Metaphrase, 9
Metre, 78–84
  dactylic, 82
  iambic, 72
Meyer, Charles F., 117

Millán-Varela, Carmen, 183
Minority languages, 36
Misfire, 151
Misleading, 152
Modality, 169
Mode, 46, 168–9
Monophthongs, 73
Mood, 153, 168–9, 171
    declarative, 153, 171
    imperative, 14, 153, 171, 180
    interrogative, 153, 171
    vocative, 14
Morpheme, 73, 88
Morris, William, 11
Move, 156, 158–9, 168
Move structure
    for editorials, 165
    interactive, 157

Nabokov, Vladimir, 12, 77
Name, 91
    proper, 91
'Name and nature of translation studies'
    (Holmes), 17
Narrative, 166, 173
Nasal, 73
Natural kinds see Kinds, natural
Natural language philosophy, 150
Newman, Francis William, 12
Newmark, Peter, 5, 71
News report, 163, 166, 181, 182
Newspaper, 158, 163–5
    broadsheet, 164
    tabloid, 164
Newspaper article, 158
    feature, 164
    non-translated, 117
    translated, 117
Nida, Eugene A., 3, 5, 28–32
Nominalisation, 183
Nord, Christiane, 35, 45
Norm, 34, 145
Norwegian, 117, 148–50
Noun, 14, 91, 93, 169
    verbal, 108
Noun phrase (NP), 91, 93, 172, 177
Novalis (Friedrich Leopold von Hardenberg), 10,
    12
Novel, 156, 182
Number, 170
    dual, 23
    plural, 23
    singular, 23, 170

Object, 169, 170, 172

Occupying a niche, 158
Offer, 171
    of information, 36
Offering incentives, 159
Offering the argument, 165
Oliver, Francisco Torres, 99–100
Omission, 66, 184
On Translating Homer (Arnold), 12
Onomatopoeia, 75
Order, 150, 153
Ordering, 153–4
Ortony, Andrew, 112
Ossian (Macpherson), 41n
Ovid's Epistles (Dryden), 9

Palmer, Frank R., 108
Parallelism, 137
Paranomasia, 15
Paraphrase, 9, 28, 111
Paris school, 88
Parisot, Henri, 95–6
Participant, 14, 177–82
Parts of speech, 59, 91–2, 93, 94, 101
Passing theory, 57
Passivisation, 183
Pattern, 14, 135
    formal, 66, 68
    metrical, 78
    of sound, 135
    semantic, 66
Pentameter, iambic, 72
Performative see Utterance; performative
Perlocutionary act, 152–3
Perrin-Chattard, Clémentine, 143–4
Perrin-Chattard, Thibault, 143–4
Perrot, Nicolas, 6, 8
Person, 170
Perspective, 174, 177, 181
Persuading, 152
Phenomenon, 177
Phonaesthemes, 76
Phonaesthesia, 76, 101
Phonaesthetic resonance, 94
Phonetic, 73
Phonetics, 70
Phonology, 70
Phrase, 70, 91, 93, 168, 169–70
    adjective, 170
    adverb, 170
    ambiguous, 107
    noun, 170
    prepositional, 170
    verb, 170
Phraseology, 122
Pindar, 7, 9

Plosives, 73
Poetry, 2, 7, 13, 14–15, 70, 71, 78, 93, 182
Politeness, 154
Pollard, David, 2
Polysemy, 108, 165
Polysystem, 33, 41n
Polysystem theory, 41n
Pope, Alexander, 6, 9
Possessive, 109
Postposition, 173
Power, 153–4, 159, 182
Pragmatics, 150
Predicate, 105
　ambiguous, 107–8
　antonymous, 106
　converse, 106
　relationally opposite, 106
　symmetric, 106
　synonymous, 106
　transitive, 106
Predicate characteristics, 106
Predicate relationships, 105–6
Predicator, 169, 171, 172, 175
Prefix, 92
Preposition, 14, 42–4, 78, 91, 123, 169
Prepositional phrase, 177
Prescriptivist tradition, 5
Presenting the case, 165
Principle of charity, 54, 56
Principle of conversational co-operation, 145–50,
　154
Principle of equivalent effect, 30
Principle of politeness, 154
'Principles of Translation' (Batteux), 7
Principles of Translation (Tytler), 9
Prior theory, 57
Priscian, 91
Process, 177–82
　material, 177
　mental, 177, 180
　relational, 177–8: attributive, 178; identifying,
　178
Promise, 150, 171
Promising, 152, 153
Promotional material, 158, 163, 181
Pronoun, 91, 169
Prose, 71
Prose rhythm, 79–84
Prototype theory, 104
Proverb, 37
Provision, 150
　legislating, 157
Pseudotranslations, 41n
Psychology, 169
　of perception, 172

Pun, 15, 27, 165
Punctuation, 19
Purpose, 35
Purvey, John, 4

Quality control, 18
Quantity, 91
Question, 153, 171
Quine, Willard van Orman, 52–6, 107–8, 109

Radical interpretation, 54
Rank, 19, 25
Rank scale, 28
Reaching the verdict, 165
Reader, 134, 142, 143, 147, 152
Reader response, 28
Reah, Danuta, 164, 165
Reality, 51, 53
Rebuke, 171
Receptor response, 31
Reckoning, 153
Recommending action, 165
Reference, 56, 152, 166n
Register, 46–7, 55, 166
Reiss, Katharina, 35, 36, 45
Relativism, 43, 46, 52
　cultural, 42, 44–5, 56
　linguistic, 42
　ontological, 42, 52–8
Relativist, 43, 51, 56, 59
Relativity
　linguistic, 11, 48–50
　ontological, 52–8
　principle of, 50
Relevance, 33–4
　functional, 27
　hierarchy of, 32, 34
Relevance theory, 89
Relevant features, 26, 33–4
Remane, Liselotte, 97–8
Remane, Martin, 97–8
Repetition, 14, 137, 140
　intertextual, 135–6
Rephrasing, 13
Representation, 168–9, 177–82
　conceptual, 89
　mental, 89, 142
Representativeness, 131
Research, 1, 132
Research article, 157–9
Review, 165
Rewording, 13
Rheme, 168–9, 173–6, 179
Rhyme, 14, 19, 71, 74, 75, 165
　feminine, 74

masculine, 74
Rhythm, 14, 70–85
Richards, I. A., 111–12
Robins, R. H., 75–6, 87
Robinson, Douglas, 8
Rodríguez, Amado Diéguez, 176
Role relationship, 46
Rolle, Richard, 3
Roman
  period, 2
  tradition, 1–2
Romans, 3
Rosenberg, Mirta, 100
Rubáiyát of Omar Khayyám (Fitzgerald), 10
Russian, 26

Saint Jerome, 3, 87
Salutation, 156, 167n
  closing, 159, 160
  opening, 159, 160
Sameness of meaning, 13
Samoilovich, Daniel, 100
Sapir, Edward, 11, 13, 48, 58–9
Sapir-Whorf hypothesis, 48–50
Schäffner, Christina, 35
Schleiermacher, Friedrich, 6, 11
Scientific report, 166
Scientific writing, 71
Scott, Robert, 97
Searle, John R., 153, 154
Seleskovitch, Danica, 88
Semantic field, 65, 66, 103–5, 109
Semantic primes, 51
Semantic primitives, 51
Semantic prosodies, 115, 130–1
Semantic relation, 137
Semantic representation, 88, 89
Semantic voids, 6
Semantics, 115, 169
  lexical, 86, 102–7
Sendbrief vom Dolmetschen (Luther), 4
Sense, 4, 87, 88, 115, 122, 152
Sense relations, 104–7, 138
Sense unit, 89
Senser, 177, 180
Sentence, 26, 168
  ambiguous, 107, 109
  declarative, 151
Sentence forming operators, 146
Set
  lexical, 23, 103–4, 109
  open, 22, 23
Shelley, Percy Bysshe, 7
Simile, 111
Sinclair, John McHardy, 130

Situation, 45, 46
Situation features, 26
Situation substance, 26
Situation type, 46
Skopos theory, 35–6
SL, 24
Slanting, 31
Slogan, 166
Snell-Hornby, Mary, 60
Soliciting response, 159, 161
Sound, 70–85
Sound–meaning associations, 76
Sound patterns, 70–1, 135
Sound representation, 70, 71
Sound symbolism, 76
Source text (ST), 117
Source text orientation, 15
Spain, 91
Spanish, 94, 99–100, 138, 141, 144, 175–6,
  180, 181, 183
  Chilean, 47
Spatial prepositions, 42–3, 51
Spatial relationships, 42–3, 51
Speaker, 147, 153, 169
Speech act, 135, 147, 150–6, 168, 171
  direct, 153
  explicit, 152
  implicit, 152
  indirect, 153–4
Speech act class, 153
Speech act verb, 152
Speech function, 26
Speech rhythm, 79–80
Speech situation, 147
SPOCA, 169
State of affairs, 151
Statement, 152, 153
Stating, 152
Steiner, George, 1, 5, 88
Stereotype, 166
Stress, 78
Stress timed language, 78
Style, 169
Stylistic analysis, 179
Subject, 169, 170, 171, 172, 179, 180
  grammatical, 170, 173, 178
  logical, 177, 178
  psychological, 173, 178
Subordination, 138
Subordinator, 174
Substitution (cohesion), 137
Substitution (translation), 66
Suffix, 92
Summer Institute of Linguistics, 5
Surprising, 152

Swales, John, 157–8
Swedish, 68, 76
Syllable, 70, 73, 74
Syllable timed language, 78
Symmetry, 106
Synecdoche, 109–10
Synonym, 105
Synonymy, 13, 105
    text-local, 106–7
System, 22–3
    closed, 22, 90

Tag question, 170
Target text readership, 143
Target text turn, 1, 15
Tarski, Alfred, 56
Task of the Translator (Benjamin), 12–13
Temporal relations, 138
Tennyson, Alfred Lord, 75
Tenor (of metaphor), 111–12
Tenor (register analysis), 46, 168–9
Tense, 169, 173
    past, 173
    present, 170, 173
Term, 107, 122
    gradable, 104
    homonymous, 107
    mutually incompatible, 103
    non-gradable, 103
    polysemous, 108
    specialised, 136
    subject specific 118
    superordinate, 104, 106–7
    technical, 118
    vague, 109
Terminological appendix, 91
Terminology, 116
    specialisation, 136
    specialist, 158
Terminology extraction system, 18
Text, 19, 134–84
    appeal-focussed, 35
    content-focussed, 35
    expressive, 35
    form-focussed, 35
    informative, 35
    literary, 13, 14, 28, 173
    non-translated, 117
    operative, 35
    promotional, 181
    specialised, 116
    translated, 117
Text act, 156, 158, 168
Text analysis, 156
Text comprehension, 143

Text function, 156
Text world, 143
Texture, 134–45, 169
Theme, 168–9, 173–6, 178–9, 180, 181
    in Spanish, 175–6
Theme First Principle (TFP), 172
Théorie du sens, 88
Theory, 17
    linguistic, 42
Theory of meaning, 54, 55, 150–1, 152
Theory of politeness, 154
Thompson, John B., 182
Title, 158
TL, 24
Tomlin, R. S., 172
Tone, 14, 73, 74
Tone languages, 74
Topic, 111–12
Tourist texts, 143–5
Toury, Gideon, 15, 18, 20, 21, 32–5, 58, 66
Transfer, 122
Transitivity, 106, 168–9, 177–82
Transitivity roles, 180, 181
Translat, 35
Translatability, 13, 146
Translating, 20, 117, 134, 185
Translating for children, 36
Translating gay literature, 36
Translating into L1, 122
Translating into L2, 122
Translation, 13, 24, 28–9, 30–1, 35, 36, 52, 56, 61, 64–5, 185
    and ideology, 182–4
    and politeness, 154
    and thematic structure, 174
    cohesion and coherence in, 147
    communicative, 71
    extent of, 24
    full, 24
    gist, 71
    grammatical, 10
    graphological, 25
    implicature generation in, 147
    indeterminacy of, 54
    interlingual, 13, 28–9
    intersemiotic, 13, 28
    intralingual, 13, 28
    level of, 24
    literal, 9, 12, 25
    literary, 14, 15
    mythic, 10
    of advertising, 35
    of attention focusing text parts, 163
    of brand names, 76
    of song, 71

partial, 24
phonological, 25
policy, 20
radical, 53
rank bound, 25
rank of, 24
restricted, 25
semantic, 71
sense based, 6
sense for sense, 3, 6, 9, 29, 87–90
technical, 18
total, 24, 25, 26
transformative, 10
unbounded, 25
word for word, 3, 6, 9, 19, 87–90
Translation accuracy, 31
Translation act, 35
Translation adequacy, 15, 33
Translation aid, 18
Translation aim, 30
Translation area, 18
Translation criticism, 20
Translation description, 35
Translation equivalence, 1, 24, 25, 26, 28,
    32–33, 34, 55, 57–8, 65, 66
  conditions of, 32–3
  theory of, 55
Translation equivalent, 25, 33, 64, 66, 145
Translation evaluation, 31
Translation history, 18
Translation industry, 91
Translation laws, 34
Translation medium, 18
Translation memory system(s), 18
Translation norms, 32, 34
Translation pedagogy, 20, 26
Translation practice, 33
Translation process, 18, 117
Translation production, 35
Translation psychology, 18
Translation purpose, 13, 30, 36, 71
Translation strategy, 18
Translation studies, 58–69, 145
  applied, 19–20
  descriptive, 59
  gender oriented, 36
  post-colonial, 36
Translation theory, 1–41, 42, 54, 55, 58–69
  general, 18
  modern, 15
Translation tools, 20
Translation typology, 10–11
Translation unit, 87
Translator, 64, 65, 90, 91, 117, 143, 145, 148,
    165

of specialised texts, 116
Translator behaviour, 117
Translator intention, 68
Translator motivation, 66, 68
Translator strategy, 91
Translator training, 117
Translatum, 35
Transliteration, 76
Transmutation, 13
Trochee, 78
Trope, 109–10, 111
Truth, 55, 56, 106, 150–1
Truth conditions, 107, 150, 151
Two Maxims (Goethe), 10
Tyndale, Willliam, 4
Type-token ratio, 117
Typicality, 104
Tytler, Alexander Fraser, 9–10
Tzeltal, 88

Über die neuere deutschen Literatur: Fragmente
    (Herder), 9
Über die verschiedenen Methoden des Übersetzens
    (Schleiermacher), 11
Undertaking, 153
Unhappiness, 151
Unit
  linguistic, 88
  of sense, 88
United Kingdom, 163–4
Universal, 43
Universalism, 43, 52, 59
  cultural, 46–7
  linguistic, 50–1
Untranslatability, 27–8, 56
  cultural, 27
  linguistic, 27
Unvorgreifliche Gedanken, betreffend die Ausübung
    und Verbesserung der Deutchen Sprache
    (Leibniz), 6
Uptake, 152
Urging, 153
Utterance, 109, 152
  constative, 151, 152
  performative, 151–2; implicit, 152

Vagueness, 109
Vehicle, 111–12
Venuti, Lawrence, 2, 9
Verb, 14, 91, 93, 169, 170
Verb-Object Bonding Principle (VOB), 172
Verb phrase (VP), 93, 177
Verdict, 153
Verdictive, 153
Vermeer, Hans Josef, 35, 36

Versification, 79, 135
Virgil, 7
Voice, 169
    passive, 170
Void (extralinguistic), 27
Voting, 153
Vowels, 70, 72–3
    tongue-high, 73
    tongue-low, 73

wa Goro, Wangui, 183
Warning, 152, 153
Warrin, Frank L., 94–5
Weather report, 165
Werth, Paul, 143
West-Östlicher Divan (Goethe), 10
Whorf, Benjamin Lee, 11, 48–50
Wierzbicka, Anna, 51
Word, 70, 73, 86–133, 165, 168
    ambiguous, 107
    content, 78, 90

frequent, 117
grammatical, 78, 90
lexical, 14
non-content, 165
nonsense, 94
open class, 91
Word ambiguity, 108
Word class, 91, 93, 169
Word classification, 90–101
Word meaning, 102–12, 115
Word order, 172
Wordsworth, William, 74
Writer motivation, 181
Writing system
    alphabetic, 70, 73, 75
    logographic, 73
    phonographic, 73
Wycliffe, John, 4

Yule, George, 142–3